N
Hamburg
Bremen
Berlin
GERMANY
POLAND
Prague
CZECH REPUBLIC
Stuttgart
July 4th
Vienna
SLOVAKIA
AUSTRIA
Budapest
LIECHTENSTEIN
HUNGARY
SLOVENIA
Ljubljana
Zagreb
Trieste
Venice
CROATIA
TALY
BOSNIA & HERZOGOVINA
Sarajevo
Florence
Perugia
Adriatic Sea
Rome

Ella in Europe

Also by Michael Konik

Telling Lies and Getting Paid

The Man with the $100,000 Breasts

Nice Shot, Mr. Nicklaus

In Search of Burningbush

MAP

CAFE

Ella in Europe

An American Dog's International Adventures

Michael Konik

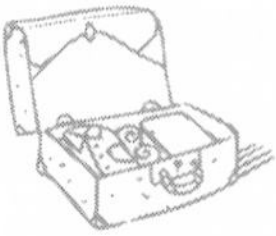

Delacorte Press

ELLA IN EUROPE
A Delacorte Book / February 2005

Published by Bantam Dell
A Division of Random House, Inc.
New York, New York

Book design by Virginia Norey

Delacorte Press is a registered trademark of Random House, Inc., and the colophon is a trademark of Random House, Inc.

Library of Congress Cataloging in Publication Data
Konik, Michael.
Ella in Europe: an American dog's international adventures/Michael Konik
p. cm.
ISBN 0-385-33851-1
1. Konik, Michael—Travel—Europe. 2. Dog owners—Europe—anecdotes. 3. Travel with dogs—Europe—anecdotes. 4. Americans—Europe—anecdotes. 5. Europe—description and travel. I. Title.

D923.K675 2005 200405611
636.7/0092/9 22

Printed in the United States of America
Published simultaneously in Canada

www.bantamdell.com

BVG 10 9 8 7 6 5 4 3 2

In memory of Eugene Konik,
who taught me to always chase my dreams,
and to Sandrine Pecher,
who made Ella's European dreams come true

Acknowledgments

The residents of Europe, almost without exception, showed me and my American mutt the true meaning of hospitality. We were welcomed into their businesses and their homes as though we were old friends. Two Europeans in particular, Yves and Janine Pecher, were extraordinarily generous with both their resources and their hearts, and I thank them for helping make a potentially difficult expedition feel as smooth and easy as a good bottle of Bordeaux.

I'm also grateful for the assiduous eye of Connie Munro, whose copyediting skills make a monolingual oaf like me look as though I actually know how to spell in Czech.

Danielle Perez is an editor of exquisite taste and great vision. Both the author and his hairy friend deeply appreciate that their story landed in her capable (and dog-loving) hands.

And just as my Ella needs a chaperone to lead her through potentially thorny journeys around Hollywood and Holland, I too need someone to watch over me and my literary ambitions. I'm thankful that the magnificent Jennifer Joel keeps me on a long leash.

Ella in Europe

Introduction

When I was a toddler, less than a year old, I had a dog in my playpen. He was a beagle named Brutus. My parents tell me he was a naughty little fellow prone to obsessive digging and tearing, as though he meant to rid the home where I was born, in Highland Park, Illinois, of troublesome rodents. I've seen old photographs of the first family dog and me crawling around together on the floor. That's how I know he was a part of my formative years (that and my parents saying so); I was too young then to retain any reliable sensory memories of Brutus. Somehow, though, the phrase "naughty beagle" has stuck in my mind. More than thirty-five years later, whenever I encounter one of his breed, I feel the words creeping to my lips whether the presumed-innocent-before-proven-otherwise creature is a well-behaved doggie or not.

I don't recall when I realized that Snoopy, the novel-writing, bird-befriending hero of the comic strip *Peanuts,* was a (naughty) beagle. But when I did, I must have instantly liked him because he would have reminded me of Brutus, my first friend. Reviewing those old photos of me in my family's picture album,

I see a preternaturally comfortable little lad. Even as a tiny tyke crawling in my playpen, I look serene and untroubled by the presence of a mischievous beagle in my padded wonderland. There's no hint of fear or consternation in my wide eyes, only playfulness and wonder. Since Brutus and I were roughly the same size, I may have misidentified him as my brother, although he had claws where I had fingers and hair where I had silky skin. His "kisses"—which, I understand in retrospect, were intended to extract whatever saltiness from my cheeks my mother's post-feeding cleanups had missed—did not alarm me. Because, after all, kissing and playing and tumbling were what two brothers did before they came to understand that, in fact, they weren't really relatives at all.

I don't recall what happened to Brutus, and I'm disinclined to ask my parents now, three decades later. But I know he was replaced at some point by another dog, a schnauzer bitch, shortly before my (real) brother, Eric, was born. And I do know my very first memory, my earliest recollection of being alive, was of her.

I was two years old, big enough to walk and big enough to graduate from a crib to my first "big boy" bed, a low mattress large enough to accommodate a wee lad and several of his favorite stuffed bears and lions and monkeys.

I remember this: My mother and I walked into my bedroom. (Where we had been previously I cannot say. Time did not begin for me until that very moment, as though the previous twenty-four months were merely a convenient fiction authored by my parents.) There, lying on my big boy bed, was Sheba, our newly acquired standard schnauzer. She had arranged herself into a crescent, a gray croissant of fur, with her muzzle tucked between her hind legs. I saw all around her a dark stain on my blue quilt, a widening circle of wetness. Had Sheba peed all over my big boy bed? Was she leaking?

I remember my mother gasping. Yet I sensed somehow she wasn't alarmed, only excited.

"Sheba!" my mom exclaimed.

And then, when Sheba raised her head to regard us, I saw what was lying in the center of the wetness, beneath her haunches: puppies! A whole pile of them!

"Oh, Sheba!" I heard my mom crying. And then to me: "Sheba had babies on your bed!"

I remember my mother cautioning me not to touch the fragile newborns just yet. But Mom allowed me to pet Sheba.

I swear Sheba looked at me from amid the moistness and quivering new life, and when I stroked her neck, she smiled at me.

* * *

Throughout my early boyhood our family had a succession of German shepherds, all of whom perished prematurely because of disease and whom I only vaguely remember. First there was Caesar, and then (a second) Brutus. (My family, I realize in hindsight, had a thing for Roman history.) I don't remember much about these animals except that they were black and tan and inexplicably frightening to strangers. Despite the pain of losing two magnificent dogs within a three-year span, my father wanted to get another German shepherd. After failing with Brutus the beagle and Sheba the schnauzer, Dad had finally gotten the knack of training dogs, particularly German shepherds—no more canine naughtiness in the Konik household!—and he came to realize that a well-behaved dog in our home was akin to having another member of the family, a son and a brother and a father confessor on four legs.

Dogs, I came to understand, were a requisite part of life, as essential as a roof above one's head and as inevitable as growing older. They were playmates and protectors, constant companions and an unpaid claque. You could do no wrong in a dog's eyes. No matter your failings as a father or son, no matter your faults of character, no matter your misdeeds and mistakes, you were still a hero to your dog.

A dog reminded everyone who lived with him that goodness was extant in the world, that redemption was available every time you walked through the front door.

Dogs helped teach me what love means.

Our next German shepherd, and the one who would accompany me through much of my boyhood in Fox Point, Wisconsin, was Mooshka, a big and regal beast with the eyes of a warrior and the temperament of your favorite uncle—the one whose inscrutable eccentricities make you love him all the more. Mooshka's great peculiarity was that he insisted on passing through the doorway between our kitchen and our dining room *backward.* He could be running at full gallop, but when he got to this one portal, he stopped abruptly, replaced his head with his rear end, and scurried through the entrance in reverse. I remember being fascinated not by the fact that our family dog had an unexplainable compulsion, but that he could swing himself around at such high speed, almost like a pirouette, and never bang his long muzzle on the doorjamb. In fact, one rainy day when I wasn't allowed to play outside, I called Mooshka back and forth between the kitchen and dining room to conduct a "scientific experiment." I discovered that no matter which direction he started from or at what speed he turned himself, the tip of his black nose always avoided a harmful collision with the wooden walls by less than an inch, as though our German shepherd were really part bat and navigated his way around the house by echolocation.

When he sat, he was nearly as tall as I, and significantly more imposing. I recall strangers clearing a wide path when we went on walks, unaware, I reckoned, that he was about the sweetest dog on the planet. Indeed, his name, "Mooshka," was supposed to be Polish, the language of my grandfather, for something noble and fierce. We subsequently learned, however, that whoever—I think it was a family friend—told us what *mooshka* meant had either committed a joke at our expense or was woefully unfamiliar with the finer shades of meaning in Eastern European languages. Our noble and fierce beast was actually named something like "little black speck."

Mooshka was the first real "people dog" I knew, the kind of canine who prefers the company of human beings to other dogs. Unlike our previous pets, he never ran away; he always wanted to be near me or my brother or my parents—so much so that he once followed my mom and me into the supermarket, having somehow extricated himself from the parked station wagon's half-open window. He found us in the frozen foods aisle, and trotted toward us with relief on his face, glad to have finally located his "lost" family.

At the time, the early 1970s, German shepherds were enjoying something akin to fashionableness in America; they were in vogue. I remember enjoying a series of British "young-adult" storybooks about German shepherds who worked as police dogs. (The author annoyingly referred to them as "Alsatians," but any kid who had a Mooshka at home could see from the illustrations that he meant "German shepherds.") I was proud that the brave breed that brought justice and peace to the world was somehow connected to sleepy suburban Wisconsin, where police dogs were needed about as much as dead-bolt locks and armed security guards. Sure, Mooshka preferred chasing squirrels to cornering bad guys, but still.

There was a Saturday morning kids' show on television called *Run, Joe, Run!,* a sort of canine version of *The Fugitive,* in which the hero, the eponymous German shepherd, had to elude an Inspector Javert-type nemesis, a mean old man who blamed lovable Joe for the mean old man's gimpy leg. Or something like that. Each week Joe would arrive in a town, perform various acts of heroism, profoundly touch myriad lives, and—just when some grateful little boy was adopting Joe as the bestest friend he ever had—the peripatetic Joe would be forced once more to hit the road, his evil pursuer sure to follow.

I came to understand the plot conceit of *Run, Joe, Run!* as a tidy allegory for the relationship between a boy and his dog. The dog quickly proves his sublime wonderfulness; you immediately fall in love with him; he soon must go.

Mooshka was epileptic, and eventually the pills our family forced down his throat no longer controlled his seizures, the onset of which I came to associate with the horrible sound of his claws maniacally scraping against the hardwood floors, vainly searching for balance and comfort. He would "awaken" from these episodes with foam around his black lips and a glazed, uncomprehending look in his brown eyes. I wanted so badly to somehow make him understand that he was still my good boy, my protector, my friend. But no amount of childhood adoration could cure my beautiful German shepherd. One day, when my dad was away on business, Mooshka's seizures occurred only minutes apart, putting him in a nearly constant state of agony.

He was five and I was maybe eleven. My mom and I drove Mooshka to the vet. And it was on that day that I became a man far sooner than I had planned.

My mother was too devastated to leave the car, so, in my father's absence, the awful deed was left to me. Even though the tears streamed down my face as I handed over my greatest pal to the vet, even though I was sure from the look in his eye that Mooshka was thankful I could bring him peace, even though the smells of antiseptic and the sounds of yelping filled my senses—I still spent the next few months utterly unconvinced that he was actually gone, as though I were in the grip of some sort of post-traumatic syndrome, a disbelieving fugue state. Previously, when Brutus and Sheba and Caesar and the other Brutus died, I was too young to fully comprehend the finality of the loss. Death was a theoretical concept.

Now I knew. I knew that no matter how much you loved a friend, a cherished member of the family, no matter how deeply you cared nor how passionately you expressed your devotion—and no matter how passionately they reciprocated—death would eventually take them away.

Which was why, I quickly learned, you had to love your dog (and everyone else you adored) with all your heart before it was time to say good-bye.

* * *

Our next dog, Max, was a collie, more beautiful in my bedazzled eyes than Lassie. He was shockingly clever—my dad had gotten really good at training our pets—and impossibly cute, and more loving and devoted than Tristan and Isolde. Max came to my baseball games. Max came to the outdoor skating rink. Max listened to my teenage angst. Max slept in the corner of my bedroom when I lost my virginity.

He was, as all dogs eventually grow to be, a real friend.

He died when I was away at college. My parents saved a lock of his splendid blond fur for me, and I made a collage with it, knowing that he, like all dogs, had lived far too briefly. Yet they never stop touching our lives with goodness, even when they've fetched their last ball or given their last wet kiss.

When my dad recovered from his heartbreak—and it took some time—he and my mother visited the local animal shelter. And just like in the movies, his eyes locked with the ugliest mutt in the joint, an Irish wolfhound/rottweiler mix with a shaggy beard and kinky fur and one misshapen back paw. And it was love at first sight.

Samson was my dad's new best friend.

He was also the smartest animal anyone had ever met, a dog who responded to spoken conversational English as though he were a literature student at Oxford. It was spooky: My father didn't give Sam commands. He merely spoke to him, as you would any other civilized guest in your home. "Sam," he would say, "would you mind excusing us while we eat dinner?" and off Sam would go, sighing heavily as he left the dining room. "Sam, please check to see who's at the door," and Samson would hop-skip-walk to the door, barking like a jackal if it was a stranger and wagging his tail happily if it was a friend. "Thank you," my dad would say. And Sam would make a little bow and return to the old man's side for his well-earned ear-scratching.

Never mind that Sam shed black hair everywhere, or that he smelled bad, or that he had the uncouth habit of licking his scrotum in front of polite company. He was the Greatest Dog Anyone Had Ever Seen. And he was a part of our family.

Shortly after my father rescued Samson, my brother Eric, living at the time in New Mexico, adopted a mean little cuss of a junkyard dog named Jerome, a chow/shepherd mix, who didn't listen, couldn't be trusted to stay on his property, and was so overwhelmingly lovable that nobody cared. The first time I met Jerome he growled at me until my brother told him I was all right. The second time I met him, he leaped through the open window of my car to kiss me—as I was *driving* twenty miles an hour down my brother's street. Wherever my brother went, Jerome accompanied him, witnessing Eric's marriage, the founding and building and selling of several wildly successful businesses, and the birth of his three children. Eric and Jerome were inseparable, the greatest of compatriots.

When Jerome died last year, at fourteen, my brother, gasping through his sobs, told me that Jerome never stopped looking into his eyes, finding a last moment of courage and contentment before departing. He wagged his tail at Eric one last time before he went.

Throughout my entire existence I have had dogs in my life. I've seen the joy they bring to life and the powerful emotions they inspire. I've watched my father find himself a best friend. I've watched my brother find himself a best friend.

I watched and I remembered, and all the time I wanted a best friend myself. Yet for much of my adult life I had to miss the inimitable pleasure of having a dog. I went to college in New York City, and after graduating I lived there for many years, and all the time I wanted badly to have a great dog. But I lived in Manhattan, in an apartment so small I had to run a string over my bed from wall to wall so I would have space to hang my clothes. I was young: I could endure whatever indignities the squalid metropolis might throw at me. But I wouldn't subject a dog—a big, full-size dog, like the German shepherds and collies my family had owned—to the cell-like prison conditions I gladly accepted. Instead, I rented dog movies like *The Incredible Journey* and bawled like a baby. Instead, I peered into the windows of pet stores, like a starving bum gazing hungrily upon a bakery's display cases. Instead, I made daily forays to Washington Square Park, where, sandwiched between the chess tables and the marijuana dealers, a civic-minded association of animal lovers had fenced off a miniature dog run. With naked longing on my face, I would pet and snuggle and kiss any dog who would let me, tarrying in the park until some of the more paranoid owners mistook me for a stalker. Indeed, it got to be that I couldn't walk down a block of New York sidewalk without imploring someone out for a stroll with their pooch if, you know, I could maybe possibly if they didn't mind, and if it wasn't too much trouble, well, could I pet their dog?

In twenty seconds or less, I'd try to explain to the owner my entire family history with dogs, the withdrawal symptoms I was suffering, why I didn't presently have a dog of my own, and so forth. As I began my monologue, heartless monsters with important things to do more or less bolted. Kind and compassionate souls didn't dash away. They walked quickly.

"I'm not dangerous!" I thought of calling out. "I just miss having a dog!"

Living in New York City helped remind me of all the things I loved about my bucolic childhood in the Midwest: the endless room to run between the forests and the lakes; yards and patios and porches; dogs.

I moved to Los Angeles ostensibly to take a job writing for a television show. But my real motivation—as all the Hollywood acting coaches might say—was to finally have a puppy to call my own.

My own best friend.

Ella at three months, with the author's parents

Chapter 1

Less than a week after arriving in Los Angeles, I was walking in Runyon Canyon, a nature preserve tucked into the Hollywood Hills, just a few blocks above the lurid electricity of Sunset Boulevard. I was in the canyon primarily for a vigorous weekend hike through unspoiled wilderness and, just as an afterthought, not because I was obsessed or anything, because I had heard that Runyon Canyon was always teeming with dogs. (And their owners, of course.) Which, in my admittedly peculiar view of the world, made it about the loveliest place on the entire planet to take a walk.

I was near the end of the loop, coming downhill on a onetime fire road, past the ruins of an old tennis court supposedly owned in the 1920s by the great Irish tenor John McCormack. It had been a fine hike. I'd seen red-tailed hawks circling the canyon, and wild mustard plants, and scampering lizards. And dogs—dozens of them. Golden retrievers and chocolate Labs and short-haired pointers, and all sorts of mongrels, and very many of them had let me pet them and nuzzle them and tell them how irresistibly beautiful they were.

I was in a joyous mood because my dad was scheduled to visit my new home in less than a week, and when he arrived we planned to visit the local shelter, where he would help me select my very first Dog of My Own. The house I was renting had a big backyard filled with fruit trees, rosebushes, and, in what I took to be a very promising sign, an old-fashioned wooden doghouse, just like Snoopy's. And in just a few days more, I suspected it might have a new four-legged tenant.

As I trundled down the path, marveling at so much wilderness hidden within a bustling city, I saw in the distance another pair of dogs, a big one and a little one, accompanied by their owner and coming my way. As I approached the trio, I could see that the larger dog was an all-black German shepherd, with a dazzlingly shiny coat. The smaller one appeared to be an all-white Jack Russell terrier, with a longer-than-usual tail. Neither dog was on a leash, but when their owner stopped walking, the big black one immediately sat at his master's heel. A few seconds later, the little white one sat down too, as though he were imitating his big brother.

I attempted my usual opening gambit. "Beautiful dogs you have," I said to the owner, a handsome and athletic man in his thirties.

"Oh, thanks," he said, smiling.

Without hesitation, I moved to close the deal. "May I pet them?"

"Sure," the man said. "Go ahead."

"Hello!" I said to the shepherd. And in classic anthropomorphic style I asked, "What's your name?"

His owner spoke for him, as often happens in these cases. "His name is Darryl."

I stroked Darryl behind his ears and told his master how many German shepherds had been part of my family as I was growing up. The man politely feigned interest.

I noticed then that no matter what Darryl did, the little white Jack Russell did too. If Darryl stood, so did the terrier. If Darryl presented his butt for scratching, so did the little white one. If Darryl became entranced by something rustling in a nearby tree, so did his diminutive buddy.

"They're very cute," I said, which is what I found myself always saying when I spent quality petting time with dogs. But I really meant it. "This little white guy. He's adorable!"

"You like her?" the man said.

"I mean *she*. She's adorable. She's so *white*. And what a face! Look at those eyes!" I caught myself degenerating into goo-goo-ga-ga baby talk. "You're so cute! You're so sweet. Yes, yes, yes, yes, yes, yes, yes!"

"You like her?" the man asked again.

"Oh, she's spectacular," I said, accepting a sloppy kiss from her across my nose.

"Well," he said nonchalantly, "do you want her?"

"What do you mean?" I said, puzzled.

"I've been looking for a home for her," he told me.

"You're giving her up?" I asked, incredulous. "She seems so—I mean, she's—oh, she's just—she's great."

"I just found her two days ago," he said. "Behind the doughnut shop over on La Brea. I figured I would bring her here, to the canyon, before I took her to the pound. You know, I figured some dog lover might want to adopt a nice puppy."

I looked at the abandoned dog, the all-white Jack Russell. And then I realized she wasn't a full-grown terrier at all. She was a puppy! Her paws were slightly too big for her body, and when I looked carefully, I could see that she still needed to grow into her ribs. "How old is she?" I wondered aloud.

"The vet says she's probably three months or less," her savior reported. "And she's basically healthy. Has all her shots and everything."

"And very well behaved," I noted. "You're so good! What a good doggie!"

"Oh, yeah! I mean, everything Darryl does she imitates. Very smart."

I asked him what kind of dog she was, if not a Jack.

"The vet told me she's a mix between white Lab and greyhound. But unless you meet the parents, I guess we'll never know exactly." As he spoke, the puppy looked up toward him, as though she understood she was being talked about. He knelt down and patted her on the head. "Good girl, Bogey." She panted as he stroked her neck. "I've been calling her 'Bogey.' But only for a couple of days. I'm sure you could call her something else if you wanted."

I knelt down on one knee, closer to her level. And just as my dad had taught me, I tested her reaction to my hand moving near her face, to see if she had been hit and taught to fear.

She didn't flinch. She licked my palm.

"Well, she doesn't appear to have been abused," I said.

"No, no, she hasn't been a stray or anything. This young girl who works at the doughnut shop has been taking care of her since she was born. But the girl's, like, fourteen, and she can't handle the responsibility. So, anyway, I just figured I would try here before she got put in the shelter, because, you know, there's no telling what might happen to her there."

I looked into the little white mutt's eyes. Without being instructed, she sat down. I leaned in close to her muzzle, close enough to see her blond eyelashes and smell her soft odor, that comfortingly pleasant smell of puppies. She wiggled her butt and cocked her head.

I said to her softly, "Hello, beautiful puppy. Are you looking for a home?"

And just then she let out a gentle bark, an excited yelp, and began to lick my neck.

"I think it's love," her rescuer said, laughing.

I wiped a tear from my eye and said, "Yes, I think it is."

Four hours later, after a breathless phone call to my daddy and an inspection of my house and yard by the rescued dog's savior, the little white puppy had a new home.

And that's how on July 1, 1994, Ella Guinevere Konik came into my life.

* * *

Ella Konik has had a good life. She's hiked through Wyoming's Absaroka Mountains in the company of llamas. She's chased squirrels through Stanley Park in Vancouver, British Columbia. She's dug deep holes in the wet sand of Venice Beach, California.

And she's loved and been loved by hundreds of people, many of whom say their life was changed when they made the acquaintance of this remarkable mutt.

Ella has kissed celebrities. She's been photographed for several magazine stories. She's been mistaken for a purebred show dog, a movie dog, and a rare and exotic and expensive possession—and all the while she's simply gone on being my mutt. And my best friend.

Ella has been welcomed into the lobby of my bank and the patio of the local Brazilian restaurant and the aesthetically bleak aisles of the nearby video store. She's voted with me (usually for the Libertarian candidate). And trained with me for the Los Angeles marathon. And revisited Runyon Canyon hundreds (thousands?) of times, never tiring of the infinite smells and sounds and inspiring places to pee.

She's waited patiently outside the supermarket and the copy store and the take-out Thai joint, since those unenlightened places have never welcomed her in as they would any other refined and well-mannered lady.

Ella has licked away my tears when I've been sad, and hopped on her hind legs with me when I've been happy, and snuggled me when I've been lonely.

Once, in the midst of my being divorced, Ella and I were involuntarily kept apart for nearly six months. I was allowed to talk with her on the phone and get reassuring weekly reports that she was "all right" without her daddy. But I knew that Ella had to be suffering. I surely was. It was agony—really, a physical pain in my gut—to not have her brilliant white fur on my clothes, her expressive ears and tail talking to me, her paws clicking on the floor. When the lawyers and the ex finally decided that Ella and I could be reunited, we met again at Runyon Canyon, not far from where I first saw her as a puppy.

I climbed the hill from my house, knowing that each step was bringing me closer to the friend I had missed for nearly half a year, the one constant source of joy in my life. When I got to the end of the street, where the park officially begins, I could see Ella sniffing the wild grass up a small hill, maybe fifty yards away. Her back was to me, but she was just as I imagined she would be, only whiter and prettier and more filled with life.

I didn't have to call her. She knew I was near.

And when Ella turned and saw me standing at the bottom of the hill, my hands outstretched toward her, she broke into a sprint, yelping and crying as she ran. I knelt down to receive my precious mutt, and she nearly knocked me over as she jumped into my arms, kissing and whimpering and entangling herself between my legs in a crazy figure-eight pattern. I cried very hard then, relieved that the darkest months of my life were finished and knowing that my future would be bright, filled with her sunny companionship. My marriage was over, but my friendship with Ella would continue forever. While the grief of losing my wife would linger for years, the salutary balm of Ella's love would make unbearable pains bearable.

Like most dogs, Ella has given me far more than I could ever give her. Yes, she's always been well fed and well loved, and in her owner's weaker moments she's been allowed to sleep on the goose-down living room couch. But there have been far too many times in my life when I've had to go places that weren't civilized enough to welcome her, times I've been forced to leave her behind to "guard the house," times she's surely felt abandoned by her supposed best friend.

I know she's probably thought something like: "How come I *always* want to be with him, yet he apparently doesn't always want to be with me?"

The truth is I almost always *do* want to be with her, especially as she grows older and our finite time together gets shorter with each sunset. But the land I live in, the greatest country in the world (and I mean that sincerely, without any sarcasm at all), does not feel about my magnificent friend as I do. To me she is a lady: elegant, smart, and endlessly amusing. To American society she's just a dog. A pretty dog, sure. But not the kind of "lady" you'd welcome into a department store or a restaurant or a library or on a golf course or at a bowling alley or a movie theater. Ill-mannered children and their obnoxious parents—come one, come all. But a dog? A *dog*? Even a perfectly behaved, astonishingly smart, ridiculously charming dog? Forbidden.

Now, this sorry state of affairs—attributable in no small part, I would reckon, to our friends The Lawyers—makes me angry, just as any injustice makes me angry. But it makes me sad too. Because I fear Ella mistakes my willingness to humbly abide by society's laws as a tacit rejection of her fabulous company. I wish I could explain to her that, despite how it appears, I'd like nothing more than to take her to play golf with me. Or to do grocery shopping. Or see a matinee screening of *My Dog Skip*. But even Ella's enormous (for a dog) vocabulary doesn't allow her to comprehend abstract concepts. She doesn't understand that good intentions do not mitigate painful results. To Ella, Daddy leaving her behind as he goes on with his life does not mean Daddy is flummoxed by a society that does not share his enthusiasm for canine companionship. It means Daddy is abandoning his alleged best pal.

Since dogs probably don't understand the concept of time—at least not in the way human beings do—when I leave our house, Ella assumes I've left her forever, that I'm never returning. This is why she goes berserk with joy when I return home—whether I've been gone three weeks or three hours. To her it's all the same absolute: Either she's with her friend or she's not. One state of affairs is good. One is bad. And every time I'm forced to create badness in her otherwise blissful life, I feel rotten. (And she knows it. When I leave without her, Ella hangs her head and refuses to look at me as I remind her how much I love her.) For an animal who is used to having her favorite companion near her far more than the average dog—I work out of a home office in which Ella has her own bolster bed in the corner—my absences sting more painfully.

Sometimes I look at Ella napping near my desk, or playing gently with her brother Sammy the cat (who likes to nibble on Ella's ears while Ella sniffs his nether regions), or having a sunbath in the garden while birds and squirrels play in the tree canopy above her. I look at her and know that she has had a happy life, a good life. She's enjoyed being a dog, and most of all she's enjoyed being my friend.

But probably not nearly as much as I've enjoyed being hers.

I see her slowing, evolving from a hyperactive pup to an

energetic adult, to an increasingly tired old lady. She's eleven now. Being a big dog—seventy-three pounds of lean muscle—she's probably entering the last years of her life. Someday far too soon I know I'll have to say good-bye to her.

Until that horrible moment, I want her life to be filled with adventure and pleasure, peace and contentment, companionship and comfort. I want her to know that she truly has been a good girl all these years. And that I love her.

I want her to know not only in words—of which she has a limited understanding—but in actions, which she comprehends completely, that I appreciate the light she has brought into my time on this planet.

I want Ella to know I'm thankful to have been her friend.

Ella proudly wearing her therapy-dog vest

Chapter 2

The most common reaction Ella elicits from strangers is unrestrained glee. Like a master comedian who needs only arch an eyebrow or cock his head to induce laughter, her mere presence produces smiles from people who might otherwise be having a bad day.

Old men strolling through our neighborhood with their grandchildren pause to pat her head and coo at her in Russian. Slacker Hollywood dudes with tattoos and facial pierces interrupt their cataloging of the world into things that are "cool" and things that "suck" to scratch Ella's butt. And aspiring actress babes who normally would try mightily not to acknowledge my presence, lest they somehow dilute their marketable allure by talking with someone who isn't a producer-agent-director-manager or a member of an indie-label rock band, drop all pretense of distant unattainableness and profess to me that my dog is the most gorgeous-cute-adorable-sweet-precious thing they've *ever* seen. (My single male friends, who frequently borrow her for walks, refer to Ella as the Ultimate Chick Magnet.) Like one of the world's great religions, Ella brings solace and happiness into people's lives—and the only holy wars she proclaims are upon the backyard rodents. She's blessed, like so many dogs, with the capacity for creating joy in this world.

One day I was listening to a recording of the great Depression-era entertainer Ted Lewis, whose bouncy signature song—"Is Everybody Happy?"—was at the time of its conception a palliative pick-me-up first and a musical number second. Here was a guy endeavoring with all his strength to "bring a little sunshine" into an otherwise gloomy time. Old Dr. Lewis had a prescription: Cheer up; life ain't so bad! (Even if you *had* lost everything in the stock market crash.) And it seemed to work for millions of dour Americans, not to mention me seventy years later. I noticed concurrently that my mutt Ella was a lot like Ted Lewis—although she didn't play the clarinet and repeatedly utter the phrase "Yes, sir!" she was adept at spreading around a little homemade sunshine.

Whenever we would run an errand, go for a hike, or loiter in the front yard, she effortlessly—and, to my mind, magically—had this salutary effect on people. After a lifetime of witnessing her good works, I eventually had an idea. Ella (and her dad) could be spreading joy to people who really needed it, not just random strangers. (It only took me about eight years to make this realization; I was a little slow on this one.) We could take "Ella in Concert" to people who couldn't otherwise attend my mutt's impromptu performances.

I had read about dogs that participated in "animal therapy," visiting hospitals and nursing homes and children's shelters, providing needy patients with health benefits as profound as rediscovering lost motor skills or as simple as inspiring a grin. Ella, it seemed to me, would be a perfect candidate for such noble service.

Researching the subject via Internet, I discovered that being an animal therapy dog wasn't as simple as just showing up at a hospital and being cute. Dogs—and their human handlers—needed to be certified by an accredited organization, which insured the animals, arranged visits, and generally promoted the cause of animal-assisted therapy. This certification involved attending workshops, passing a home study course, and successfully completing a fifteen-task behavioral test.

When I went to an orientation session at Create-a-Smile, the Santa Monica–based nonprofit group that oversees therapy animals in the Los Angeles area, I learned that Ella would be a perfect candidate for their program. Except for one thing: I didn't think there was the slightest possibility that she could pass the behavioral test.

Fourteen of the fifteen tasks would be easy for her. But the other one—socializing comfortably with other therapy animals—would be impossible.

Ella, like every tragic hero, has a flaw, a defect that mars her otherwise perfect character. She's very mean to other dogs.

People? Nice as can be. Babies, children, boys, girls, men, women—couldn't be sweeter. But dogs? Well, if they stay off her territory and far, far away from her dad, she'll ignore them. But if they come close to her garden or, even worse, within a few yards of me, Ella gets insanely aggressive.

It's only with me. I suspect she thinks she's "protecting" her owner from interlopers who might disrupt our pack. Or maybe she's just a jealous bitch.

Several years ago I rescued a stray mutt who was wandering the neighborhood tired and hungry. To Ella's chagrin, I welcomed this fellow into our home and named him Louis. It was not a duet she appreciated. Used to monopolizing my attention, Ella was furious that she was now being asked to share everything—her water bowl, her food, her dad's affection. And in the language of canines, whose vocabulary includes hackle-raising and fang-baring, she suggested to Louis that she did not consider their relationship "A Fine Romance." If she had her way she would propose "Let's Call the Whole Thing Off."

Ella shed no tears when Louis departed our home a few months after he arrived. In fact, when he left for another owner, her demeanor noticeably brightened. But she became permanently unpleasant to other dogs, fearful that any one of them might be the next unwanted intruder on her sovereign turf.

When I posed the quandary to my father, who knew all the tricks to get a dog to behave properly, he suggested a kind of immersion therapy in which I was supposed to take Ella to Runyon Canyon every day and force her to socialize with all sorts of strange dogs—and every time she snarled, growled, or snapped, I was supposed to impress upon her the extreme badness of her conduct. That training method lasted exactly one day. No matter how much I scolded and cajoled and punished, Ella resolutely refused to get the message. In fact, she seemed to be sending a message to me: "Accept me as I am, pal. I'm not going to change."

Damn that infernal unconditional love! I brought her home from the canyon, muttering all the while how she could never be a certified therapy animal with her rotten attitude. She wagged her tail at me.

Like most people who play the game of golf, I'm an optimist at heart even when my optimism is entirely unwarranted. (Unless you're a dedicated masochist, you can't play golf unless you retain some hope, no matter how slim, that it's all eventually going to get a wee bit better.) I convinced myself that though Ella and I would surely fail the behavior test, our otherwise kind dispositions would somehow earn us a waiver into the animal therapy program and we would redeem ourselves with good works and cheerfulness. Or a variation on that theme.

So I went ahead and did the home study course and attended the boring workshops and signed up to take the test—reminding the poor receptionist who was booking the appointment that Ella was actually a really very nice and sweet dog who made many people smile and whose lifetime of unintentional charity should somehow be rewarded by a passing grade even if she did, you know, sometimes sort of act toward other dogs as though she were Cujo.

The Thursday morning we were scheduled to be evaluated at the Create-a-Smile headquarters, Ella nearly propelled herself through the antique iron fence that surrounds our front yard in an attempt to express her displeasure at a great Dane who had the gall to walk on the sidewalk in front of our home. My optimism was waning.

When we arrived in Santa Monica, the first thing the evaluator, Daniella, asked me was "How's Ella with other animals?"

"Well," I said, trying to come up with the right phrase that wasn't exactly a lie. "She's . . ."

"Because we have a lot of cats here," Daniella explained. "Is she all right with cats?"

"Oh, she's great with cats! She lives with a cat. No problem whatsoever with cats!"

"Good. So everything should go smoothly."

"Right," I said, swallowing hard.

We cruised through the first bunch of exercises. Sitting, staying, lying down—this was child's play for Ella. Heeling, walking through a crowd, remaining in place despite loud noises—easy for an old pro like her. Rough petting, ignoring a misplaced dog cookie, being approached by someone on crutches—all part of Ella's standard repertoire.

Then, while Ella was demonstrating her ability to stay for two minutes on one side of the room while I waited on the other, Daniella said to me, "She's doing great. After this I'll go get Doctor Buddha, my pug, and we'll finish up."

"We're ready," I said perkily, hoping that Buddha's small stature would somehow present less of a threat to Ella's seventy-three-pound ego. Maybe my mutt would understand that the good Doctor wasn't going to come home with us because he was a purebred and we were a home of mongrels. Maybe Daniella would interpret Ella's patented lip peel, in which she steadily drew back her jowls to expose her incisors, as a smile. Maybe the Mohawk of hair down her spine would seem to our evaluator an innovative new doggie coiffure.

When Daniella left the room, I knelt on one knee and put my lips near Ella's peach-tipped ear. "Listen," I told her. "This is really important. I'm begging you: Please be nice to this other dog. I really need you to be a good girl now. Please, Ella. Please be a good girl for me."

Ella's brown eyes met mine and she licked my chin. I didn't

know if that meant "Okay, just this once," or that I was excreting tasty nervous perspiration.

Daniella returned with Doctor Buddha, who panted and gasped in that peculiar pug fashion, as though he had emphysema. He was on a leash, but he never left Daniella's heel, and he seemed only perfunctorily interested in the presence of a huge white Lab-greyhound beast in his playroom.

Ella sat at my side, feigning aloofness.

Daniella and Buddha walked toward us and stopped two feet away. "Hello!" Daniella said, extending her hand. "I'm Daniella, and this is my dog, Doctor Buddha."

"Hello!" I said, shaking her hand. "My name's Michael, and this," I said, looking cautiously at the impending disaster sitting beside me, "is my dog, Ella."

Ella looked straight ahead, still as a portrait model. Buddha looked up at her; she glanced down at him. I felt as though I were standing between two gunslingers waiting for the other guy to blink.

"Good," Daniella said. "We'll just stand here chatting for a little while and see what happens."

"Sure," I said, watching the clock on the wall behind her as though I were holding my breath underwater.

Doctor Buddha sat and panted, pausing once to investigate an itch near his butt. Ella watched, outwardly placid as a high-stakes poker player.

I took great care to focus my gaze on Daniella, and not the other dog—a self-preservation technique I've learned from walking around Hollywood with a former girlfriend. It seemed to work well with Ella too. She was convinced—or agreed to play along—that I had eyes for no one but her, that the panting pug sitting two feet from her powerful jaws represented nothing but a potentially interesting new thing to sniff.

"Wow. She's *really* good," Daniella commented. "I'm impressed."

"Me too," I thought out loud.

"That went well." Daniella extended her hand again. "Nice to meet you. We're going to go now. Bye, Ella!"

"Good-bye, Daniella. Bye, Buddha. See you soon!" I watched them walk out of the room.

I turned to look at Ella. She smiled at me.

"Thank you! Oh, God, you are so good. What a good girl! I am so proud of you." I felt like I might giggle, so I stopped gushing, fearful we might get downgraded for emotional instability. Ella wagged her tail and accepted a behind-the-ear scratch.

Daniella returned from her office clutching papers, sans Doctor B. "Congratulations," she said, "you guys passed. Great job. You're now an animal-assisted therapy team. Both of you did very well."

I knelt down and hugged my mutt. "Way to go, partner."

Ella licked my face from chin to forehead. "We did it," I whispered to her.

And by the way she was licking my cheeks up and down, you would have sworn Ella Konik was nodding and saying, "Yes, we did!"

* * *

Being all white, Ella looks good in almost any color. She has a collection of bandannas that she wears as scarves, including a fetching leopard-spot number that matches her eyes and lips, an American flag motif that expresses her patriotism, and a menagerie of solid colors that match the schemes of whatever sports team her daddy happens to be rooting for on a particular day. But I thought her new red service vest was especially flattering on her—and even more so with her title embroidered across the back and an "I Work for Hugs and Kisses" patch sewn onto one of the side pockets.

After getting certified, I acquired all the accoutrements an animal therapy team needs to look and feel its best: official Create-a-Smile T-shirts; laminated identification cards (featuring Ella sitting on my lap); and, of course, the red therapy-dog vest, which made my mutt look very much like a professional guide dog or a waiter in a schlocky Italian restaurant.

After an orientation visit to observe an experienced therapy team, Ella and I were on our way to our first solo assignment at a Westwood nursing home optimistically called the Country Villa, despite its proximity to a Santa Monica Boulevard gas station and industrial furniture outlet. I was more nervous than she. Our training had covered nearly every circumstance that could arise, every catastrophe that could occur, and I was supposed to know how to handle all of them. But I wondered if all this joy-spreading business was worth all the anxiety. Ella, I figured in a moment of panic, probably would prefer to be playing in her backyard, spying on tightrope-walking squirrels.

Then I looked at her in the backseat of my car, wearing her official red vest, looking preposterously cute, and I couldn't help grinning.

Making people smile, I decided then, was definitely worth the trouble.

When we arrived at the Country Villa, I realized that much of my angst wasn't about Ella. It was about me.

I have, among other quirks, a profound fear of death and decay, of mortality and decline. Places like hospitals and nursing homes scare and depress me, possibly more than they do the average sensitive type. As far as sites go, they're not my first choice at which to do volunteer work. But I knew that they're also the places that most need a dose of canine happiness.

When Ella and I first walked up the stairs and into the facility, we were confronted with the Boschian specter of badly disabled septuagenarians, many of them in obvious states of dementia, sprawled across mobile hospital beds and wheelchairs, staring into the distance, searching for their memories. I felt a wave of panic. Ella, though, regarded these people as a group of potentially affectionate human beings who might be fun to visit—which, I realized, was probably how they would like to be regarded if neurotic young men could be as egalitarian and kind as a ten-year-old dog.

"Thanks for being here with me," I said to Ella, who was preoccupied with sniffing the Country Villa's carpeting.

The activity coordinator, a smiling Filipino man, greeted us near the entrance and invited us to wander the hallways, popping into rooms with open doors. He didn't think we needed an escort or supervision. "Everyone will be happy to see you," he promised.

I adjusted Ella's red vest and checked her collar, and then I took a deep breath. "Okay, old girl. Let's go meet some new people."

In less than a minute, I knew we were doing a good thing.

The first patient we encountered was parked outside his

room, propped upright on a wheeled gurney. His mouth was frozen agape, probably from a stroke, and his arms dangled at his side, paralyzed. He was bald and pale, and his blue eyes were rheumy. He did not look happy.

Ella and I approached the side of his bed, and just as the Create-a-Smile people had trained me, I cheerfully exclaimed, "Hello! I'm Michael, and this is my dog, Ella. She's very friendly and loves to meet new people. Would you like to say hello to her?"

The man's eyes moved infinitesimally in my direction, but he didn't move.

"Oh, Dick doesn't talk much," a uniformed nurse said, coming out of Dick's bedroom. "Do you like the doggie, Dick? She's very nice."

"This is Ella," I said.

"Can I pet her?" the nurse asked.

"Of course!"

The nurse knelt down and stroked Ella's back while I stood beside her. Ella seemed unusually calm.

We exchanged the usual pleasantries about my dog—what breed, how old, how long have I had her, how did she get trained—and then the nurse took Dick's left hand in hers and rested it upon the top of Ella's head, slowly moving Dick's palm back and forth across Ella's brow.

He didn't move. But when the nurse removed Dick's hand from Ella's soft fur, I saw something change in his eyes, as though a flicker of recognition and light had pierced the murkiness. "Nice dog," he croaked.

The nurse gasped. "Dick!" She replaced his hand. And to me she said, "He almost never talks!"

"Wow," I said, stunned.

The nurse cooed to Dick, "Do you like the doggie? She's nice, isn't she, Dick?"

Dick never moved. But the smile he couldn't form with his mouth flashed in his eyes.

"You're a good girl, Ella," I told her. "You're a very good girl."

She looked up at me with a face that said "I know."

Indeed, Ella displayed a calm confidence, an assurance in this unfamiliar environment that I found oddly inspiring, as though she were trying to impart a lesson her companion needed to learn. When we encountered a manic woman in a wheelchair, who was orating in a language of her own invention that included bits of English, Spanish, French, and possibly Latin—I picked up a few references to Satan and the number 666—I was momentarily nonplussed, and more than a little concerned. The woman seemed, well, crazy, and perhaps prone to upsetting outbursts. I looked to my mutt. As the babbler wheeled past, Ella sat calmly at my side and barely twitched an eyebrow.

We spent the rest of our hour at Country Villa meeting residents like Dahlia, a 102-year-old dog lover who accepted Ella's kisses on her hands as though they were a magic arthritis balm. We met Leonard, who was so overjoyed by Ella's visit that he occasionally broke into silent sobs. (First I thought he was laughing; then I thought Ella might have somehow hurt him; finally I realized that Leonard's emotions were as mysterious to him as they were to those of us not employing wheelchairs.) And we had the great pleasure of chatting with Mr. Strauss, who confessed he couldn't possibly remember my or Ella's name, but who, nonetheless, could still play virtually every Chopin nocturne and Beethoven sonata from memory—and proved it on a portable electronic keyboard he kept beside his bed. We sang "Someone to Watch Over Me" together while Ella, by now immune to her daddy's warblings, reclined at Mr. Strauss's side. "She's a sweetheart," he said. "I hope you'll come back again soon with her. I'm sorry—what's your name again?"

Before we departed, one of the nurses asked if we might look in on Johnny, who, she whispered, was "not doing very well."

I was not prepared for Johnny's condition. He appeared to be a man in his forties who had somehow aged into an octogenarian. His face resembled a concentration camp victim's, so sunken were his cheeks and so drawn his skin. Indeed, his entire body, tucked into a hospital bed, was not much larger than Ella's.

"He's got cirrhosis of the liver," the nurse informed me. "He's in bad shape."

I looked to Ella for comfort and steeled my nerves. "Hello, Johnny!" I said, cheerfully as I could muster. "My name's Michael, and this is my dog, Ella. Would you like to meet her?"

He screwed up his brow, apparently in great pain.

"Johnny loves dogs," the nurse said, stroking his bony shoulder. "Don't you, Johnny?"

Johnny moaned.

I positioned Ella beside his bed. "Would you like to pet her, Johnny? She loves being petted."

Johnny nodded slowly and moaned again.

"He has trouble moving his hands," the nurse explained.

I remembered from my training a technique employed by highly experienced animal-assisted therapy teams. Although it was our first day in the field, I knew Ella could do it and that somehow she'd be happy to have met the challenge.

"If you'd like," I said to Johnny and his nurse, "Ella can get in bed."

"Oh! Well!" the nurse exclaimed, looking at my seventy-three-pound partner. "Would you like that, Johnny?"

He nodded slowly and moaned.

"Okay. Sure," she said.

I traced my hands over the sheets, feeling the outline of Johnny's withered frame underneath the fabric, clearly delineating where his legs and torso stopped and where open space began. "Do you want to pet the doggie, Johnny?" his nurse implored.

Johnny screwed up his brow, evidently in great discomfort, and squeezed out the word "yes."

I led Ella to the foot of the bed, keeping one of my arms between her and Johnny's frail appendages. "Okay, Ella," I said, tapping the mattress. "Get up!"

In one powerful bound, she leapt onto the bed.

At home, when Ella comes to bed she normally circles herself two or three times in that peculiar canine fashion, making a nest among the comforter and blanket. On this day, somehow sensing the delicacy of the circumstances, she reclined immediately, directly at Johnny's side.

"What a good girl," I reassured her. And then, without any bidding, Ella gently placed her muzzle across Johnny's torso, beside his hands.

His brow unfurled momentarily and he stroked her white neck with his knuckles and his wrists. Ella sighed.

"You like that, Johnny?" his nurse asked. "You like the doggie?"

Johnny nodded and closed his eyes, resting his hands upon Ella's warm fur. A certain peace enveloped him, and his breath seemed to slow.

The nurse and I watched them rest together, and I felt like a very proud papa.

When it was time to let Johnny have his nap, I asked Ella to stand straight up, and then, cradling her under her butt and her shoulders, I carefully lifted her down to the ground, where she gave a prodigious full-body waggle, the kind that usually accompanies my announcement that we're going on a walk.

"Good-bye, Johnny," I said, knowing this probably would be the last time I would see him. "I'm very glad we got to visit with you."

Johnny took a few labored breaths and said, "Thank you."

When we said our farewells to all the residents of the Country Villa and arrived at the parking lot, I threw my arms around Ella and finally let myself cry. As I removed her vest and her collar, leaving her in her natural "naked" state, impossibly white and irresistibly pettable, I said to Ella, "You were great today, old lady."

Ella licked my chin and wagged her tail, and I got the feeling that she knew she'd done what my late grandma would have called a mitzvah, a simple act of kindness, even if she couldn't quite define in human language what that word meant.

* * *

Once or twice a week, Ella and I visited nursing homes and hospitals, battered women's shelters, and abused children's sanctuaries—anyplace where joy was usually a rare commodity. Allowing dozens of strangers to pet and pat and poke her, Ella dutifully visited human beings in need—even when she probably preferred to be in Runyon Canyon, sniffing old urine markings in the dirt.

One morning we went to a clinic in Culver City that treated Alzheimer's patients. There, in a community activity room, Ella performed some of her best tricks: playing "dead" until I told her that some guy with a net (the dogcatcher) was going to lock her up in the pound, at which point she awoke from her coma and jumped up into my lap; refusing to eat a dog cookie I proffered as "junk food" but gobbling it up when I assured her it was "healthy food"; demonstrating the difference between her right paw and her left, and then taking a bow. The patients adored her, and seemed to understand everything Ella did; indeed, they asked to see her tricks again. And again. And again—until I figured out that they were not so much impressed with Ella's antics as they were unaware that they had made the same request five minutes earlier. (Ella didn't mind. She got extra cookies.) When I offered a soft-bristle brush to one smiling lady, hoping she would enjoy helping me "groom" Ella (an animal therapy technique that encourages fine motor skills and the completion of a goal), she nodded vigorously and began to style the silver hair of the perplexed gentleman sitting next to her.

Working with the elderly and the confused, Ella (and I) became accustomed to repetition. Repetition of questions (How old is she? What kind of dog is she? How long have you had her? Is she nice?), repetition of activities (petting, grooming, kissing), and repetition of troubling visages (disfigured limbs, damaged skin, demented faces). Confronting unwell people every week was much harder on me than on Ella. I found it exhausting to remain upbeat and positive while surrounded by so much misery. Ella never seemed perturbed. She seemed to find it comforting and reassuring to have a weekly visitation routine, even if the strangers we were encountering were unlike the people she was used to playing with back home.

I think she came to understand that when I brought out her red therapy-dog vest it meant we were going to work, and that work required her best behavior and most serene temperament. Usually, any journey outside our front door, whether to the dry cleaner around the corner or for a bike ride into the hills, inspires in Ella the kind of jiggling paroxysms generally seen in pubescent girls at a Justin Timberlake concert. But when it was time to leave the house to be a therapy dog, Ella seemed to understand that unrestrained exuberance wasn't appropriate. She seemed to know it was time to be a lady.

Her placid demeanor was put to a stern test one week when we visited a facility (hereafter referred to by the acronym ECF) that provides day care for severely developmentally disabled adults, people society used to refer to as "retarded." Populated by dozens of men and women with Down syndrome and other maladies, the ECF campus, near downtown Los Angeles, provides supervised activities such as personal grooming, games, and art to fill the days of citizens who otherwise cannot function in society. Nonetheless, to a visitor who has been conditioned by decades of media exposure to produce a relatively narrow definition of physical beauty and normalcy, a place like the ECF can be frightening in the magnitude of its Dickensian institutional suffering. Many of the clients had simian features and were no larger than an elementary-school child. Many of them had severe dental problems and lacked oral communication skills. And many of them had vision problems and weight problems and, not the least of it, severe emotional traumas that someone like me could never fully understand. Despite the therapeutic activities the ECF staff had arranged for the clients, many of them spent their days staring uncomprehendingly into space, mute and seemingly present in body only.

Into this horrific atmosphere entered Ella Guinevere Konik.

Even as her dad struggled with the shroud of sadness that threatened to envelop his heart, she did what she knew she ought to do: bring some joy, regardless of how fleeting or permanent, into the life of everyone who seeks it, no matter what they look like or how they scream or any other irrelevancy that distracts us from the essential truth that dogs seem to know—that every human being has a soul, and every soul needs some sunshine.

We visited every client of ECF that day, all 118 of them. One man, Alex, appointed himself Ella's official leash-holder. Another fellow, Claudio, whom the staff claimed had not previously interacted with his peers, took great care to instruct every new person we encountered how to "properly" pet Ella's back. (It involved stroking in a certain direction and pattern of his choosing.) And one high-energy woman, Linda, who inexplicably vacillated between screams of exuberant pleasure and abject agony, made sure Ella got a fresh hug around her neck every five minutes.

At one point, Ella was in the "senior center," where ECF's

older clients congregated. At the behest of their counselor, the entire group—about a dozen—swarmed around Ella in a tight semicircle, alternately laughing and crying at her, chanting phrases I could not decipher. I looked to my mutt for signs of distress—nervous panting and tail-wagging, hair-raising, pinning her ears back—but she looked as regal and calm as a grand dame taking her seat at the opening night of the opera. These were people, after all. And though they were misshapen and monstrous to the prejudiced eyes of someone like me, to Ella they were simply another group of two-legged creatures who wanted to touch her and talk to her and maybe play a game with her, just like every other two-legged creature she had ever met. That was her mission, wasn't it? To be the locus of attention, the furry outlet for the human impulse to express affection and feel sensual pleasure. She was just doing her job, and doing it without the bigotry and judgmentalism that infect so much of our human intercourse.

As Ella sat at the center of this crowd of observers, a little man named Rodney emerged from the pack with his arm extended and a huge grin on his face.

"You want to pet the dog, Rodney?" his counselor asked.

Rodney nodded vigorously and lumbered toward Ella on increasingly unsteady legs.

"Watch out, Rodney!" his counselor warned, moments before Rodney tumbled sideways.

He crashed on the floor inches from Ella's feet and tail.

She never moved.

Instead, as Rodney struggled to his knees and threw his arms around Ella's broad shoulders for support, she served as an anchor to which Rodney could attach himself and regain his equilibrium.

Once righted, Rodney hugged Ella for a long and loving time.

I scratched behind one of her ears and looked her in the eye. "You're so good, Ella," I whispered to her. "I love you."

And I decided then that my therapy dog, my inspiring teacher—my friend—deserved a reward, however small and inconsequential when measured against a life spent bringing happiness to all she meets. She should have more than dog cookies and extended fetch-the-ball sessions. I decided then that Ella should, if only temporarily, experience the world not as a hairy beast but as an elegant lady.

I watched her accept Rodney hanging around her neck and Alex pulling her leash and Linda screaming in her face and all the rest of the mystifying strangers surrounding her, and I knew Ella had earned everything I wanted to give her.

HOTEL

Ella discovers the local cuisine in Antwerp, Belgium

Fraternizing with the locals and watching the World Cup in an Antwerp bar

Chapter 3

The World Cup of soccer (or, more properly, football, as everyone but Americans calls the sport) is a once-every-four-years event that unites the entire planet—if you can call simultaneous mass screaming at television screens unification. The World Cup final is the world's most watched broadcast, reaching billions of people in every time zone and latitude, many of whom follow their favorite players and teams with the kind of devotion usually reserved for anointed saints and heavily promoted rock bands.

Hundreds of countries that otherwise lack a presence in the world's athletic consciousness—Honduras, Iceland, Mali—field national teams that compete against other national teams, and after several years of qualifying matches, thirty-two finalists congregate for a nearly month-long tournament to decide the World Champion of the most popular sport on earth.

It's a big deal to almost everyone except the residents of the United States, who as a rule prefer their football players to weigh 325 pounds, wear gladiatorial shoulder pads, and inflict grievous bodily harm on the opposing team.

I myself am not a regular soccer fan. But I like the idea, possibly fanciful and spurious, that, at least quadrennially, the disparate principalities of our war-torn world can come together in peace, competing fairly and honorably on nicely mown grass fields. And I like the idea, also possibly fanciful and spurious, that gross inequities in national wealth and education and opportunity in general can somehow be brought into balance when twenty-two men from opposite sides of the planet run around together and try to kick a ball into a net. Cameroon triumphing over France. Bulgaria thrashing Saudi Arabia. Costa Rica beating anyone. At the World Cup, it's possible. And it happens amid the pomp of colorful uniforms and unfamiliar anthems and unpronounceable names, all of which seem outlandishly entertaining—mostly because everyone outside of America who *does* recognize the uniforms and anthems and names seems to care so much about the results.

I realize, of course, that the World Cup is a grand marketing opportunity for the behemoths of commerce, who pay millions of dollars to have, say, their sugar-water named the "official soft drink of the World Cup." But, naively perhaps, I like to concentrate on the beautiful athletes playing a beautiful game, competing furiously in a cross-border conflict in which no one dies. It gives me the hope, however foolish, that we human beings can conduct fierce and passionate rivalries without resorting to AK-47s and cluster bombs.

Watching the World Cup final in America is okay, especially if you're able to access one of the Spanish-language channels, where the announcers famously work themselves into an apoplectic lather whenever someone scores: *"Goooooohhhhhhllllll!"*

But it's more fun to be somewhere outside of the United States during the tournament. I like watching the games in the company of people who live in a country where time stands still for football, especially if their brave lads are in the contest. During past World Cups, I've cheered for my outclassed red-white-and-blue American compatriots (and sung along to "The Star-Spangled Banner") in the north of Thailand, on a big-screen television set up in the town square of a small hamlet near the Burmese border. I've sat mute and slightly frightened in a pub along the Thames, an interloper among passionate English fans, who were alternately refined and dyspeptic (depending on the bounce of the ball) when their squad faced archrival Argentina. And I've been drenched with celebratory beer and genuine man-tears in a tiny fishing village on the Ayrshire coast when the Scottish team scored a goal against Colombia.

In the 2002 World Cup final, Brazil is playing Germany and I'm surrounded by a crowd of rabid Irish football fans in a smoky beer house near the central square of Antwerp, Belgium. With an American dog at my side.

Did I mention that the World Cup manages to momentarily and instantly unite our planet's disparate nationalities?

On this sunny Sunday afternoon, everyone is fixated on the drama being beamed from Japan to the wall-size television screen here in the old section of Antwerp. So no one notices I'm grinning like a teenaged boy who's just discovered girls.

I'm watching the World Cup—the *Coupe Mondiale*—in Europe, with my dear friend and traveling companion, Sandrine, who grew up less than ten minutes from Antwerp's central square. And with Ella, who didn't.

This is too cool.

Sandrine lives near my house in Hollywood, where she composes film scores. She speaks what seems like ninety-four languages, has visited nearly every country on her home continent, and adores Ella. She's the perfect guide: one who can explain and translate and generally smooth the way for an American dog (and her dad) experiencing Europe for the first time.

The pub is packed with fans simultaneously singing, hooting, moaning, dancing, and generally yelling at startling decibel levels, utterly hypnotized by the historic action occurring live via satellite. Despite the riotous throng, loud and unruly as headbangers at a Metallica concert, Ella is customarily placid. She seems demonstrably more interested in the deep-fried snacks on my plate than in the stamping strangers ululating all around her.

I figure she might be slightly jet-lagged. We've only been off the long plane ride from Los Angeles for one day, and if her internal body clock is anything like mine—and I'm not sure if dogs have such a thing—she's probably feeling like it's still early in the morning, not yet time to grumble at the cat and patrol the yard for squirrels. Or howl at soccer games involving South American fellows with strange haircuts.

On the other hand, her obliviousness to the mob could simply be the product of her utter infatuation with "people food." My dad exclusively fed our family pets dry dog food on the theory that if they got wet food or table scraps, they would refuse to eat their nutritious kibble in hope of getting something more delicious. I've raised Ella on the same principle, and she's become like a crack addict for anything that's *not* her normal dried lamb-and-rice-meal pellets. If it's different she wants it. And if it happens to be composed mainly of ground meat, she *really* wants it.

Today, I can't blame her. During the World Cup, Sandrine has introduced me to *bitterballen,* petite orbs of unidentified battered animal flesh that, despite the Flemish name, aren't at all bitter, just astonishingly tasty, addictive, and shamefully bad for the arteries. I'm also munching on a serving of french fries, or "frites" as the locals prefer to call them here. Belgians take mild umbrage at the term "french" fries, since they, the Belgians, consider themselves the inventors and leading consumers of potatoes drowned in hot fat. (When you're New Jersey to France's New York, you cling to every available distinction, no matter how dubious.) Though I'm not exactly a fries connoisseur—at least not since my last cholesterol test—I find the Belgian version dangerously superb. They're crispy on the outside, fluffy inside, and unashamedly suffused with lard. The real Belgian innovation, however, is the panoply of sauces available for garnishment. In Antwerp you don't get plain old ketchup. You get three different kinds of ketchup, including a spicy curry concoction. You don't get plain old mayonnaise. You get several kinds, including a pungent garlic emulsion. There's also tartar sauce, béarnaise sauce, and *stoof vlees saus,* a creamy beef stew that would do well over a serving of egg noodles. Fries in Antwerp are an event.

Confronted with the zenith of snack food artistry, I understand my mutt's enchantment. She's like a shipwrecked sailor who's suddenly washed ashore on a temperate island filled with freshwater springs and caregiving mermaids—and *bitterballen.* Paradise!

At the risk of portraying my furry friend as a creature who thinks primarily with her belly, I should say that Ella's extensive therapy dog work has served her well. Here in Belgium she's surrounded by dozens of unfamiliar grabbing hands and staccato exclamations, and she remains preternaturally serene. She can be serenaded by a symphony of unfamiliar war cries and hardly twitch her ears. Indeed, when Brazil finally scores in the sixty-seventh minute and the crowd erupts in full-throated yelling that would drown out the Three Tenors, Ella sleeps at my feet. I'm sure she hears the shouting. But since it doesn't contain recognizable and important words like "walk," "outside," and "cookie," she's not particularly interested.

In Flemish, "Antwerpen" translates loosely to "thrown hand." Amid the cobblestone streets, beneath the towering cathedral at the city's nexus—a short walk from a statue of native son Peter Paul Rubens—there's a much-photographed statue of a heroic little fellow who mythically cut off the hand of an evil giant and threw the appendage, discuslike, into the water. The giant was supposedly suffocating the port with usurious taxes. The joke these days is that taxes in socialist Belgium are higher than ever. Which is why, perhaps, Belgians really like their beer. A typical Belgian bar serves more than a hundred kinds of beer, and each one, it seems, should be sampled during the course of an afternoon. (It helps that beer in Belgium costs less than half of what it does in America, and that it tastes better, too.) The mild inebriation—all right, drunkenness—that such imbibing produces causes the patrons to pay about as much attention to Ella as she does to them. Which is all to say that everyone in our Antwerp pub gets along marvelously and focuses every cell in their body on the thing that really matters: the World Cup final (and my plate of fries).

I figure obliviousness equals normalcy. No one here is shocked, awed, or startled by the presence of a sleeping dog in their midst, as they would be back in the States. No one cares that there's a canine off her leash, lying on the floor, chewing on the occasional Belgian fry. No one makes much ado about how cute or lovable or sweet she is. A dog is like a glass is like a fork is like a screaming Irishman, all part of the natural order of things during an afternoon of televised football. *Of course you can take your mutt to a bar in Antwerp,* their behavior seems to suggest. *Why wouldn't you?*

So I continue to grin.

I also root rather forcefully for the Brazilians, for two reasons. One, I have a small wager riding on them. Two, I have a chip on my shoulder against the Germans—and not for the usual reasons harbored by someone of Polish Jewish ancestry.

Germany, according to my Internet research, is one of three backward European countries that do not allow dogs on trains unfettered. Germany, so say the regulations, requires dogs on their trains to wear muzzles. (England and Spain do not allow dogs on board at all. Toward those two I have an armada-size chip. These barbarians have been pointedly left off our itinerary.) So I cheer loudly and lustily when the Samba Gang punches two goals past Deutschland's Aryan god of a goalkeeper, Oliver Kahn. Ella, of course, pays no attention whatsoever to my applause, since it doesn't involve fried meat.

Her behavior in a congregation of strangers is unlike that of any other dogs I've known. At a dinner party given by Sandrine's parents in honor of their prodigal daughter's return from the culturally bereft precincts of Hollywood to the civilized climes of continental Europe, Ella is surrounded in a fifth-floor apartment by a mob of Delphines and Alains and Jean-Michels, all of whom express amazement—*c'est incroyable!*—at the dog's tranquility, especially when tempted by plates filled with herring and ham, salmon and sushi. "Monsieur," they ask in charmingly accented English, "explain please how it ees possible he does not eat zee fish? You have made him educated at a university?"

When Ella performs a few of her standard tricks—refusing to eat "junk food"; "sleeping" in a deep coma until she hears the word "dogcatcher"; demonstrating the difference between *la droite* and *la gauche*—the Belgian partygoers howl with uninhibited joy (much like the disabled adults we visit back in America) and declare, *"C'est merveilleux!"*

She really is marvelous, and a perfect lady, content to bask in the spotlight when it shines upon her and happy to doze under the piano when everyone's chatting about the vicissitudes of the euro.

Brazil is winning, and I'm continuing to grin, silently repeating to myself *Ella is in a bar. Ella is in a bar.* Every time I say it I feel gently tickled. I imagine the sensation is similar to what a parent might feel seeing his child on a movie screen. *"That's my kid! Up there with Pacino!"*

Well, it's my dog! Mingling with dozens of drunken European soccer fans!

Now, more than a few friends, playing devil's advocate, have suggested to me that most dogs aren't as well behaved as Ella. Therefore, they argue, our American penchant for keeping dogs out of bars—and almost everywhere else—is a necessary protection against wild canines who can't be trusted. "Ella," my friends insist, "is the exception." The dogs that make up the rule, they say, would only cause trouble.

I've heard this argument a million times. It's the same line of reasoning that prevents beer being sold at Paul Brown Stadium in Cleveland, where a few inebriated, bottle-throwing idiots once caused their football team to forfeit a game. Since we know there will always be a couple of "rotten apples" whose rancidness might potentially spoil the fun for everyone else, the thinking goes, we shouldn't trust the vast majority to police themselves (and to prosecute the miscreants). Instead, we just throw the entire "barrel" into the rubbish. Instead of revoking the privilege of the abusers, we punish everyone.

My response to this wrongheaded methodology usually goes something like: The vast majority of dog owners know if their pet is well behaved enough to mingle in public, and if the dog isn't well trained they generally have enough common sense to leave him at home. It's like parents with children. If you know your child is prone to fling his spaghetti at other diners, you're probably considerate enough to leave him with a babysitter when you go out to eat. If, however, you've raised a well-mannered youngster, you're fairly certain he won't do anything that might compromise the enjoyment of those who do not find pasta projectiles amusing, and so you gladly (and proudly) bring him along. Likewise with dogs. A naughty mutt who likes to chew on tablecloths and the pants of strangers should be left to do his damage at home. A good dog who obeys commands and likes being around people should be welcome to join the party.

Furthermore, I suggest, cultures that include dogs in the events of everyday life tend to breed better-behaved dogs. It's a benevolent circle. Since dogs are expected to be part of the social fabric, they're generally more sociable.

To all this my friends—a contentious lot, don't you think?—say, "Well, that's *there.* Here in the United States it's different. You can't just start socializing dogs who don't have any experience with going out in public. There's no way of differentiating a great dog like Ella from a bad one."

Well, actually there is. America is very big on licenses and accreditation. You need a special license to sell watercolors at the beach, a special license to drive a taxicab, a special license to serve bottles of beer to thirsty music fans. And, technically, in most American cities you're supposed to have a license to own a dog. Let's take it one step further. The American Kennel Club awards a "Canine Good Citizenship" certificate to dogs who can pass a thorough but fair behavior and personality test. (Ella has one.) Good Citizen dogs, I have found, are usually nicer and exhibit more predictable behavior than the average singles-bar patron or preadolescent child. So I say we ought to encourage owners to make Good Citizens of their pooches and allow such exemplary Dobermans and dachshunds, Pomeranians and Pekinese, increased access to places other than fenced dog parks.

Then again, I'm against motorcycle helmet laws and for the legalization of drugs and prostitution. Maybe I'm just a crazy libertarian whose belief in the sanctity of civil freedoms has turned him into an annoying crank with a peculiar obsession.

Maybe taking dogs everywhere is, like my friends suggest, a generally bad idea.

But in the specific case of Ella Guinevere Konik, I can't see the harm—and I definitely see the pleasure.

In Antwerp, a few of the patrons absentmindedly pet her when the on-screen action flags. But mostly they merely acknowledge her presence as a natural part of the scenery, as commonplace as pints of lager and deep-fried potatoes. *Ella is in a bar!* And no one minds at all.

I'm grinning because I'm overjoyed—and slightly stunned—to see my mutt in a public watering hole. I'm grinning because I'm confident some officious twit won't ask, "Sir, is this your dog?" and insist that she must be taken outside where she allegedly belongs.

Injustice and famine and cruelty still mar our world every second of every day. And avoidable sorrow and misery afflict countless souls. But in this tiny outpost of the planet, a really nice dog is hanging out with a really nice group of people during the broadcast of a really nice sporting event. I'm grinning because right now, at this isolated moment, in a negligible and almost entirely irrelevant way, the world is how I believe it ought to be.

* * *

On the night we depart Belgium, Sandrine and I take her parents to dinner in Brussels, at Le Grand Sablon, a charming plaza near the royal palace. Lacking a reservation, we make an informal survey of restaurants in the neighborhood that welcome dogs in their dining room. After receiving five affirmatives out of five inquiries, we get the message—*"Mais oui!"*—and settle on Philippe's, a bistro that by American standards would be considered "nice" but not formal (modernist steel tables, tinted glasses, handsome waiters). I keep Ella on an exceptionally short leash—like, three inches from my thigh—mortified that suddenly, at this revelatory moment, centuries of breeding and a lifetime of training will be shorn away by an ancestral yearning for animal flesh. I'm scared she'll turn into a rapacious wolf.

I feel short of breath and vaguely nauseous. My palms are sweaty. My legs feel weak. I can't believe it: I've got stage fright!

The hostess shows us to a table for four in the front of the dining room, not far from the entrance. Instead of having a languorous, triumphant stroll, I dash with Ella in tow to the banquette, prod my mutt between the chairs, and unceremoniously plop down above her before anything bad can happen. Exactly what I'm so worried about I cannot say. That Ella will disgrace her species? All of America? Me and my theories? I don't know. It's just that I've never done this before.

Ella has enjoyed patio dining at modest restaurants in Los Angeles, but here in Brussels we're inside, beneath a roof, in a place where they have candles and a wine list. To my relief, Ella assumes her usual position—reclined elegantly, with muzzle on front paws—and refrains from pouncing on the steak tartare appetizer being brought to the table behind ours.

I want to savor the moment. After all, I've waited a lifetime (Ella's) to dine in a good restaurant with my faithful mutt. I want to commemorate the triumph—the achievement?—with a pithy toast, or an apposite song, or something, just as I plan to do the first time I break par on the golf course, or get published in *The New Yorker*. But I'm still stunned, still trying vainly to comprehend that my dog is *in a restaurant*. I mean, I *know* she is. All the obvious signs are there: a kitchen, tables set with silverware, tempting aromas suffusing the air. And, yes, there's no denying that the white pile of fur at my feet is indeed Ella. But still. These things don't go together, do they?

A waitress approaches and the muscles in my neck stiffen. I feel like I've been trying to get away with something not quite legal and I'm about to be caught. *My dog is inside a restaurant. On the floor. Next to other diners.* Surely they'll realize a mistake has been made and ask us in haughty French to depart immediately before the police are summoned. Surely I'm about to be cited and fined.

Not long ago, two extremely hardworking Los Angeles County sheriff's deputies patrolling the mean streets of West Hollywood, where you're more likely to see a man in a dress than a heroin-addicted mugger, wrote me a hundred-dollar ticket for having Ella off her leash. Never mind that I was standing at a corner of Santa Monica Boulevard waiting for the light to change and Ella was sitting in place—*sitting*—less than a foot from my left heel. Never mind that when they got out of their squad car, Ella immediately assumed her *down* position on my command. And never mind that I was dressed in jogging clothes and she was wearing a vest to carry my keys and money. These assiduous law enforcers recognized in my recumbent mutt an imminent danger, a time bomb that could explode at any minute. And their quality police work kept the main West Hollywood thoroughfare safe for unsuspecting Judy Garland impersonators.

The waitress at Philippe's hands out menus, takes drink orders, and recites the evening's specials. I nod and smile dumbly, comprehending about a third of what she's saying. Sandrine whispers discreetly to me, "She's asking if you want water for *le chien*."

"Ah! Oui, oui. Merci, madame. C'est parfait!" I say, along with whatever other vaguely intelligible French gibberish I can think of.

Now I'm grinning again, and breathing almost normally.

We're not tolerated. We're welcomed.

I look down at Ella. She looks up at me expectantly, like she might be getting a treat. Her ears, which convey her emotions and her moods almost as effectively as the sounds that come out of her mouth, are cocked and alert, on full surveillance mode. I lean over, kiss the smooth top of her forehead, and tell her she's the best dog in the world. "You're in a restaurant, Ella. Do you understand that? I can't believe we're all here together." Then I kiss her again and reemerge from beneath the table. Ella's ears droop back to normal position, dismayed that I've merely given her the sentiments of my heart and not something fried in pork lard.

Surveying the restaurant, I note that no one fusses over the *mutt Americaine* beneath the table. Neither the staff nor the other diners seem particularly impressed by Ms. Ella's presence. I'm relieved, but I'm also a little disappointed. Surely a little fawning wouldn't hurt. Then I notice there are at least two more dogs here that I can see, and one that I can't. The unseen one, hidden beneath a corner table, isn't nearly as taciturn as my jet-lagged hound; his occasional yips earn him a good-natured French shushing from his owners. The other two, a spaniel and a terrier, loll at their owners' feet, blissed out on table scraps. The dogs nap; the humans drink wine and murmur seductively. The sun sets on Belgium, and more wine is poured. I hear the legato music of French and the guttural rhythm of Flemish, and I see a happy sight: dogs accompanying their best friends in a nice restaurant. This unfamiliar (but delightful) tableau seems so natural, so unforced and effortless and inevitable, like a Rubens angel. Like curry ketchup on fries.

As I feast on *chèvre* and *crevettes,* I think of life back home in California. How preposterous and funny it seems at this moment that Ella may not enter my neighborhood Denny's, where pimps and homeless Hollywood street hustlers gorge on Grand Slam breakfasts. How absurd it seems that she must be parked outside on the sidewalk, like a hairy bicycle. Ella has spent her life gazing at me through grimy plate-glass windows. On this blessed night in Bruxelles she's inside, where it's warm and safe.

My mutt gets a few fries from me, and a dish of water from the waitress. A couple of Belgians comment on her cuteness and her whiteness. And the business of the restaurant goes on as usual, the way, I reckon, it ought to be in a more perfect America, where a customer is judged on the content of her character, not the amount of fur upon her back.

An American dog at what remains of the Berlin Wall

An afternoon's refreshment in front of a museum in Berlin

Chapter 4

I'd like to state unequivocally that I have no chip whatsoever on my shoulder when it comes to Germans and their astonishingly wonderful train system. I would also like to proclaim in no uncertain terms that it's a pitiable shame that some benighted countries—like, say, for instance, England and Spain—cannot see the wisdom and grace in Deutschland's sparkling example of how to run a railway.

Ella, I should add parenthetically, was *not* made to wear a muzzle on the German night train from Brussels to Berlin. Nor was her master made to pay a separate steerage charge. She was welcomed on board by the conductor, who resembled Ben Kingsley in *Schindler's List,* with a smile and an avuncular pat on the head.

How strange and somehow glorious it is to board an international train with your American dog—especially when the train has elegant sleeping compartments reminiscent of black-and-white movies starring Clark Gable. Well, it happened one night to me, and once I overcame the cognitive dissonance of Train + Ella in the same mise-en-scène, I was able to appreciate the civilized comforts of traveling in a sleeper car with a glamorous woman vaguely suggestive of Claudette Colbert, and my seventy-three-pound dog (whose resemblance to movie stars ends with Lassie). After the helpful German conductor showed us to our berth and took our orders for the next day's breakfast, both ladies immediately availed themselves of the fold-out mattress. The four-legged one, however, was banished to the floor, where a plush green travel mat decorated with a pattern of paw prints was designated "bed"—as in "Go to bed, Ella, and don't bother me until we cross the Elbe."

Employing her enviable talent for sleeping anywhere and at any time, Ella didn't move from her spot the entire night.

If it's true that a sound sleeper possesses a clear conscience, then Ella must surely be a guilt-free canine. Yes, she terrorized a few rodents in her youth and barked somewhat threateningly at delivery people trying to do their jobs, but I don't recall her ever doing anything that would banish her from Heaven. (Masturbating in the dining room during a dinner party doesn't count.) That she is more than six thousand miles from the familiar comforts of her yard doesn't trouble her. Of course, that she doesn't have any conception of distance or time zones or continents probably helps. Faced with an environment that neither looks, sounds, nor, most important in her hierarchy of sensual signs, *smells* anything like her bed at home, Ella simply does the doggie pirouette and arranges herself into a vanilla croissant.

Our sleeper car is an exemplar of German engineering, in which every available space is used smartly and efficiently, everything enclosing and containing something else. They've ingeniously managed to fit an entire New York City apartment into a space that's at least ten percent smaller than a New York City apartment. And yet, for all the clever design tricks, the most comforting thing about being on a train traveling through the night to Germany is having my Guard Dog sleeping near the door, ready (I think) to snap out of her dreamy slumber should any jackbooted thugs appear at our compartment asking to see our papers.

My only real concern—and it's a small one—is whether Ella will be able to "hold it" for the duration of the trip, approximately ten hours. She got a "last call" in Brussels, and she normally can control her bladder for a good twelve hours, but I wonder if the vibrations in the floor and the rocking of the train car will produce a tragic spill. I've set out her pink plastic travel kit, which caters her usual meal of tap water and Nature's Choice lamb-and-rice pellets. She ignores it, possibly sharing my leakage concerns.

Early on in this journey, I'm finding that my main obsession during our tour of Europe isn't that Ella has any life-altering and indelibly joyous experiences, but that she doesn't do anything to offend, disrupt, or dismay the residents of foreign countries, who, after all, never expressly invited her to visit their sovereign soil. I'm so worried she might do something wrong that I fear I'm overlooking countless opportunities for her to do something right. Like bring a smile to a train conductor's face.

In the morning, Mr. Kingsley knocks on our door bearing coffee, juice, bread, and, to Ella's gratitude, an unidentifiable liver concoction that smells suspiciously like what Sam, my cat, gets as a treat when he comes inside the house without a mouse in his fangs. I check the dog's haunches. They're dry as a kaiser roll. If that's not worth a treat, nothing is! I toss her a dollop of mystery liver, which disappears down her gullet faster than the cross-border express.

When we arrive in Berlin, at the Bahnhof (train station), Ella relieves herself on the first scraggly patch of grass she can find outside the terminal. Then we find a taxicab.

There's a line of cream-colored Mercedes 320s at the ready. I take a deep breath and approach the first in line, gesturing theatrically to the luggage and the dog. Instead of the hesitancy or complaint I feared would be forthcoming—*ein Hund in mein Taxi?!*—I get a warm smile and what I think is a *ja*.

We three clamber into the backseat, and I grapple with another dose of What's Wrong with This Picture. *Ella is in a Berlin taxicab.* German is one of the many languages Sandrine speaks (and one of the several hundred that I don't), so she and the driver chatter about things I can't understand while I try vainly to explain to my dog that she's in Berlin. "German shepherds? Black, tan, somewhat menacing? This is where they come from," I tell her. She attempts to lick my face. Ella has no grasp of history, or geography, or cultural differences—or any of the other abstract concepts that allegedly elevate human beings above the less learned beasts who share our planet. She knows only this: She's somewhere that's not her home and she's with her dad, the latter of which is probably consolation enough for the former.

When we arrive at our hotel, an ugly relic of East German functionality, the Fräulein who checks us in neither charges us a "pet supplement" (the reservation, booked online, confirmed that the hotel would accept dogs for a modest extra fee) nor comments on Ella's adorableness. The clerk's phlegmatic demeanor seems to say "Fact: That's a dog. Fact: We accept dogs as readily as we do babies in strollers and Americans in jeans. Now take your key and make room for the next tourist."

We traverse the lobby to the elevator, and all the time I'm expecting someone to tap me on the shoulder and quietly ask me to "step this way, please, to the interrogation room." I still haven't completely accepted that everything is okay, that traveling in Europe with a dog, an American dog, isn't in violation of any law, municipal code, or social convention. Anticipating that somewhere along our odyssey I'll be confronted by someone who gets paid to enforce arcane regulations, I've packed a bulging dossier of health certificates, veterinary declarations, and therapy animal commendations, all of which attest to Ella's strong moral fiber and dearth of communicable diseases. So far no one has asked to see a single document. But I'm skeptical of my good fortune and on alert for the inevitable annoying complication that surely must attend any ambitious international travel project, particularly one involving a large greyhound-Lab mix. Nearly four decades of life in the United States have conditioned me to expect a confrontation, an inspection, a hassle, from someone who is "just doing his job." Yet here we are, in Berlin, where people notoriously adore their rules and regulations, and no one has said a cross word.

I can think of two explanations: First, incomprehensible as it seems to me—me who's having a hard time accepting the truth even as he's basking in it—is that, *aha!* we're not breaking any rules and regulations! Second, and less logical but altogether more lyrical, is that the normally rule-loving Germans are on this particular day suffering from a countrywide malaise that has inspired them to collectively say "Oh, hell, what's the point."

Yes, it's the day after the German national team lost 2–0 to Brazil in that little football contest that some people watched on television. To be honest, the nation seems to be taking it well, hardly acknowledging the defeat, except maybe for the modest gesture of draping the entire Brandenburg Gate in fabric upon which is a picture of German football players. They're depicted from the knees down, in clean socks and polished shoes, and they bear a message of encouragement from Deutsche Telekom wishing everyone best of luck in 2006.

* * *

Back home in Hollywood, Ella is what naturalists on Animal Planet might call "territorial." A fence of rosemary, lavender, and rosebushes, with a wrought-iron gate that I keep closed during the day while I work, surrounds our house. The front door, however, stays open (except during mail delivery hour), and Ella's free to wander around the front yard, which, along with the backyard, the driveway, the porch, and the sidewalk in front of the house, she considers her personal domain. She amuses herself—or maybe she thinks she's performing a valuable service—by barking ferociously at other dogs who make the mistake of walking near her sacrosanct borders. If you didn't know her, you would think she was a vicious killer. In fact, she's a gentle sweetheart—but she wouldn't want any of the other dogs in the neighborhood to know it. Especially Rufus, a black great

Dane the size of a Shetland pony, who finds all the shouting when he ambles past with his bodybuilder owner mildly unsettling.

If Ella isn't exactly physically aggressive to other dogs in our neighborhood, she's not particularly nice. In other words, she can be wickedly loud and obnoxious if she suspects another canine might pee on her grass.

Which is why I'm fascinated to see how consistently *kind* she is to dogs in Germany. When we walk on the wide boulevard known as Unter den Linden, Ella encounters several local dogs—bassett hounds, golden retrievers, poodles—without international incident, just the standard nose-rubbing and butt-sniffing. She seems determined to represent her country well, to be a civilized diplomat abroad instead of the raging diva she can often be on her home turf. The language differences that an ignorant monolingual like me encounters on a multinational tour of the European continent don't afflict my dog. (At least I don't think they do.) Hers is a universal code with a lineage extending to wolf-pack days. Dogs don't need a dictionary for translation; they communicate effectively among each other without uttering a word. The canine nonverbal signals—posture of tail and ears and neck—say everything that human handshakes and eye contact are meant to convey. Dogs can tell if the approaching stranger on four legs is cordial or nasty, and they can silently announce to the world their intentions and interests.

So as we walk I observe the hair on Ella's back, which she often arranges into a comical Mohawk when she's trying to pass herself off as tough. I keep an eye on her elastic black lips, making sure she's not curling them upward in a sneer to expose what's left of her teeth. And I confirm that she's not slinking, crouching, or tugging on her leash, preparing to pounce.

In fact, she's wagging her tail and letting her big red tongue fall out of her mouth, looking very much the picture of contentment, the happy pup oblivious to anything but all the good smells on the sidewalk.

It's times like these when I fervently wish I could understand how she thinks. Is she consciously attempting to foster international peace, or is she momentarily distracted by the newness of what she's experiencing and forgetful of the Queen Bitch persona she likes to project to other dogs? Does she genuinely like German dogs, or is she holding out an olive branch to unfamiliar members of her species, eager to mend the wounds of the previous century? Does she even know what a German dog is?

These philosophical conundrums intensify when we visit the Reichstag, the enormous and intimidating edifice in which, shall we say, many bad ideas were planned. Ella, of course, has zero inkling of the building's historical significance. All she knows is that there are hundreds—thousands?—of people in line, the majority of them Germans, waiting to tour the structure. They spill out the doors and down the stairs, wide and long, like a stream rushing down a mountainside. Some of them want to pet her and coo at her in an unfamiliar tongue. And that, as far as Ella is concerned, makes the Reichstag a pretty cool place to spend a morning, regardless of the Nazi memories.

I take a couple of "Where's Waldo?"-esque photos, placing her on one of the high steps, surrounded by the German throng, a tiny speck of white against the gray stone. From nearly fifty meters away, I snap funny photos of her posed in the barely recognizable distance, a symbol of animal innocence sitting motionless upon a place that, one time not so long ago, embodied human evil. When Ella comes scampering back to me, past the patient queue, I tell her what a good dog she is. And this time I mean it in a way I normally wouldn't.

On the plaza level, beside the streets that surround the Reichstag, we find an exhibition of billboard art made by idealistic creators from around the globe. The common theme these South African and Guyanese and Danish artists explore is "coexistence." Many of the images feature people of different colors and ethnicities sharing an embrace, or a handshake, or even common space, and many of these hopeful billboards move me deeply—maybe because of what they say and maybe because they're exhibited where they are. The images have inspiring quotes inscribed across the bottom, epigrams from Jefferson and Churchill and Gandhi, which all say more or less the same thing: that we *can* coexist, and that we *must* coexist.

I look at my American mutt, who's standing at my side, waiting for me to take her someplace less emotionally charged, preferably one that has some grass. She can't read, and she certainly can't decipher the semiotics of conceptual art. (Half the time I can't either.) But here in Germany, Ella seems to have instinctively understood the vital message that, after centuries of vain effort, we humans are still trying desperately to hear.

* * *

Berlin being Berlin, it's difficult to be a sentient traveler without bumping into historically provocative sites, graphic reminders of a civilization momentarily gone wrong. Being here—even in the company of my naive dog, the equivalent of Chance the Gardener on four paws—forces me to think about events I would prefer to ignore, or at least defer to a later date, when I have the strength of constitution to stare the truth in the eyes. For example, I want to see what remains of the infamous Wall, but when Ella and I arrive at the spot where two hundred meters or so of the thing has been preserved, I'm confronted with another outdoor exhibit, this one entitled "Topography of Terror." And this one's not uplifting art. It's a documentary in words and pictures, maps and news archives, of the debasement and psychosis in German thinking that led to the permanent taint upon modern humanity we know as the Holocaust. What's left of the Berlin Wall stands in the shadow of the former headquarters of the SS.

Though I feel something like a duty to bear witness, an obligation to remember and, as the slogan goes, never forget, I don't like looking at such stuff. (Does anyone?) We're faced with nearly constant reminders, transmitted through the daily news, of mankind's ability to visit cruelty upon mankind. Suicide bombers, Scud bombers, nuclear bombers—they all have varying degrees of righteousness and rectitude on their side, but at the end of the day they all accomplish the same result. What happened in Germany is simultaneously a reprisal of past atrocities and a rehearsal for future ones. We like to think "Never again." But unless we start behaving more like dogs and less like human beings, we're destined, I fear, to eventually exterminate ourselves. Viewing exhibits like "Topography of Terror," unpleasant as it is, acts like a sobering slap in the face for complacent heirs to the world's mistakes, willfully oblivious Jews and Christians and Muslims alike, drunk on the potent liquor of material affluence.

As I force myself to fathom the unfathomable images, mounted on the same ground where not long ago desperate Easterners were literally dying to get in, Ella walks by my side, solemnly shuffling a few feet forward as I move from one awful document to the next, working laterally through the dark memories. She's not supposed to be here. (There's a NO DOGS sign posted not far from the entrance.) But I need her to make this walk with me. I need to occasionally look down into her brown eyes, framed by white-blond lashes, and I need to see undiluted innocence, an unknowing and blithe beast untouched by the destructive impulses harbored in the human soul.

Dozens of other people, some German, some American, many with translating headsets held to their ear, make the walk with us. No one seems to notice Ella, and she doesn't ask for attention. She knows somehow that her job at this moment is simply to be.

When we finish I give her a kiss on the muzzle and take a photo of her in front of what's left of the Berlin Wall.

* * *

One gloomy afternoon, when rain persistently threatens the skies yet never comes, we visit the former Checkpoint Charlie. There's a big museum at the site, but I'm tired of looking at images that make me sad. Instead, I want to do something happy and light, like drink German lager and talk nonsense to my dog. Across the street from the museum, in view of the little Charlie hut and piled sandbags that serve as a constant memorial, I find an inviting café that doesn't appear to prohibit Western dogs from crossing the front-door border. In keeping with my long-held commitment to eat whatever the locals eat, I order wurst and sauerkraut, staples, I figure, of traditional German cuisine. (Then I look around the restaurant, filled with businesspeople on their lunch break, and notice that everyone's having salads and omelets.) My eat-like-the-indigenous-people ethos has, in the past, forced me to choke down wild boar in Panama, snake in Hong Kong, and deep-fried haggis in bonnie Scotland. So sausage and kraut don't look so bad at the moment. Besides, to Ella, sausages are the doggie version of beluga caviar, an ineffably sublime delicacy that haunts her culinary dreams, despite her penchant for bolting them down with nary a savoring chew. If she's a good girl throughout the repast—and she had better be; we're inside a smart German café!—she'll get an under-the-table reward of the minced pork variety.

Although it seems to me that the other patrons consider Ella's presence on the wooden floor of Café Checkpoint utterly normal, I'm still nervous. She's the only dog in the dining room this afternoon, and I'm the only American, and, well, I don't want myself and my hound to become to Berliners a lasting symbol, as the pile of sandbags in view through the window has become.

To my relief, Ella behaves impeccably, employing her talent for narcolepsy with great effectiveness. The other diners, at least those who even notice there's a sleeping dog in their midst, take her for granted—just as we Americans too often take our bountiful blessings for granted. I'm eating lunch not twenty meters from a place where the tenuous line between freedom and enslavement once was drawn. And I'm feeling grateful to be a citizen of a country where I may travel freely, speak openly, dissent passionately, worship individually, associate widely, and sleep securely, content in the knowledge that the vast imperfect democracy I live in cherishes the principles that made a place like Checkpoint Charlie necessary.

Even steadfast patriots, though, realize that the United States of America is no utopian paradise. It's a grand experiment, a work in progress that sometimes disappoints, often infuriates, and occasionally depresses. It's a country I'm proud to call home—even if I can't take my dog into American restaurants.

After lunch, the conclusion of which includes Ella's first (fleeting) taste of authentic German pig innards, I walk across the street and take the same commemorative photo all the other tourists take of Checkpoint Charlie: standing or sitting on the sandbags, looking ironically vigilant. But I do mine with a white mutt who dreams not of freedom and peace, but of constantly replenished plates of boiled meat.

For a country that has suffered through totalitarianism and National Socialism, Germany, to my surprise, has a refreshingly progressive attitude toward man's best friend. In Berlin, Ella experiences her first ride on a public bus. (And without a muzzle.) Waiting at the stop near the hotel for our bus to arrive, I'm hopeful I'll have a charming story to tell about her virgin journey on European municipal transportation, something involving the bridging of language and cultural differences. (I'm also hopeful my irrational nervousness isn't too obvious.) But the truth is Ella simply gets on the bus with me, lies on the floor at my feet, and gets off with me ten minutes later. That's it. One excited little girl, a blue-eyed dumpling about five years old, babbles to her father about the pretty *Hund* across the aisle. But that's all the action I have to report.

When we take the subway—*the subway, the Berlin subway!*—later that evening, the scene (if you can call something so undramatic a scene) repeats. We get on, we sit down, we get off. No icy stares, no frowns of disgust, and conversely, no laughs of amusement and no handshakes of congratulations. The prevailing attitude I'm able to perceive from the average Berliner is: *Dog on the subway. So?*

It's a common sight, apparently. I might as well have brought on board a shopping bag filled with bratwurst and sauerkraut.

Despite the absence of a big deal being made, I'm jacked up on adrenaline, like a kid after his first roller-coaster ride. Standing on the sidewalk aboveground, I want to go back down and do it again.

"Ella," I fairly shout at my startled mutt, "you were on the subway!"

She blinks at me.

"Do you have any idea what that means, Smelly?" (Smelly is one of my affectionate nicknames for Ella, although on paper it doesn't seem half as loving as it actually sounds.) "Do you realize where you are?"

She pants a few times and starts walking in between my legs, which is what Ella does when she's happy and excited.

"You are so unbelievably good I can't stand it!" I exclaim, scratching her behind the ears. "You know how to ride the subway."

Ella's face seems to say *I have no idea what you're fussing about, but it's fun nonetheless. And, oh, by the way, can I have another sausage?*

Down the street from the rebuilt (in 1988) Berlin synagogue, which stands under the constant guard of the local police, we find a late-night restaurant that specializes in bagels and milkshakes. Eager to celebrate, and no longer nervous about traipsing into a classy joint with my mutt, I take Ella inside, where she curls up on the soft carpet. We've entered an art deco sanctuary, an airy den with red velvet furniture and sumptuous black drapes. Young couples snuggle in the corner, and impulsive laughter fills the air. One wall is covered with ancient golf memorabilia, and another with vintage jazz photos.

Not forty meters away, in front of the Jewish temple, men armed with machine guns help prevent the sins of the past from disgracing the present. Here in our funky German paradise, Louis Armstrong, musical libertarian and patron saint of the American spirit, smiles down from the wall on me and my dog. What a wonderful world, indeed. Ella has a bowl of water and I have a dish of chocolate ice cream to commemorate a minor triumph that, I've got to admit, neither man nor dog fully comprehends.

Traveling in style on the Berlin-to-Prague train

Near the central square of Prague

Chapter 5

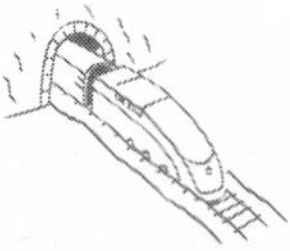

The Czech Republic exists in a peculiar existential limbo, situated both literally and figuratively between Western and Eastern Europe. On one hand, when we visited, the Czechs didn't participate in the European Union's unified euro currency; on the other hand, you can find an Internet café on every other street in Prague. On one hand, the Czech national diet—goulash, sausages, and potent black beer—resembles the fare served in Stalin-era work camps; on the other hand, you can find inexpensive restaurants serving every imaginable cuisine from around the globe. And most telling, although the Czechs cherish the renaissance in Western-style freedoms their country presently enjoys, they also cling to a Soviet-era respect for having all of one's papers in perfect order.

On the train from Berlin to Prague, I get my first taste of what it might have been like to live under the watchful eye of Central Party supervision. Between Bad Schandau, the last railroad stop in Germany, and Děčín, the first one in the Czech Republic, I hand over my documents for inspection three separate times.

First my papers undergo examination by a burly bear of a man in a lime green shirt and a blue cap who packs a small pistol. Then, five minutes later, a slender, clean-shaven man wearing a navy blue shirt (and no official cap or sidearm) gives them a thorough looking over. Finally, a very unhappy-looking fellow with a baby blue blouse, toting handcuffs and a large semiautomatic weapon, performs the inspection. I'm not sure what they're all looking for exactly, but they all seem to have a particular interest in the white bundle of fur reclined at my feet.

All three functionaries ask to see Ella's papers—or at least what sounds like "papers" to my unfluent ears. I feel mildly vindicated for being an obsessive worrier: Finally, her personal dossier is being put to vital use! I dutifully show each one Ella's State of California Agriculture Department Health Certificate for Interstate Travel, and her rabies vaccination certificate, and proof of various blood tests—all of which are in English, and none of which, it appears, the armed officials can actually read. They riffle through my dog's documents wordlessly. They seem dissatisfied, unconvinced. But then, to a man, when they come to the last item in Ella's file, a laminated identification card indicating her membership in our American therapy-dog society, they frown slightly (the universal "Okay, I give up" sign) and return to me her dossier, mumbling something that sounds like "thank you." (Or they could be telling me I'm lucky not to be thrown into a fetid jail cell. I go with the happier interpretation.) Laminated identification cards carry a lot of weight in Eastern Europe, even if they show a panting dog wearing an embroidered red vest and sitting on her dad's lap.

The last of the officials—the one with the biggest gun—

points at Ella snoozing on her travel mat and he mimes breathing through a gas mask. I can imagine all sorts of nefarious intentions in his charade, but I take his gesture to mean "She should be wearing a muzzle." I briefly consider telling him I'm a big fan of Václav Havel and Jaromir Jagr. Instead, I smile and nod dumbly, rapidly repeating the phrase "Yes, thank you, sir" until he shrugs heavily and leaves in search of more laminated identification cards.

Later, as we approach Prague, a fourth functionary appears at the door of our compartment. This uniformed official, I eventually deduce, would be the train's Czech conductor. (Apparently, the German one got off at the border.) He examines my tickets assiduously, as though searching for a hidden code among the letters and numbers. Then he demands to see the *hund*'s papers. (The conductor optimistically assumes I speak German, a notion I unintentionally reinforce by understanding the word for dog.) I produce Ella's extensive health file once more, but he shakes his head vigorously and says something in German. Sandrine tells me he wants Ella's *ticket*.

"Ah, her ticket!" I say to the conductor. "You want her ticket. I see. Well, actually, I no have ticket for *hund*." We didn't need one for Belgium or Germany, so I wrongly figured we wouldn't need one for the Czech Republic, either. Plus, everyone thinks she's so *cute*.

"Jksulej minedjhpr," he replies.

"Right," I say, nodding. "I no have."

After ascertaining that I no have Czech money, either, he performs a complex set of calculations involving timetables and regulation books, and finally determines that Ella's passage to

Prague will cost the euro equivalent of six dollars—which is one dollar and fifty cents less than a bowl of tasty (but extravagantly priced) vegetable soup from the dining car, where the chef stands over the grill with a cigarette dangling from his lips.

I decide we're officially in Eastern Europe.

Looking out the train window, I see that all the words on the signs we pass have crazy accent marks I don't get, little apostrophes and upside-down triangles missing their hypotenuses. Our immediate future, I suspect, will include an abundance of pantomime and a dearth (I hope) of local jails designed to accommodate regulation-breakers and their formerly innocent mutts.

I remind Ella that she's probably the only dog on her Los Angeles street ever to have been in the Czech Republic. She blinks at me twice and goes back to sleep.

* * *

Not long before departing for our European journey, Sandrine and I met an older couple at the Los Angeles Music Center. They had just returned from a fabulous opera tour of the continent, where they had been especially charmed in Prague by a folksy beer hall they remembered as "Ooh-flecker." They said locals and tourists sat elbow to elbow at communal wooden tables, getting sloshed on the home-brewed stout. "A marvelous place," they insisted. "You've got to go there!"

I wondered aloud if Ooh-flecker would be the kind of joint that allowed dogs to grace the sawdust floors.

The Opera Couple thought for a moment. "I think I saw dogs in there," the wife said unconvincingly.

"Yes, I think there were dogs," the husband agreed.

But I got the feeling that the quantity of beer they had imbibed made their memories of their night in Prague less than reliable. Now, a couple of months later, half a world away from the refined hallways of the Dorothy Chandler Pavilion, where Placido Domingo and company do honor to the great bel canto repertoire, we're standing at the entrance of the Opera Couple's favorite beer hall.

At least I think we are. According to the personable taxi driver, who offered extemporaneous commentary on the major Prague tourist attractions as we sped by them in his car, *this* must be the place our friends were talking about. (Of course, his labored English combined with my nonexistent Czech could have led me and my dog to the local abattoir, and I wouldn't have known the difference.) The restaurant he thinks we're looking for is actually called U Fleku. (Every other person I ask, including several startled pedestrians I accost on the street outside our hotel, seems to think so too.) From what I can gather, in Czech *U Fleku* means "Den of depravity where they get you falling-down drunk on homemade black brew and Becherovka, a spicy (and ridiculously strong) liquor of unknown origins and insidious effects."

The second thing I discover about U Fleku is if you try to refuse any of the beverages they bring around on trays, the waiters insist in hypnotizing accented English that "it's tradition." And who am I to fly in the face of tradition?

The first thing I discover is that the "tradition" here—and everyplace else in Prague—is to extend a warm welcome to dogs. It's a beer hall, after all, where people sing and shout and smoke like Gary, Indiana, factory chimneys. Living in California, where people can't light a cigarette anywhere in public, including bars(!), I've become conditioned to nightlife with "fresh" air (a funny concept in Smogville, USA). I've also become accustomed to a pronounced puritanical streak among the proprietors of adult watering holes, none of whom seems to appreciate the pleasures of having a furry mutt lying on his floor. In Prague, I quickly determine, nobody gives a damn. They're too preoccupied with the dark nepenthe emerging from the U Fleku vats.

The beer here, black as tar, and with a toasty cereal aroma, is part beverage, part meal. It's very easy to drink several frosty flagons of the stuff without remembering that you've had several frosty flagons of the stuff. And yet, this beer is somehow unforgettable, the liquid essence of Prague.

I feel likewise about the sauerkraut. Compared to the German variety, the Czech version—*kysané zelí*—is insanely sweet and pungent on the tongue. You forget the staple ingredient is cabbage, and like the beer, you want more, more, more, as though you were confined to a Victorian orphanage. If I sound more than a little obsessed with the seductiveness of my first Czech dining experience, I should say I am not the only one. Ella, in fact, I am certain, will never again eat her doggie nuggets after having been exposed to a sample of Flekovian goulash and a taste of my *vepřová plecko*—a dish whose composition I cannot say authoritatively, other than it must contain something highly attractive to canines.

The gregarious waiters bring Ella a big plastic bowl of water, and they bring her daddy way too many *pivo*s, which, the next morning, I think means "beers." When we finally stumble out of the babel-like din—the air is crowded with Czech, German, Dutch, French, and some English voices—my mutt and I stroll beside the Vltava River, disproportionately happy to be a man and man's best friend, respectively—though after a night at U Fleku, I'm not certain I can tell the difference.

I'm not surprised to learn subsequently that the residents of Prague consume more beer per capita than any other municipality in the world. There are more bars in this city than anyplace I've ever seen, including my hometown, Milwaukee, Wisconsin, Beer Capital of the United States. Every twenty meters we encounter another drinking establishment from which issues forth the sounds of laughter and Slavic chatter. Ella is attracted to the unfamiliar noise and intermittently pokes her nose into the doorways, sniffing for stray wursts and half-eaten *moučník*—which I think means "dessert." In Prague, my American dog walks without a leash. The stone streets are narrow and mostly free of traffic, and the ones that accommodate cars and trams have wide sidewalks suitable for a zigzagging sniffer.

I look at Ella sucking in the new aromas she's discovering on the streets of Prague, filling her nostrils with sublime smells beyond my human olfactory capabilities. She's having a swell time (I think).

One of the great joys of travel is having all of one's senses piqued by the extraordinary, the unusual, the new. But as anyone who has been flummoxed by unfamiliar languages and customs and foods can attest, the very reason we travel—to see what the world is like beyond our provincial routines—can often be the very reason we long to go home. Too much difference absorbed too quickly can be frightening. I recall the first time I visited Southeast Asia, in my early twenties. After the day and a half of flying, the navigation of the Bangkok airport, the negotiation with the taxi driver, the astonishing strangeness of everything I saw and smelled and heard, I arrived at my cheap hotel, closed the door of my tiny humid room, and promptly broke into uncontrollable tears. I looked at my return ticket and wondered how I could possibly endure the four awful weeks of sensory overload awaiting me before I could return to the comforting sameness of life in the United States.

Over the years I've become better prepared for what's commonly known as "culture shock," and I don't collapse nearly as much upon arrival. But, still, although I've now been to nearly sixty countries in my life, I understand why some people have a profound distaste for travel. It can be scary.

Watching Ella sniff every square inch of Prague sidewalk she can manage before getting scolded for not heeling, I wonder if perhaps dogs feel a similar sense of dislocation. Am I exposing her to too much newness, subjecting her to more raw sensual data than her little brain can handle? Does she like all the curious signals she's receiving through her nose, or does it unsettle her? Is this fun, or just way more stress than an elderly mutt needs?

Do I imagine it, or is she noticeably more fatigued than usual at the end of the day? Is the flagrant disruption of her daily patterns causing her distress? Or, like everyone, man and beast alike, is so much extra walking and doing and experiencing—so much *traveling*—naturally exhausting? Surely, not being able to relieve herself whenever she wants, as she can when she's back home in her garden, must be upsetting. And not finding one of her three bolster beds awaiting her tired paws at the end of the day must be mildly disconcerting. But, then again, I tell myself, she's with me. That's supposed to be the great trade-off.

Racked by momentary guilt, I promise Ella that when we stop for a *moučník* on the way back to the hotel she'll get a tasty treat that makes all the hardships worth it.

* * *

Walking through the ancient Prague streets at night, I notice that the city fathers have thoughtfully provided doggie-cleanup-bag dispensers at many intersections. I also notice that the residents of Prague largely ignore them. When I take Ella to a park beside the Vltava, near the famous medieval Charles Bridge, she does her business in a clump of high grass. I immediately rush to scoop her droppings into a specialized cardboard-and-plastic package designed and sold in the United States, and which I'm conscientiously schlepping around the continent, morbidly afraid of being an ugly American befouling the postcard-worthy streets of the great European cities.

The Czech dog owners at this riverside park observe my fastidiousness with barely concealed amusement. None of them, I notice, stoops to scoop. In fact, one young man in the company of a handsome Airedale terrier studies me toting my disposable package to a trash bin, fascinated and puzzled, it seems, that I should be willing to transport such objectionable cargo.

I don't mind. I've convinced myself that I'm not only representing the American population in general but American dog owners in specific. I can't say what exactly I'm crusading for, since I'm quickly discovering that American dogs are quite welcome in Europe. But though the legitimacy of traveling with my mutt may be moot, I'm determined nonetheless to be as good a boy as she is a good girl. Besides, everyone is so damn *nice* to tourists in the company of a rather large all-white-with-peach-colored-tips-on-her-ears-and-tail greyhound-Lab mix that I want to ensure neither I nor my pup do anything remotely untoward, anything that might make all these delightful strangers stop smiling at us. (Even when Ella loudly passes gas in our hotel elevator, the Czechs on board laugh and pet her back, subtly encouraging a behavior I'd just as well she not repeat.)

The residents of Prague, I observe, seem generally happier than the residents of Berlin. There are exceptions, of course. (Every society needs their misanthropes for balance, I suppose.) But as a whole, the Czechs strike me as noticeably jollier than the Germans. This may have something to do with the indigenous black beer—and I aim to conduct a full investigation before departing. It may also have something to do with the exhilaration that rushes into hearts and minds that finally, after extended darkness, are filled with the light of freedom.

Many of the buildings in Prague are painted in the pastel colors of St. Petersburg. But Praha, as it's called in Czech, seems brighter, demonstrably more alive than its Russian cousin to the north. A visitor can get lost wandering among the ravishing old apartment buildings, and one day that's what Ella and I do. We stroll through the gorgeous walking lanes, each one of them crying out for a snapshot, until I'm not sure where I am—and don't mind at all. I love that I can walk around Prague without an itinerary, without even a destination, and still feel engaged and provoked at every turn. Ella loves that she's welcome on all the streetcars and, as we're discovering throughout Europe, in all the cafés and restaurants, where, unbidden, every waiter brings her a bowl of water and a pat on the head. We're able to do almost everything I'd like to do *together,* and without feeling like an imposition or a scofflaw—although in Prague we manage to unwittingly commit two crimes within one hour.

Well, actually, *I'm* the one who deserves jail time, but my dog could be convicted as an accomplice.

Our first misdemeanor occurs when we jump on board a streetcar, assuming we must pay in transit. In fact, passengers are supposed to obtain a ticket *prior* to boarding, like on an airplane. (Where one does this I've not yet discovered.) I spend the interminable ten-minute journey from the Vltava River to the art nouveau Public House, the *náměstí Republiky,* looking over my shoulder, fearful a ticket-checker guy will throw me behind bars and impound my pup. Tortured by horrific visions of what they might do to my innocent-at-heart but guilty-by-association four-legged partner in crime, we get off two stops early and make three right turns to be certain we haven't been followed.

Then, on one of the pretty walking streets whose name I cannot pronounce, I pay for twelve postcards at a street vendor's stall and discover subsequently, when I sit down at a sidewalk café to write everyone back home, that I've actually taken thirteen.

"We're in big trouble, young lady," I inform my accomplice. "Do you have any idea what they do to dogs in the Prague pound?" (I certainly don't.)

Ella gets up from her spot beneath the table, places her front paws in my lap, and tries mightily to look as cute as caninely possible.

I kiss her on her black nose and scratch her behind her floppy ears. She smiles.

A wave of sadness passes through me. How I'm going to miss those smiles when they're gone. I try not to worry about the end—about Ella's, about mine, about everyone's I know and love. But how can I not? The trick, I suppose, is not to pretend that the inevitable won't happen; it's to use that morbid fact as a call to action, an inspiration to commit oneself to enjoying every blessed and too-brief day. To live while we can live.

On that note, instead of concentrating on Ella's obvious aging, the general slowing that all once-rapid animals endure, I focus on the profound amusement she's still able to generate simply by being an adorable dog. I watch her and Sandrine traverse the Staroměstské náměstí, the central square of Prague, and I giggle like a child watching a cartoon. I see her part a sea of pigeons as though they were an avian Red Sea, and I chuckle. I watch her sniff the ground where only seconds before so many Czech birds once sat, unaware that such a thing as an American dog was extant in this world, and I laugh. I laugh because although I know she won't be with me forever—and damn the omniscient power who forgot to arrange that!—right now, today, she's with me in a strange and distant land, effortlessly making me feel like we could be at home anywhere.

When we wander into the Jewish Quarter, where Franz Kafka lived, I labor to keep my mind on the present, not the inexorable future or the permanent past. It's a challenge. There's the Spanish Synagogue. An Old Synagogue. A New Synagogue.

Thanks to events that cannot be undone, these aren't merely architectural wonders; they're historical footnotes. (Ella commemorates the gravity of it all with a pee in the kosher bushes.) Canny travel agents offer daily bus tours departing from the Jewish Quarter to Terezín, the former concentration camp outside of Prague. I don't want to go. I don't want to be confronted with more reminders of anything that isn't about the magic of *right now*. If I have to die, I want to drown in beauty, in Prague's stone and bronze, in yeasty black beer, with my faithful doggie at my side.

It's late afternoon, when the sun is hottest in this part of town, and we plan on pausing for something Czech and Jewish and typical. But Ella is panting hard and beginning to fall behind—and not just because she's been detained by a fascinating smell that's got an iron grip on her attention. She's exhausted from all of our aimless walking and, unlike me, finds no invigoration from timeless architecture. I look for an appropriate resting place for her to recharge—maybe a restaurant that specializes in Czech-style gefilte fish—but instead we encounter an outdoor café put down in our path by providence. It's called Zíznivý Pes: the Thirsty Dog.

My *zíznivý pes* and I spend the rest of the day doing the things tourists are supposed to do when they visit an ancient European capital: viewing castles and cathedrals, palaces and monuments, all grand and noble edifices that initially stun the onlooker with their majesty and then leave him numb from astonishment overload. As I dutifully snap photos of the overwhelming beauty, my mind wanders again to larger questions of equitable wealth distribution, and the usurping of power, and persistent illusions of immortality. Ruminating on such concepts normally sends me spiraling downward into an existential funk worthy of a teenager upon his first reading of *The Trial*. But having my white mutt strolling beside me this day makes everything seem light and gay, as though everything around us were part of the airy set of a Fred Astaire musical. Off her leash (but on alert for motorized traffic), Ella visits all the cathedrals and castles and palaces in Prague and never once complains of boredom, let alone existential malaise.

Which gets me wondering. Is Ella happy here? Sure, I know she likes being with me, especially outdoors. But are granite buildings, no matter how ingeniously designed and sublimely gilded, a source of joy to a dog? Of course not. Yet here I am dragging her around the great capitals of Europe under the pretext of seeing new sites together. Might she be happier home in her garden, patrolling for squirrels and napping in the sun? Wouldn't she prefer to hike in Runyon Canyon, marking hundreds of chaparral bushes with her urine, instead of dashing from taxi to train to streetcar? Probably yes. But then I also wonder if all animals wouldn't be happier in their wild state, roaming in ancestral packs and following only the command of Nature. It's the rub of domestication (and antiterrorist schemes): liberty sacrificed for comfort and security.

Animal "rights" fanatics deny this trade-off, absurdly assigning house pets the same inalienable privileges as a sentient human being. This pathetic fallacy undermines those of us who do not confuse dogs with voting citizens. We don't think dogs—or cats, or circus elephants—are people, too. We merely believe that well-behaved, hygienic, four-legged friends ought not be discriminated against because they occasionally lick their nether regions in public. I disagree equally with the fanatics at PETA and puritanical moralists like the average American shopkeeper, and I disagree with them for the same reason: We're all animals; but some of us are smarter and stronger than others. Once both camps come to grips with that fact, you'll start seeing a lot more dogs in public places *and* a lot less cruelty toward innocent beasts.

Though these are concepts I assume Ella can't understand—and, hey, I could be totally mistaken about that—I explain them to her anyway, because I want her to know the rationalizations behind why she's going to be made to tramp around Prague, whether or not she finds the city the least bit amusing.

The next day at breakfast, during which Ella receives some ham surreptitiously slipped beneath my chair, I lay down the law. Since Praha, along with Paris, is one of the great walking cities on the planet (for humans, anyway), I tell Ella that she should be prepared to cover at least six miles in one long day of sightseeing. Sandrine and I will pause every couple of hours for refreshments and rest. But I'm not carrying her.

She sniffs my palm, her head spinning from *eau de pork*.

During all our perambulations, Ella seems to most enjoy our visit to the renowned Charles Bridge. While Sandrine and I browse for cheesy watercolors of the Prague skyline (to augment my collection of cheesy watercolors from around the world, which adorn the upstairs bathroom back home), Ella mingles with hundreds (thousands?) of peculiar-smelling (and thus fascinating) tourists. We visitors swarm here to take pictures of statues, appreciate the vista across the Vltava, and, most important, acquire officially licensed souvenir flotsam from the Czech vendors lining both sides of the bridge. These local salespeople aren't great conversationalists, but they do seem well versed in the English phrase "Good price for you!" There are also many dogs (not for sale) on the Charles Bridge, and Ella enjoys a few internationally flavored butt-sniffs. To her, this Big Attraction must feel like a carnival—not that she's ever actually been allowed to attend a carnival back in America. There's music and laughter and amusement. Old Satchel Mouth Louis, bless his heart, keeps following us around Europe, and as far as I'm concerned, that's always a good thing. While a Czech band plays Mr. Armstrong's "Chinatown" (with a Czech vocalist singing Slavically through a golden megaphone), Ella consumes the sensual gumbo of first-time sights and sounds and smells, truly gleeful, it seems, to be part of such a large and eclectic congregation.

Her other favorite spot is a café located on a terrace beside the Prague Castle. The standard tourist menu is no big deal, but the terrace has a spectacular view: It overlooks a garden infested with cats and kittens. As Ella stares and drools at the activity twenty feet below her, one intrepid feline reconnoiters, sneaking up on the water bowl a nice waitress has given her canine customer. When Ella finally notices the interloper, a staring contest ensues, complete with mutually raised hackles. The smaller beast eventually retreats in a blaze of hisses, while the bigger one maniacally sniffs the ground she has "won," searching frantically for a scent that might identify and explain the temporary visitor. Now, that's European fun!

At the end of a very long day, we're looking for a typical

Czech restaurant near our hotel, walking slowly, perusing menus, peering through windows. Then, suddenly, a rainstorm of biblical proportions fills the night sky, pelting so much water down upon us it hurts. (When the destructive flooding that covers much of Eastern Europe hits later in the summer of 2002, I can understand how such a disaster is possible. The rainfall here is *hard,* violent in its severity and quickness.) Trapped without an umbrella, we duck into the doorway of the first place we see, an absurdly swank establishment called Café Pod Kridlem, which, a sign announces, specializes in something called "New Age cuisine," an innovation that I imagine involves organically grown macrobiotic foods accompanied by Yanni music. It's one of the few dining establishments in Prague to sport such Western accoutrements as linen tablecloths and a wine list replete with first-growth Bordeaux. The prices, by Prague standards, are astronomical. Dinner for two could easily cost forty dollars here.

The Pod isn't the authentic beer-and-stew joint we were seeking, but the rain is intensifying and I've got two tired ladies on my hands (which can be dangerous). The only problem I see is that this restaurant obviously fancies itself one of the more refined culinary institutions east of the Vltava, and I'm having trouble picturing my wet mutt curled up on their art deco carpet. The wood floors of a beer pub? Sure. But such a *nice* place?

I enter the front door, where a man in a tuxedo and bow tie greets me. I ask him in German if he speaks English. In English, he says yes and asks me if I speak Czech. In French (what the hell am I thinking?), I tell him no and ask if we can talk in English.

"Of course," he says.

"Oh, thank you," I say. "There's two of us, no reservation. And, um, we have a dog. She's very well educated!"

He looks over my shoulder at the Belgian and the American.

"Of course," the host says. "This way, please."

We're led to a quiet table near the front window, a cozy spot from which to watch the storm raging outside. I point to the carpeted floor beside the table and direct Ella to "go to bed."

She . . . doesn't.

"Hey, Ella. Go to bed!" I say sternly.

She puts her tail between her legs and rubs against my thighs. I look to the host, expecting he'll throw us out. "Please enjoy," he says, and floats away on patent leather shoes.

I sit down and order Ella to do the same next to my chair. Instead, she puts her paws on my lap and tries to tuck her head underneath my arms. She's trembling.

"It's okay, Ella," I say soothingly, petting her back. "It's okay."

We're in what may be the finest restaurant in Prague, and I've got a seventy-three-pound mutt on my lap, quivering like a gelatin mold riding the subway.

Ella Konik isn't frightened of United States postal workers, meter readers from the gas company, or evangelical Seventh-Day Adventists spreading the good news door-to-door. Larger canines don't intimidate her, nor do aggressive blue jays swooping down on the backyard birdbath. And she doesn't find Wes Craven movies all that scary. But the unseen menace of thunder is enough to send her running for Daddy's arms. Ever since the cataclysmic Northridge earthquake, when Ella was just a wee lassie, she's been terrified of atmospheric rumblings.

I don't begrudge her irrational fears. We all have them. I just wish she weren't in the throes of a panic attack at this politically sensitive moment, when a crab-claws-and-candelabras joint is making the magnanimous gesture of letting a (slightly wet) American dog enter their gastronomic palace.

"Honey, I know you're scared," I tell her. "But you've got to lie down, or we're all going to the pound. Come on, Ella. It's okay."

She reluctantly leaves my lap and curls up beside my chair. A flash of lightning splits the night and a crack of thunder rumbles the windows. She jumps back to my lap. I hug her to my chest.

Just then, the host reappears to get our drink order. (Apparently he also serves as headwaiter for troublesome foreign visitors who can't control their spasmodic mutts.)

"She's scared of the thunder," I explain.

He nods. "Maybe a glass of wine?"

"For the dog?" I ask.

"That maybe is not a bad idea," the host says, chuckling. And then he tells us about the evening's specials.

When it becomes evident that my shivering puppy and I aren't going to be evicted, I'm able to relax enough to examine the menu, which features an eccentric synthesis of California-French-Slavic dishes. What's most strange about the chef's offerings, however, is that chicken, the most humble of meats back home, seems to be considered the supreme treat in this part of Europe. Every concoction involving the lowly fowl is nearly twice as expensive as those containing beef, pork, or fish. (I noticed this in Germany, too.) My curiosity aroused—and also because the most extravagantly priced item on the menu only costs about fourteen dollars—I order a chicken breast stuffed with prosciutto and wild mushrooms. It sounds delicious. But even more important, I'm fairly certain that the very frightened animal cowering on my lap will find this dinner distracting enough that she'll forget the unseen threat and behave like the serene lady I imagine her to be.

It works. After a few small tastes of chicken (when no one in the restaurant is looking) she retreats to the floor, where she stays for the rest of the meal, even as the storm continues to pound the cobblestone streets of old Prague.

The waiter comes by several times to check on us, and he notices that Ella is no longer making a spectacle of herself. He smiles and nods silently in her direction.

"She was just scared of the thunder," I overexplain. "Actually, she's a very well-behaved dog, a very good *pes*."

The tuxedoed gentleman raises his thick brows. "A good *pes*. You speak Czech!"

No, of course I don't. But if I did, I would tell him that both I and my doggie appreciate his kindness and tolerance, his willingness to ride out the storm, as it were. Lacking the skills to say as much, in Czech I merely tell him, "Thank you."

He seems to understand what I'm trying to communicate, despite my comic ineptitude with his native tongue. Though about nineteen people have explained to me the Czech phrase for "thank you," I keep saying it incorrectly. Sometimes it comes out *Chihuly,* as though I were touting a popular American artist whose blown-glass sculptures decorate casino lobbies around the world. Sometimes I inadvertently say *patooey,* as though I were spitting. When I'm thinking about chocolate milk I say *yoohooey.* When I'm wondering how I'm going to open the door to our hotel room I say *duh-keya.* And when I'm reading about New York's baseball team in the *International Herald Tribune* I say *yanqui-ah.* Only when we're on the train out of the Czech Republic do I finally say the word correctly. (And I still don't know how to spell it.)

But on this night, surrounded by good food, refined decor, and a momentarily contented dog, I say to our Czech host *dookuey*. He looks at the rain outside and the white mutt at my feet and he seems to understand everything I'm trying to say.

En route from
Prague to Vienna

At Mozart's grave in Vienna

Chapter 6

We arrive in Vienna on July 4, Independence Day. Ella wears her celebratory American flag scarf. (Her modest collection of neckwear includes the classic red-bandanna look, which makes her look butch, and the fetching leopard-print number, which doesn't.) Yet, though she's sporting her stars-and-stripes nationalistic garb, I suspect few of the natives believe she is, in fact, a visitor from the United States. This is because, by now, in her fourth European country, she's walking confidently off the leash, almost swaggering with assured brio. (Or maybe it's just me, ridiculously proud of my extraordinary hound.) Despite the newness of everything she encounters, Ella seems utterly at home on a continent that's six thousand miles from her Hollywood garden.

At the sidewalk café of the Hotel Sacher, eponym of the beloved chocolate torte that has added untold inches to the waistlines of diners everywhere, a genteel, mustachioed Viennese man named Karl stops at our table to tell me he noticed Ella on his way inside. "She vas beheffing just pufuhetly, lying there, so shtill. Und ven I came back, she vas in the same place! I vould say this is un exceptionally vell-behaved dog. Ya?"

I affirm Karl's assessment with as much modesty as I can muster—which, I confess, isn't much when it comes to Ella. When Austrians I've never met take a moment from their day to sing Ella's virtues, I feel like a father who's just been told by the homeroom teacher that his daughter was a particularly compelling Mary in the elementary school Christmas pageant.

She's by no means a person, a point gracefully reinforced on the train ride from the Czech Republic to Austria, during which Ella was charged half the human second-class fare—the dog rate. But she's not a stupid beast, either. In fact, she's a really smart beast who possesses a plethora of human virtues we humans too often neglect. Like, for instance, being kind to strangers. I grew up being taught one shouldn't even talk to strangers, let alone befriend them. But Ella, bless her heart, seems incapable of prejudice or innate distrust. Unless given solid evidence to the contrary, she likes everyone—and everyone likes her, especially in Europe.

What a charmed state of affairs, I think, savoring a last bite of Sacher torte. Normally I'm introverted, slightly awkward in social situations. (So was the Nobel Prize winner John Steinbeck. And when he set off across America in a mobile home in the 1960s, he famously brought along his poodle Charley to help.) Despite my natural reticence, following my sweet mutt's example, I resolve to henceforth open my heart to whatever European I may randomly encounter in my trek across their continent. Like Ella, I'm going to assume everyone, no matter how different or unfathomable, is a potential friend.

This ethos, I know, will be particularly difficult in Austria, which holds for me a panoply of historical associations, many of them ominous and dark. But then I remind myself that my dog and I are able to stroll freely and happily and safely through what was formerly a Nazi stronghold, formerly the official residence of people like Kurt Waldheim. Meanwhile, back home in the allegedly evolved city of Los Angeles, California, innocent fliers on El Al are being shot at the airport check-in counter by a crazed gunman filled with hatred for all the "infidels" who worship a different deity than he does.

It's the summer following the 9/11 terrorist attacks. Yet, here in Vienna, I'm accompanied by a white dog with an American flag around her furry neck, and somehow I'm not terrorized at all.

* * *

As a modest reward for canvassing the entirety of Prague on foot, and without complaint, I treat us all to an extravagant tour of Vienna via horse-drawn carriage. The city has *fiaker* ranks (horse limousine stands, which you can smell from some distance) situated around the important tourist magnets. Instead of making the ladies—especially the seventy-year-old one with four paws—walk from palace to theater to palace to cathedral and then to another palace (Vienna has a lot of palaces), we three pile into a chariot, camera at the ready.

Ella seems supremely comfortable perched upon a blanketed bench. I imagine she feels a vague sense of kinship with Frederick, the horse that's pulling her around Vienna, since, like her, he's all white, with light brown markings at the tips of his ears. I doubt Ella fully comprehends the difference between, say, a convertible automobile and a fiaker, except that the latter moves much more slowly. But in the carriage she seems to affect a queenly attitude, a regality, as Frederick clip-clops her around his city. It's as though she were examining her loyal subjects—residents of Vienna and the people who come to take photos of their buildings—from a majestic pulpit.

"Hey, your Royal Highness," I call out to her. "Before you get too carried away with yourself, don't forget I still have to pick up your poo with a plastic bag."

Ella cocks her head at me.

"Yes, you."

She blinks twice and returns to viewing her duchy.

Serenaded by the hypnotic rhythm of Frederick's percussive hooves, we roll from one magnificent edifice to another, astonished at the accumulated wealth and unabashed pulchritude that occupies the center of Vienna, south of the Danube. (Well, I'm astonished. Per her usual custom, Ella eventually falls asleep.) The city's splendor reminds me of the series of Sisi movies, starring Romy Schneider, popular with European girls who dream of marrying rapacious princes. (The actual Empress Elizabeth palace, the Schönbrunn, is about thirty minutes out of town, to the southwest.) If you can conveniently forget that the Sisi legend utterly whitewashes her husband Emperor Franz's brutal reign, the cinematic gowns and sparkling chandeliers and glamorous state balls are simply divine. Likewise, if you can make yourself ignore some of Austria's troubling past, it twinkles in the tourist's eye like a sequined silk dress. As we traverse Vienna, decades of ugly history seem to vanish beneath the corrective brush of baroque architecture and golden monuments.

The palaces, the cathedrals—yes, they're all so beautiful you can hardly believe they were built by mere mortals. But after so many glorious structures viewed in close succession, I find myself becoming numb and immune to their appeal. Call me a simpleton, a fool, an aesthetically challenged heathen. But I admit the pretty buildings eventually start to bore me. I'll also admit I'm greatly amused by a battalion of Japanese tourists streaming out of their bus toting videocameras, all of them murmuring excitedly and advancing on our carriage like well-drilled soldiers. They aim their recording devices at us, laugh heartily, and fire away. They're overwhelmed, I gather, by the irresistible cuteness of Ella Guinevere Konik riding behind a gallant steed, impersonating the Duchess of Fiaker. Yes, all the hand-carved gargoyles on St. Stephen's Cathedral are nice. But I'm more excited to know that my American mutt is now an integral part of several dozen souvenir videotapes being watched in Osaka family rooms.

* * *

One night we dine not far from Frederick's fiaker rank at the evocatively named Bierklinik restaurant, which, as the sobriquet suggests, promotes a deeper understanding of malted hops and barley. Not only is Ella welcomed warmly at this classic Viennese brew pub, she's lucky enough to be seated—okay, lying on the floor—next to the restaurant's owner, Erika Kos, who's entertaining some friends. Frau Kos proclaims herself a *big* dog lover (in German, with a strong Austrian accent that reminds me of Arnold Schwarzenegger) and, on her own accord, brings her esteemed canine visitor a bowl of water and a heaping plate of cold wurst. To my dismay, Ella inhales the sausages like a whale devouring plankton, hardly pausing to chew. Frau Kos shrugs and exclaims, "She likes our wurst!"

"That wasn't very ladylike," I tell Ella, who's already arranging her facial features into beggar mode, hoping for more handouts. "You're supposed to be a dog, not a swine."

Her expectant expression suggests, *Yeah. Okay. Whatever. Do I get any more sausages?*

One of the things that separates man from the beasts—besides opposable thumbs—is our ability to savor sensual experiences, to prolong or even delay pleasure; indeed, to find the pleasure inherent in everyday acts. Unlike my voracious dog, I linger over a plate of Wiener schnitzel—ordered on Eat Indigenously grounds—marveling at the simple goodness of a perfectly prepared portion of breaded veal. The American version to which I'm accustomed resembles the authentic Viennese version only in name. The Wiener schnitzel at Erika's Bierklinik is impossibly delicate and devoid of grease, as though it were prepared in not a frying pan but a tandoori oven. Paired with a dark beer (and the magnanimousness of our host), the Bierklinik seems at the moment the most perfect place on earth for a man and his hound to have dinner.

And I'm not the only one who thinks so. There are four wooden tables in our section of the pub. Three of them have dogs lying beneath them. And all three animals are asleep, sated on Erika's wurst.

Slightly tipsy from my advanced studies at the Bierklinik symposium, I begin to muse out loud on what the white doggie beneath my table might be thinking.

"What are you thinking?" I ask Ella, who opens her eyes momentarily, heaves a dramatic sigh, and returns to slumber.

"No, really. Tell me." I half expect her to answer me.

I whisper to her. "Are you happy? Do you know where you are?" I feel myself getting weepy, and at the risk of embarrassing myself (not to mention Sandrine and Ella), I halt the imaginary colloquy.

But silently I wonder: *Does Ella miss her home? Does she pray the Bierklinik is her new home? Does she assume we're going to relocate every few days, like a band of nomads, for the rest of our lives?*

Then I let my mind wander down the peculiar paths of the subconscious, into murky territory we usually visit in dreams. Or when we've had too much beer. I wonder about impossible-to-answer questions that have vexed philosophers and poets throughout the ages. What Does Life Mean? What's the Nature of a Soul? Does My Dog Have One?

I look at my sweet hound, asleep on the floor. *Does she even comprehend that life itself is finite? Or is she unconcerned, thanks mostly to her devout belief in reincarnation? Who, in fact, was Ella in a past life? Anyone I might know? Mozart, maybe? Is Ella/Mozart finally returning to her/his real "home"?*

I snap out of my reverie and pull myself together long enough to express my thanks to Frau Kos and to trundle Ella onto a streetcar back to our hotel. She's made to pay a "kinder-fare"—the child's price. I take that as a subtle signal that maybe I'm on to something with this reincarnation business. In this grand and confounding universe we inhabit, anything, it seems, is possible. Later, thinking about it in bed, I decide I've just had too much to drink.

Despite the patent absurdity of imbuing my pet with the same made-up history claimed by countless residents of state psychiatric facilities, I've got the idea in my head that Ella Konik isn't *just a dog*. I mean, yes, I know she's a dog. All the obvious signs are there. But also, if you look closely, all the other signs are there too. Her comprehension of conversational English. Her sensitivity to emotions and moods. Her problem-solving aptitude. This is not a normal dog. Everyone says so.

I realize that what I'm about to report sounds like the mad hallucination of a lunatic. So I should preface my remarks by saying I am of relatively sound mind and can tell the difference between right and wrong, good and evil, reality and fiction. (I do not, however, profess to understand string theory, past lives, or even the enduring popularity of music composed and performed by Kenny G.) It's all beyond my meager ability to make sense of a universe that's too big and beautiful and complicated for my wee brain. I would modestly suggest, therefore, that I'm not crazy. I'm just a little confused and uncertain—which, if I'm to believe W. K. Heisenberg and a lot of other people far smarter than I, is a natural state of affairs.

This is all to say that the next morning I take Ella to visit Wolfgang Amadeus Mozart's grave, just to see if anything weird happens. Anything spooky and suggestive.

Nothing does. (At least nothing I'm able to detect.) But for me it's still a transcendent experience.

Even if he and my dog are not one and the same—*What the*

hell was I thinking?—I'm still struck by the magnitude of the gifts he left behind, and that they were given to us by a person who once really and truly existed. Standing at Mozart's grave, I realize almost palpably that this immortal genius isn't merely a legend, a historical figment that we read about and marvel at, but a real man—a human being who lived and died and whose remains now lie beneath a floral plot of dirt in a sylvan cemetery.

Ella isn't supposed to be inside the gates; there's a sign posted that says *HUNDE VERBOTEN.* But here on the outskirts of town, far from the beautiful opera house and concert hall where Mozart's music originally rang out, the cemetery is nearly deserted. Aside from a workman painting a fence, we're the only ones here. (This is never the case at the grave sites of Jim Morrison or John Lennon, but never mind.) So we stroll through the entrance undisturbed. I walk beside Ella through the headstones of Vienna's prominent burghers and socialites, neither leading nor following, but secretly hoping she'll direct me to her/Mozart's resting spot. To my dismay, she doesn't react as though the cemetery is a sacred nexus that sends magnetic vibrations through her body. To Ella, apparently, it's just a pleasant place to sniff and find some shade.

I locate Mozart's grave myself. A discreet green sign points to the prodigy's resting place, in a small semicircular arbor. For a man whose creations are a constant source of pleasure to all of humanity, his burial site is remarkably humble. I recall Shakespeare's Richard II: "And my large kingdom for a little grave, a little little grave, an obscure grave." There's a modest stone cross, broken and crumbling, looming over a simple headstone: "W. A. Mozart 1756–1791." An angel stands beside the monument, his hand on his brow, disconsolate that the music has been silenced.

From 1756 to 1791. Thirty-five years! That's all. Franz Schubert even less. Yet can we say these residents of Vienna didn't live a full life?

I gaze at Mozart's grave, with Ella sitting demurely beside it, and I wonder what, if anything, I'll leave behind. What work of lasting value? What meager contribution, even? Books about golf and gambling? A book about traipsing through Europe with my dog?

Maybe Maestro Mozart will inspire me, I think. Maybe there's a reason I can't yet comprehend for being here this morning with my American dog in a deserted Viennese cemetery.

I crouch down on my knees and lay my hands upon the ground covering the great composer. I don't know what I'm hoping for. Osmosis? A message from beyond? But I do it anyway, and I wait.

I wait for a minute. Ella curls up next to me.

We wait together some more, silently.

I can hear the birds singing a simple melody and the wind rustling the trees, and though Wolfgang Mozart does not speak to me through the dirt, the symphony of life, the music of being alive, fills my ears. I give Ella a long hug and rise to go.

Sometime later, talking with an erudite friend, I discover that "Mozart's grave" may not, in fact, be where Mozart is actually buried. (There's some controversy on this issue. But according to my friend, many historians report that the composer was ignobly interred in a mass paupers' grave.) I originally intend to ring up a few musicologists I know and research the question myself.

But I never do. Because I realize, in retrospect, that it doesn't matter. Habeas corpus be damned. It's irrelevant.

We humans all have more or less the same bodies, anatomically speaking. We're all the same mix of chemicals and proteins and minerals. It's the mind—and what's contained there—that distinguishes one man from billions of others. Which is why Mozart's decaying body may or may not lie beneath the ground in a leafy Vienna cemetery that my dog and I can visit—but his *spirit,* the thing I was foolishly looking for in Ella, lives forever. It might presently reside in another human form, or in a bird that sings childlike songs. (Or, who knows, in my hairy white dog.) But I can say with certainty that Mozart's spirit lives eternally in his music, singing out in symphony halls and skyscraper elevators, from parlor pianos and college choirs. Every time we hear what his mind created, he is there.

I look at Ella, resting peacefully beside Mozart's headstone. I hope when death comes to call I will feel likewise about her. The body shall pass on. But the joy and the love she gave will continue interminably. When Ella departs the physical world, I hope I will remember this day we spent together at Wolfgang Amadeus Mozart's resting place. And I hope I will find in the memory some small measure of consolation.

* * *

Vienna's cultural richness makes a man who lives in Hollywood, birthplace of aesthetic detritus like *Scooby Doo* and *My Wife and*

Kids, feel mildly retarded, as though having a home so near to where America vomits forth its popular culture could infect you with stupid germs. Hollywood: Home to Anna Nicole Smith and Steven Seagal. Vienna: Home to Mozart, Schubert, Beethoven, Schoenberg, Freud, Klimt, Schiele, and the entire Vienna Philharmonic.

Cognizant of their city's rich artistic legacy, the Vienna tourist commission—or whoever designates certain sites worthy of promotional literature—prints pocket-size maps with the birthplaces, resting places, and all-the-time-in-between places of Vienna's illustrious citizens. (The maps also show where tourists may find the casino.) It's possible to survey the important epochs of serious music in one frantic day, dashing from one composer's home to another, from classical to romantic to atonal, pausing briefly to admire original scores and antique furniture.

Ella, however, is not quite the music lover her daddy is—though she does frequently situate herself underneath the grand piano at home when I commence to play (badly) my (extremely limited) repertoire of sonatas and nocturnes. So I make her a deal, which, conveniently, she can't refuse even if she wants to. We'll go to just one or two of these famous Viennese cultural landmarks. Then we'll find a nice lawn—preferably at the former palace of a horrible despot—and play with her squeaky monkey toy.

I'm especially keen to see Sigmund Freud's place, in an artsy district not far from the Zentrum. I associate Freud, like Mozart, with grand, consciousness-altering intellectual achievements that make their creator feel somehow fictitious, made up. (I also like seeing where important writers did their writing.) Plus, there's a park nearby in case Ella grows bored with Dr. Freud's interior decorating.

When we arrive at the entrance, on the third floor of an apartment building, a soft-spoken young man with intricately shaved facial hair greets us at the door and says, in Austrian-accented English, "Italian? Spanish? English?"

"American," I say. "We're from America."

"Und so you speak English, ya?"

"Yes. English. I mean, the American version."

He looks at me impassively and hands me an audio handset. I briefly suspect the doorman is a doctoral student in psychiatry and my presence is an impromptu opportunity for him to do some fieldwork. Finally, he says, "Ah, yes. And I velcome you."

"Danke schön," I reply, drawing on my vast knowledge of Wayne Newton lyrics.

"Yes. But is dis your dock?" he asks, indicating Ella, sitting beside me.

"Yes. She speaks English, too," I say, smiling at my own feeble joke.

"I see," he says. "But den dis is a problem." He shrugs. "Duh dogs, dey are not allowed inside."

"But she's very well behaved," I say genially.

"Yes. Dis I cun see. But I am sorry. It is a problem."

"She's a big fan of Dr. Freud," I tell him.

He almost laughs. "I am sorry."

It's taken me less than two weeks in Europe to forget that dogs aren't invited everywhere their masters go. I had sublimated this psychological trauma.

I make arrangements with the elaborately barbered doorman

to leave Ella outside Freud's apartment. I tell my mutt I'll be back shortly and tour the place myself.

Dogs not allowed. I mutter silently in my head. *Dogs not allowed.* My diagnosis: anal retentive disorder exacerbated by white-hair neurosis. Just a few sessions on the couch and I could have these people completely cured.

Investigating Dr. Freud's former study and examination room, his family quarters and patient waiting room, I'm struck, as I was at Mozart's grave, by the irrefutable confirmation, the tactile *realness* contained in an old walking stick, a top hat, an ashtray. This man really did live (and die). He worked and loved and ate and slept. He isn't merely a theory for feminists and Marxists to argue about; he was a man with an apartment—an apartment through which I may now walk, albeit without canine escort.

I could linger here for hours, studying the faded photographs, the handwritten letters, the knickknacks. But I'm expected outside. On the way out, I note with delight a Freud family film of old man Sigmund playing with a chow named Jo-Fi, a dog he reportedly adored beyond any rational explanation.

Freud was crazy about his dog, I muse. *Hmm.*

Does this say something about my relationship with Ella? Does it somehow excuse whatever psychological quirks my love for my mutt potentially masks?

I don't know. But seeing the good doctor playing with his Jo-Fi as though they were two children on holiday makes me think Sigmund Freud might not have been such a difficult character after all.

Now, Ludwig van Beethoven I *know* was a troubled soul. (Or

at least I think I know, based on prevailing biographic wisdom.) But I'm thrilled to report that anyone who wants to can visit the Vienna home in which he wrote his Fifth Symphony and *Fidelio,* among other masterpieces. You can drop in without an appointment—and you can do it with your dog. ("As long as she doesn't pee everywhere," according to the small museum's curator.) And what a magical experience! How awe-inspiring it is to stand beside the two-hundred-year-old pianoforte Beethoven used to compose some of his greatest quartets. How stupendous it is to tread the same floorboards the maestro once paced, laboring to find the perfect motif for his Seventh Symphony. How magical indeed to realize the music that enriches and inspires life *today* was made—was born—*here,* in these rooms.

And how wonderful it is to enjoy the experience with your dog.

After passing inspection at the door—"She seems very cultivated," the curator, a tall Austrian man, comments in perfect English—Ella joins Sandrine and me inside Beethoven's modest apartment, on the fourth floor of a building that still houses dozens of local families. Sandrine herself composes classical music, and she is more or less reduced to exclamations along the lines of "Wow" every time she encounters another Beethoven keepsake, another original score, scribbled madly in barely intelligible notations. I, too, am stunned. Beethoven's creations alone make life worth living. I adore the sublime and intensely human art he gave to those of us who are able to do what in later life he could not: hear. I vaguely understand now the impulse that makes stalker freaks break into a celebrity's estate and sleep in his bed. To be in Beethoven's home, to touch his walls and look out his windows and, when no one is looking, place my fingertip upon his piano—I'm flabbergasted and giddy.

Ella is slightly less impressed. The floors are all polished wood, and her nails make a soft clicking as she moves from room to room, slipping slightly when she tries to turn a corner too quickly. Beethoven's piano, which occupies the center of a sunlit room and is surrounded by protective velvet ropes, does not strike my dog as an instrument out of which was wrought immortality. No, it's a nice spot of shade perfect for a nap. The curator doesn't seem to mind. Only two other couples, both Japanese, visit the Beethoven apartment this afternoon, and our host seems eager for us to stay, to linger over the exhibits and engage him in everyone's favorite classical music parlor game, "Who Was Beethoven's Immortal Beloved?" (The curator points to a not-very-good oil painting on the wall and says with startling certainty that it was the woman in the picture.) I listen to recordings of the *Eroica* symphony and the *Emperor* piano concerto, trying vainly to comprehend how the music I'm hearing in my headphones made the strange and glorious journey from the mind of that fellow there—the one whose portrait hangs on the wall, the one with the wild eyes, petulant mouth, and untamed hair—to brittle sheets of paper, and then onward into the light of day.

Floating in what feels like a fugue state, I summon my dog from the floor and return to the mysteries of quotidian life.

Chief among the enigmas I consider on this fine Austrian afternoon is the inconsequential yet niggling question: How can Ella go to sleep anywhere? No matter the circumstances, when she wants to rest she merely has to put her muzzle on her paws, and away she goes. The magic hardwood floors of Ludwig van Beethoven's apartment, the cool marble of a centuries-old café, the rumbling floorboards of an electric streetcar—Ella gets comfortable and, moments later, she's off to dreamland.

Unlike Hamlet—or any of us less eloquent, less royal dreamers—for Ella Konik there is no rub. Dreaming is what she does when her dad keeps her from grass and dirt and fun things to sniff.

What she dreams of I can't say, although sometimes her paws and lips twitch as though she were picturing herself running, chasing after uncoordinated rodents who can't evade her lightning strides. Does she envision herself as a champion racer? A hunter? The leader of a (domesticated and completely housebroken) pack?

I can only imagine. I do know, however, that in Vienna, Austria, one of Ella Konik's dreams finally comes true.

One morning, we three stand on the banks of the mighty Danube. Sandrine and I are singing Strauss's waltz in unintentional harmony, and Ella is teetering on the edge of the river, trying to filch mouthfuls of the not-at-all-blue water. (It's actually closer to a shade of transmission-fluid green.) She's about two feet above the current. I've discouraged her from jumping in—a drawn-out "noooooooo" does the trick—since I'm not convinced she'll be able to clamber back out.

But then, as they say on American television shows that specialize in shaky home videos of car crashes and tornadoes and children falling into elephant habitats at the zoo, "disaster strikes." During our second chorus—*da-na-na-na-na . . . plink-plink, plink-plink*—a mama duck and a trio of her ducklings paddle past us.

Ella can't help herself. This is like having a side of beef placed in her plastic bowl. This is like having her own Schönbrunn Palace filled entirely with grass and fire hydrants. This is like having her own St. Stephen's Cathedral stocked to the spires with rawhide bones.

She springs toward the flock with one pantherlike leap, crashing into the Danube with a prodigious splash. The mama duck squawks furiously and the babies scatter. Ella dog-paddles—what else?—behind the mama, but far too slowly to catch the alarmed bird, who periodically looks over her shoulder to shout obscene curses at the white beast swimming in her wake. (Not that Ella would actually *do* anything if she could overtake her quarry; for her it's not the thrill of the conquest but the sport of the chase that seems to arouse something in her greyhound-Lab constitution.)

I let Ella have a few seconds of fun and fantasy fulfillment, and then I sharply call her back to the bank—which, as I feared, is too tall for her to climb onto. She reluctantly paddles back to shore and struggles to get her paws over the edge without sinking back into the river. So I grab Ella by the nape of her neck, as her own mother surely did many years ago, and I drag her onto dry land.

She performs an odd prancing dance, half rodeo bull, half Lipizzaner stallion.

"Ella! You were floating in the Danube! What's a dog from

Los Angeles doing in the Danube?!" I'd kiss her, but I don't want to get splashed from the inevitable full-body dog shake.

My dog doesn't realize she's just swum in the Danube, muse of Johann Strauss (and subsequently of Stanley Kubrick and countless salad dressing and fabric softener commercials). All she knows is she got to chase a duck.

My dog also doesn't realize that she's in Vienna, home of Mozart and Beethoven and Sigmund Freud, where art and thought and music are just as important as a plate of wurst. But, I suspect, she understands intuitively, with a special innate sense—which maybe only dogs possess—that simply by being herself, having the soul she's always had, in this life and possibly others, Ella has somehow made her silly old dad a very happy man.

Riding the quintessential Venice mode of transportation

Chapter 7

Traveling from Austria to Italy on another overnight train, I prepare myself for all the obvious differences we're sure to encounter. Language, cuisine, architecture—the hallmarks that distinguish one culture from another. I'm also readying myself for any temperamental differences between the local inhabitants, the gradations of emotional expressiveness that allegedly distinguish one nationality from another. Austrians are one species of exotic animals; Italians are another. Trying to be an "observant traveler" sensitive to the vast variety of national characters that comprise the European continent, I'm unwittingly fortifying my prejudices.

Vienna and Venice couldn't be more different places. Their names both start with the letter V, and, let's see . . . well, they're both cities.

Dragging along a canine ambassador to both places, though, tends to obviate the starkest cultural contrasts. At the risk of sounding like a not-very-convincing greeting card, dogs teach the observant traveler that we're not elementally so different after all. (At least when it comes to cuddly animals that crave our affection.) Germanic or Italian, American or European, when we're around creatures like Ella, our best qualities, undiluted by nationalism, radiate outward. We're one tribe of nice people, in spite of the hackneyed stereotypes.

Now, although the inhabitants of Venice may be spiritually interchangeable with their brethren in Danzig or Dubuque, the place where they live is a singular oddity. Islands traditionally present a unique set of challenges to their inhabitants—getting stuff on and off chief among them—but Venice's oldness and compactness, and its dearth of unoccupied square footage, make it an especially challenging place to accomplish the ordinary tasks of everyday life.

That's the charitable way of putting it. A slightly less nice way would be: Venice, Italy, is an absurd, ridiculous, utterly impractical city that survives in spite of its fundamental wrongness.

Venice is also one of the most sublime metropolises on the planet, a place that everyone in the world (and his or her dog) ought to eventually experience. So there you go.

Here's another viewpoint, from a lifetime resident: "Venice is a great city for lovers. But Venice is not a great city for dogs." Case in point: One morning, walking through the Piazza San Marco with Ella, we encounter a piano tuner at work at an outdoor bandstand in front of a café, readying a keyboard for the ninety-six renditions of "O Sole Mio!" that will be played upon it before the sun sets. *"Che bella!"* he exclaims, admiring the hound. And then, I gather, he asks if he might pet her. (As this is communicated in rapidly delivered Italian, I can only make approximate guesses.) Naturally I agree, and another Venetian love story begins.

While the Piano Man exchanges kisses with Ella, I ask him if he knows a place, maybe a park, where *mio cane* could relieve herself. In what must strike some of the early morning tourists as a peculiar Venetian custom—*Look, Harold, how the Italians talk with their hands—and their arms and their legs too!*—I pantomime squatting and lifting my leg.

Because of early obedience training, Ella has got it in her head that urinating on stones or sidewalks is bad. She needs grass to go, even if it's a one-meter-square patch. Unfortunately, 99.9 percent of Venice is composed of rock.

The Piano Man enthusiastically recommends a nearby garden, adjacent to the water-bus stop for Calle Vallereso. I bid him *arrivederci* and he actually does the kissing-fingers gesture, seen only in television commercials for restaurant franchises and bad Hollywood movies featuring stereotyped Italian characters.

I speed-walk my desperate dog to what I hope will be salvation. As ravishingly gorgeous as Venice is to the human eye, it's something like a medieval torture chamber to Ella. Sure, there are countless public fountains from which she's welcome to drink. But then where may she rid herself of the by-product? Similarly, there are dozens of seemingly refreshing canals, beckoning her to swim in them. But her dad won't allow her in the foul, obviously polluted waterways. So much temptation, so little satisfaction.

The garden suggested by the Piano Man turns out to be a gated park conveniently located a mere fifteen-minute walk from our hotel on the Rialto, a distance that adds an element of suspense to our morning constitutionals. Will Ella be able to hold it, or will I be faced with the unenviable task of trying to clean a puddle off the narrow sidewalk in front of some elegant haberdashery, armed only with an ineffectual plastic bag and the ability to constantly repeat the phrase "I'm sorry" in Italian?

For reasons that become obvious within our first few hours in town, Venice is not home to many canines. (We see just a few, including a notably naughty beagle dragging his fashion-model owner through a small square while she attempts to talk on her palm-size cell phone.) The last thing I want is for Ella to be considered further evidence for keeping dogs out of this surreal city. This ancient community, with hardly a single "modern" building, somehow functions in the twenty-first century. (A constant rain of tourist dollars, euros, and yen doesn't hurt, I'm sure.) In Venice, seeing a dog out for a walk is itself a surreal sight. The image of Ella at the prow of a water taxi, puttering down the Grand Canal, is, to my disbelieving eyes, perhaps the strangest sight of all.

Given the rarity of her species, Ella is herself something of a minor tourist attraction in Venice. Everywhere we walk, the sounds of "oohs" and "aahs" echo through narrow alleys. I briefly consider setting up a stand near the vendors in San Marco who sell grain to feed the pigeons: "Only One Euro! Have Your Photo Taken with the *Cane Molta Bellissima*!" A couple of busy afternoons and I could have my bar bill paid. (Almost.)

Venice is truly an "international tourist destination," a label many places like to flaunt but few can actually support. Venice draws everyone who cherishes beauty, history, and pigeons.

Now, I don't presume to call Ella Konik an "international tourist destination" just yet, but I note that she tends to effortlessly attract everyone who cherishes cuteness, sweetness, and soft fur. In one Venetian day alone we meet travelers from England, India, Japan, Malaysia, Mexico, South Africa, and Bergen, New Jersey—not to mention fourteen different Italian cities (before I lose count). We meet painters and real estate developers, psychiatrists and vintners, interior decorators and engineers. We meet a rabbinical student from Moscow named Moishe (whose persistent invitation to Friday night services I'm able to decline on having-a-dog grounds). We meet a retired couple from Barcelona, whose repeated question of "How much?"—they might mean "How long?"—I mistakenly understand as an offer to purchase my dog. And we meet children, dozens of children, from all walks of life, whose eyes widen in wonder at the friendly white beast who meets their smiles and giggles with a tranquil wag of the tail.

In Venice, I feel Ella is even more of an American ambassador than usual, and I'm proud that she creates so much joy, no matter how fleeting, for the strangers she encounters. I'm also proud that on the day she wears her American flag scarf she does so with dignity and grace, that she doesn't visit shame upon our country by peeing in an inappropriate spot. Like, say, one of Venice's seductive *osterìas*.

She may not be able to find many open fields, but Ella has no problem locating dining places that welcome her inside their air-conditioned precincts. The proprietors of Venice's bars and trattorias embrace her presence—literally. (She gets lots of hugs and kisses, in classic emotionally demonstrative Italian style.) They're used to having locals and tourists alike lounging for hours, drinking cool glasses of wine, sampling an array of *cicchetti* (snacks), and talking loudly (with and without hands) about important issues of the day, like soccer. But because Venice has far fewer doggies than the average European city, the restaurateurs here aren't accustomed to seeing *cani* in their establishments. When one does turn up, particularly one that they deem *molto tranquillo e molto educato,* they can barely contain their delight. (Which, of course, takes me, Mr. Proud, to several astral planes beyond delighted.)

One night we pop into an *osterìa antica* during a violent rainstorm that rivals the one we endured in Prague. Normally, Ella would find a spot underneath the table, determine that she's not getting any scraps until the plates are cleared, and promptly go to sleep. But tonight epic thunderclaps are in the air again, and no matter how much I reassure her with "good girl"s, she trembles like an underdressed Californian visiting Reykjavík in January. She refuses to drink the bowl of water the nice waiter has brought and even forsakes the Holy Grail of Begging: antipasti. I dangle salami before her snout.

But she's having none of it. Ella's inconsolable.

Then the unthinkable: A few minutes after Sandrine gets up from our table to use the restroom, Ella stands up out of her "down" position and, in a most un-*tranquilla* and un-*educata* maneuver, leaves the table to look for her. Before I can call her back, to my horror and shame Ella wanders into the kitchen. It's one of those semi-open *cucine,* with a one-meter-wide slot in the wall, where the chef can hand the waiters plates of carpaccio and tagliatelle. Thus, I can see the whole terrible tragedy unfolding: Ella, frightened and confused, meanders among simmering pots of bolognese sauce, sautéed vegetables, and semolina pasta. Her investigation takes her past open containers of cuttlefish filets, platters of prosciutto, and scaloppini of veal. My dog is loose among the food!

I rush to retrieve her before the chef and owner, Marcello, calls the *polizìa*.

To my great relief, Marcello refrains from chasing the dog out of his kitchen with a broom and a cleaver. He doesn't even yell at her in an apoplectic frenzy.

No, instead, sounding like Roberto Begnini at his most endearing, Marcello exclaims, *"Aaay! Bellissima! Un bacio per Marcello!"* Then he bends down from his chopping and stirring to accept a lick on the nose.

"Aaay!" he calls out to the rest of his staff. *"Il cane è in cucina!"*

The entire staff gathers around and begins gesticulating in the much-lampooned but incredibly charming way Italians gesticulate, as though they were all simultaneously conducting the triumphal march from *Aida*. And none of them can stop laughing—or kissing—my still-confused but incrementally less frightened dog.

To the best of my knowledge, none of the diners at Marcello's *osterìa* contracts a fatal canine-borne disease that night. And I can say with some certainty that the Venetians in attendance, on both sides of the kitchen counter, enjoy one of the restaurant's most memorable visitors.

This scene, minus the kitchen invasion, repeats itself at every place we go to eat, as well as some we merely pass on our itinerant strolls. In Venice, Ella isn't tolerated; she's celebrated. At one *gelaterìa,* upon spying Ella on the sidewalk outside, one of the ladies who serves the addictive treats puts down her scooper, dashes out from behind the counter, and throws her arms around Ella amid high-pitched squeals of (Italian) ecstasy that border on the erotic. (Several English tourists look on with compulsory disapproval.) The gelato lady's unabashed joy—her nearly orgasmic howling—makes me laugh (and also blush a little). But it also reminds me that whether in America or Italy, Ella has the rare and priceless ability to generate smiles in others. I don't know if she feels good about this talent of hers; she might mistakenly assume that every human being she has the pleasure of meeting just happens to be a really happy person. But I certainly do. Traveling with Ella is like having a fur-covered flask containing a constantly replenished magic elixir.

One morning at our hotel, the breakfast waitress, Luisa, actually exclaims *"Mamma mia!"* when she first sees Ella in her dining room. (Until this day I was under the misguided impression that one only heard such pronouncements from bad improv comedy groups pretending to be Italian.) Luisa makes a frothy cappuccino and sits down next to our table, where, partly in English, mostly in Italian, she regales us with an epic tale of her papa and his house full of dogs and children, the rough translation of which goes something like this:

Luisa's daddy, Bepe, was a man of large tastes. He had twelve children, including Luisa, the youngest of the girls.

Bepe also had as many as half a dozen dogs at one time, which, thanks to the shortage of space caused by an abundance of children, were forced to sleep outside. For years, Luisa would see a procession of dogs come and go. Some would run away. Some were banished. Some died. And Bepe never shed a tear.

He was a hard man. Even when Luisa's mother passed on, she never saw her father cry.

At this point in Luisa's oration, I have a strong sense of where the narrative is going, and I sort of wish Luisa would stop before she gets to the sad part. But I don't know how to say so politely. So onward toward tragedy we rush.

Among the pack of canines that occupied Luisa's childhood home, Ingro, a noble Doberman pinscher and Bepe's favorite dog, got the special treatment. He was allowed to sleep inside, at the foot of Bepe's bed. The two "men" were inseparable. Bepe would talk to Ingro like he was a person and Ingro would always seem to understand. It was really quite amazing.

One day Ingro was hit by a bus.

Uh-oh.

He died that night. For the first time in her life, Luisa saw her father weep. He cried for what seemed like three days straight. Nothing anyone could do or say would bring him comfort. He would just repeat, again and again, how much he loved his Ingro.

And for the last fourteen years he's never owned another dog. Bepe says he never could, not after Ingro.

Bepe's a very old man now. When Luisa goes to sit with him, in the same house she was raised in, he seems so lonely. She suggests maybe he should get another dog. For company. "No," he says, "never another!"

Luisa doesn't push it. She doesn't want to see her father cry any more.

Luisa wipes a tear from her face and lets Ella lick her salty finger. The other diners peek over their coffee cups. "Then I see your *bambina,*" she says. "And I think maybe *padre mio . . .*" Her voice trails off.

"It's very hard to lose them," I say unhelpfully. "They're like family."

Luisa nods affirmatively. *"Sì."*

I say to Ella, "Give Luisa a kiss. Kiss, Ella." Ella points her black nose beneath Luisa's chin and gives the Italian woman a hearty lick on the neck. Luisa cries out joyfully. *"Aymiodiocaramore!"* and embraces Ella around the neck, allowing the dog to lick her face as though it were a gravy-stained plate. The other diners try unsuccessfully not to gawk.

"Good girl," I tell my affectionate mutt. "You're a good girl." I look at Ella, in the breakfast room of a Venetian hotel, a world away from the nursing homes and runaway shelters of Los Angeles. Whether she knows it or not—and sometimes I'm not sure—she's still doing her therapy work.

Luisa declares emphatically that she is in love with Ella. With slightly less certainty, she declares that it might do her father

Bepe some good to meet this nice *cane*—or at the very least have a photo of her. Maybe it would awaken something in him that's been asleep too long. Maybe he'll smile.

"Sure. Of course!" I tell her.

"Domani, domani!" Luisa declares. We'll take pictures tomorrow—with Luisa and Ella.

In the meantime, Luisa innocently inquires if I wouldn't mind, if it wouldn't be too much trouble, could she maybe give Ella a *piccolo* piece of Parma ham?

Ella would consider her a friend for life, I say. "Of course, signora."

I take this dog-meets-pork moment to show off Ella's "junk food" trick, performed in translation. Luisa's eyes widen in astonishment when Ella refuses to eat a slice of ham that I've told her is *alimente male*—and then devours the same piece when I call it *buono*. From the way she carries on, you would think Luisa had just witnessed a miracle along the lines of a weeping Madonna statue. (The virgin one.) The other hotel guests want to see what all the fuss is about, and we do the trick again. Luisa makes Italian exclamations that sound vaguely religious, something about blessings and divinity. (Clearly she's never seen Ella lick her own hairy butt.) Then she embraces the dog again, unwilling to let her go.

I explain to Luisa that Ella's junk food trick is no miracle. She's just a very smart dog, capable of learning just about anything that doesn't involve trigonometry or biophysics. To illustrate my point, I ask Luisa's colleague, Tira, who hails from Albania, how to say the words "up" and "down" in Tira's native language.

I don't know how to spell the words, but within thirty

seconds, my putatively monolingual mutt is hopping up and lying down when commanded in Albanian.

The dining room erupts in laughter, and Ella gets a compensatory slice of ham. Everyone's happy. Particularly me. I'm ashamed to admit what a stage father I am when it comes to my white hound, but it's true. I live vicariously through the love and affection Ella generates with her simple yet effective performances. Pathetic? Perhaps. Yet I can excuse my impulse to be my dog's impresario with this rationalization: She makes people feel joy. And I figure that's always a good thing.

The next day, when we arrive for breakfast, the room looks different, rearranged, almost as though it has shrunk overnight. Then I realize someone has commandeered four of the tables in the rear of the room (and the chairs that go with them) and concocted a makeshift stage, organizing the furniture into a platform with pedestals.

"Buon giorno!" Luisa calls out, striding purposefully from the kitchen. *"Mi amore!"* she cries at Ella, her arms outstretched for a hug. If I didn't know better, I would say Luisa was wearing heavy makeup.

With an evocative combination of hand movements and Italian, Luisa makes me understand that she hopes to make an official "portrait" of her and Ella—which she will in turn present to her father, Bepe.

With an audience of a few straggling guests picking at their croissants and melons, Ella leaps up onto the podium, and with one more hop, she settles onto a chair. Luisa sits beside her—two princesses on their thrones.

Using Luisa's camera, I snap three images of the two friends.

One picture, Luisa says, she'll send to us in America. One will go in her childhood home. And one, Luisa promises, will hang permanently in the breakfast room of her quaint Venetian inn.

If you have a cappuccino and a *pane* at the little Graspa de Ua Hotel on Venice's Rialto, you might see the Ella monument there today.

My dog is in good company. Venice is filled with monuments—to Marco Polo, to Casanova, to Carlo Goldoni. All real men in an unreal city. Monteverdi's tomb rests in a Venetian church, the Basilica di Santa Maria Gloriosa dei Frari, not twenty meters from a stunning Titian altarpiece that the locals gaze upon every time they kneel to pray. Testaments to great artists and architects and writers dot the city. And though the only "Venetian blinds" I see during our visit are on the train into town, the great wooden doors and stately statues—and the canals and the colors—remind faraway travelers that they're in a city like no other.

Venice, Italy, feels like an amusement park. Delicious food stands on every concourse tempt the palate, "water rides" beckon from every canal, and outlandish "characters" in familiar costumes roam the movie-set streets. The city is a friendly labyrinth from which one has no inclination to escape. To human beings, anyway. To Ella, beautiful Venice probably seems like every other place we've visited, i.e., not her grassy home. I wish I could explain to her that, for dogs, the Venice on the Pacific Ocean, twenty-five minutes on the freeway from her Hollywood garden, is not remotely as welcoming a city as the Venice in Italy. Even though the one back home in Los Angeles County was loosely modeled on the original in Europe, the

California version is notoriously antidog, with stringent leash laws and a draconian no-canines-on-the-beach policy that prevents four-legged Frisbee chasers from frolicking in the surf while their masters make sand castles.

Similarly, the Venice, Italy, version of Venice is a far nicer place (for dogs) than the Las Vegas equivalent, the Venetian Hotel and Casino. Like the original, this American version also features a Grand Canal, gondoliers, and tacky souvenir merchandise. But the Vegas Venetian has significantly more slot machines and blackjack tables. (The Las Vegas Venetian presents a semiotic enigma that I'm not nearly smart enough to unravel: How does one deconstruct the meaning of a completely "unreal" place which is modeled on a previous "unreal" place? I'm sure a diligent doctoral candidate somewhere in academia-land is tackling the problem as I write.) Do I even have to mention that, while the Vegas Venetian has a roster of celebrity chefs and more marble in the bathrooms than the average museum, it does not allow dogs to grace its polished floors?

To be fair, some attractions in Venice aren't as dog-friendly as I had hoped. The churches, for example. Not all the masterworks of Renaissance art hang in the Louvre and the Metropolitan, or for that matter, in museums at all. Many of them are exhibited in relative obscurity, tucked into dim corners of five-hundred-year-old Italian churches. Not grand cathedrals. Neighborhood churches. In Venice, at La Scuola Grande di San Rocco, an art lover can look at dozens of Tintorettos—he was a parishioner here, and San Rocco is sometimes called "Tintoretto's Sistine Chapel"—as well as brilliant Giorgiones, Bellinis, and Vivarinis. But you can't do it with a mutt.

Ella doesn't get fine art anyway. (She's unfamiliar with the Bible stories and early historical figures many of these old masters chose for their subject matter.) Still, I had harbored an unspoken fantasy that maybe on this side of the pond she'd be granted some kind of hall pass, a cultural exemption, and join me on my picture-gazing expeditions. When we get to San Rocco, however, and I ask the nice lady at the door if my *educata e tranquillo cane* can come look at the Tintorettos with me, the lady shakes her head, says something in Italian, and smiles in a way that communicates the rhetorical question *What, are you insane?*

So while I marvel inside at the art, Ella stays with Sandrine at an outdoor café. When I emerge from the church, slightly buzzed and slightly winded from both the quality and quantity of what I've just witnessed, I take Sandrine's place while she has a look. Sitting there in the shadow of San Rocco, I realize there may be as much pleasure in sipping cool red wine and sharing a *panini* with your dog as there is in viewing ancient legends rendered in colorful pigment.

* * *

Some things in life are compulsory. You can avoid them on grounds of iconoclasm, originality, or sheer obstinacy. But at the end of the day it's often much easier to just give in and do them. When in Venice, for instance, hiring a gondola for a tour of the canals is so predictable, so usual, so *touristy.* But, really, how can you go to Venice and not hire a gondola?

This is what I'm thinking, strolling the crowded sidewalks of the Rialto, wondering what I'm going to do with Ella while Sandrine and I do what the traveler's life dictates we must. I can't leave the dog parked on the shore while we paddle away. (Well, I could, but she would probably dive in after us.) And surely the famous Venetian gondolas are like the famous Venetian churches: pretty, popular, and off-limits to canines.

As my mom is fond of teaching her bright and inquisitive third-grade students, there's no such thing as a "dumb" question. Or, expressed as another cliché, it never hurts to ask.

That's the thing about clichés: The ideas they express turn out to be true so often that they become, well, clichés. Thus, I've become a big fan of doing a job myself when I want it done right, treating others the way I want to be treated, and, yes, asking because it never hurts.

Usually that last practice is easy: You just ask. But I find my principle gets sorely tested when I have to do the asking in a foreign language I'm no good at, and when the question seems so silly I can already hear the derisive answer.

"Excuse me, sir," I inquire of the first gondolier I see. "We'd like to hire your gondola for a ride. The two of us and, um, our dog. She's very well educated and tranquil. Is that possible?"

The gondolier, a muscular fellow outfitted in the standard gondolier uniform of horizontally striped shirt and straw boater with a sash, tries to decipher my halting Italian. "You wanna come in gondola, yes? With dog, yes?" he replies, not at all offended by my request, it seems.

"Yes! *Sì!*" I throw out my magic phrase. *"Un cane molto educata e tranquillo!"*

The gondolier nods. He looks at me and Sandrine. Then he looks at Ella. She looks back at him blankly.

"Okay. You come with me."

"All three?" I ask, worried I may not have made myself properly understood.

"Sì, tutti tre. Andiamo."

We negotiate the price for an hour-long cruise, a process I normally relish for the let's-play-a-game quality. Some cultures, I've learned, expect haggling and bickering to be part of the deal; without it, the transaction feels incomplete. If you don't dicker a little, the local merchant feels mildly offended, albeit financially better off than had you made a fuss. The Italians have one of those cultures. Everything is up for discussion. In this case, however, I'm not going to press my luck—and I think the gondolier (Gino is his name) knows it. Perhaps every gondolier in Venice readily accepts American dogs on their gondolas. But I'm not willing to investigate that possibility on the slim chance that Gino is, in fact, the only boatman in town who doesn't object to canine customers.

It's dusk, that magic time when the sunlight bathes Venice in orange-pink light, painting the already gorgeous old buildings with a patina of warming hues. Gino wants to hurry. It will be dark soon, and, if I understand him correctly, he was supposed to be home for dinner half an hour ago.

We file into the gondola. Sandrine and I recline on a low couch. Ella lies at our feet. And Gino assumes his position in the stern, pole in hand. I'm waiting for the Mario Lanza soundtrack to begin, for Merchant-Ivory productions to call out "Roll 'em!" But the life of Venice carries on normally. Waiters light candles at canal-side restaurants; tourists laden with shopping bags return to their hotels; and boats, hundreds of boats, putter to and fro on the Grand Canal, like so many cells in a drop of plasma.

I look at my dog. She must have a vague idea that she's on a boat, because the floor moves in a rocking, boatish kind of way. But she can't possibly understand that she's *in a gondola. In Venice, Italy.*

She lifts one of her hind legs and invites me to scratch her pink inner thigh. I whisper to her, like it's the biggest secret ever. *"You're on a gondola!"*

The impossibility of the moment is lost on Ms. Educated and Tranquil. But everyone else in Venice, it seems, appreciates what they're seeing. As we float beneath petite walking bridges, fellow tourists flock to snap photographs of me, Sandrine, and Ella, lounging in our waterborne chariot like three contented pashas. If they don't get the shot they had hoped for, many of the amateur paparazzi run ahead to the next bridge for another chance. We must be an amusing sight: an awestruck American, a grinning Belgian, and a pettable white mutt trying vainly to stay awake.

We cruise through narrow canals flanked by stone buildings painted pink, yellow, and green, and faded by centuries of air, light, and water. So ancient; so implacable. Venice looks like all the movies made about it, only better.

As Gino silently paddles his trio of mesmerized passengers into the interior of the city, back through time, back into an increasingly mystical place, I quietly sing a few Italian songs (by request) to the ladies at my side. Some Verdi, some Puccini, a little Donizetti. The sound of immortal melodies echoes off the stone fortresses surrounding us, blending with the gentle splash of Gino's paddle in the water. The eternal sun begins to set. The air cools rapidly. I snuggle closer to Ella, and I try to inhale the moment.

My sweet little puppy, now a stately old dame, falls asleep at my feet, rocked to slumber in her floating cradle. She's off in a land of her imagination, writing happy stories in her head. I, too, feel as though I'm in a dream, a delicious and fantastic dream, from which I never want to wake.

A "good luck" kiss
in Florence

Sleeping off an Italian lunch on the
Venice-to-Florence train

Chapter 8

The proprietors of our hotel in Florence are having a vociferous argument, shouting furiously at perceived injustices and flagrant stupidities they've been made to endure. (I can hear all this from my room, one flight above the reception desk.) After more careful listening, I'm able to determine, in fact, that nobody downstairs is actually angry. They're rehearsing the latest absurdist comedy by Dario Fo.

But after some more careful listening, I determine that, in fact, the "acting" is far too natural to be the product of subversive playwriting. They're actually all hearing-impaired. (Strange. I didn't notice this when the nice man at the front desk checked us in thirty minutes ago.)

My curiosity piqued, I put on some shorts and creep down the stairs to investigate.

What I discover are three normal Italians sharing a few simple stories—but at an operatic volume (and with an abundance of pantomime) that, when viewed live and in person, somehow seems not excessive in the least.

The lusty, passionate expressiveness of Florence makes no

impression whatsoever on Ella. She could sleep through the *Surprise* symphony—and often does. The architecture, the statuary, the *Italian-ness* of Firenze does not seem to mean much to my phlegmatic hound. Loud Italians, old carvings: Apparently they're all the same to her.

Still, Florence is an exciting place for a dog—because it's a little dangerous. Buzzing Vespas pay no heed to American mutts (or Italian ones for that matter). This is the first city in Europe where I'm scared to let Ella walk without her leash. Florence's spacious parks (with infrequently mown grass) are nice. But she can't enjoy them if she's constantly being run down by speeding motor scooters. The challenge here, I quickly ascertain, isn't finding fun things to do with my dog. It's keeping her alive.

Ensconcing Ella within the sturdy walls of a museum would surely do the trick, except, as I discovered in Venice, she's not welcome among the Tizianos and Raphaels. Too bad, because like most of the major Italian metropolises, Firenze, Italy, is home to more great art than can reasonably be seen by anyone with less than a year to linger. I'm determined, however, to try, even without the assistance of an expert guide dog.

While the girls cavort together in a nearby park frequented by local terriers and shepherds, I walk a few doors down from Hotel Joya—whose name gets me singing the last four bars of an aria from Verdi's *Otello: "Oh, joyyyyyy-aaaaaah!"*—to the entrance of the Gozzoli chapel, the ancient personal praying place of the de' Medici family. I'm not there five minutes before I begin to miss Ella's sunny presence. In the courtyard leading to the upstairs art collection, I see immense statues of several ideal(ized) young Adonises, the fifteenth-century equivalent of *Men's Health* cover boys, standing naked and proud—each with his trusty dog posed obediently at his flank.

Inside the chapel, whose walls Lorenzo and family had decorated with wraparound frescoes depicting the Medicis' civic excellence and spiritual holiness (a neat little trick most modern politicians seem to have trouble pulling off), I stand in awe before Benozzo Gozzoli's craftsmanship. The frescoes impress with both their grand scale—they fill the room—and their meticulous detail. I could stand for hours admiring the mastery in the vibrant brushwork, but, alas, there's an American mutt and a Flemish lady waiting for me outside. It's sad, because although I think Ella is completely color-blind (or maybe I've got her confused with my cat, who's home in California with a house sitter), I suspect she would appreciate the Gozzoli frescoes for their content, if not their execution. Among the noblemen and supplicants, the plebes and the patricians, the artist depicts at least eight hounds (that I counted), several of which are in the act of taking down a wild deer.

Would Ella consider this image a profound inspiration or an abiding mystery? Would a visit to the Gozzoli chapel awaken ancient impulses or confirm, instead, what a good and easy life she has? (Good and easy, of course, except when her dad is dragging her around Europe.) Regrettably, since she must play by the entrance rules, I'll never know.

Between museum visits, we take a walk through Florence's narrow streets, careful to avoid decapitation by Vespa. Not far from the Uffizi Gallery, my next stop, there's a statue of a wild boar. The idea, I gather from observing other tourists, is to make a small donation in the fountain at the pig's feet and then touch his nose for good luck. For some reason this seems to me like a good thing for Ella to do, although I can't think of a single instance where good luck (or a lack thereof) influences the outcome of her day's activities. (If she were a luckier dog, would previously sure-footed squirrels slip off the overhead wires that traverse Ella's yard? Would every thunderstorm bring with it a torrent of filet mignon from the heavens?) I encourage Ella to give the boar a kiss, but she's having none of it. So I scoop her into my arms and lift her to the lucky proboscis.

The moment of communion between dog and statue provides one amusing photo for me and about three dozen for other tourists, who ask me to repeat the maneuver with my seventy-three-pound load so they can get a souvenir picture. I gladly comply for another minute of posing—which is as long as my biceps hold out.

Florence in July is crammed with tourists (just like me, minus the dog). We come for the timeless art and the enduring architecture, the plates of penne and the *cornéttos* of gelati. But especially the art. In America, I'm accustomed to seeing the lengthy lines outside the Uffizi (two-hour wait) and the Accademia (ninety minutes, minimum) at the arena box office when Bruce Springsteen tickets go on sale, or at shopping malls when a daytime television star is signing copies of her low-fat cookbook. I take the queues of tourists waiting to look at Michelangelo's *David* and Botticelli's *Birth of Venus* as powerful and hopeful evidence that Western civilization is not yet irredeemably dead—despite the inexplicable popularity of Britney Spears, Carrot Top, and the entire cinematic oeuvre of Vin Diesel. I myself despise waiting in line for anything. But in Florence the treasures lurking at the conclusion of the tedious loitering makes the wait almost worth it. Even if you have to leave your pup outside.

The truth is, the next time I visit Florence—and I hope it's soon—I'll probably leave Ella at home. Lingering before Leonardo's *Annunciation,* I feel a brief pang of disappointment that I have to rush away from such sublimity because there's a white mutt waiting for me who doesn't care for Caravaggio, acts bored with Borromini, and would rather play the lotto than review the work of Giotto. This city, I think, speed-walking back to the hotel, has too many spectacular museums—and none of them admit dogs, American or otherwise.

When I'm reunited with my philistine friend after a morning of abbreviated art appreciation, I inform her that she's "going to the pound." This is my all-purpose expression of exasperation, which, after nine years of repetition, Ella has correctly translated into "I love you so much I'll never leave you!"

Sandrine tells me about Ella's "adventures"—dogs she met, places she surreptitiously urinated. High-drama stuff.

I tell Ella that it's a shame she's so hairy and flea-bitten and smelly, because she would have liked one of the pictures at the Uffizi Gallery. Veronese's *Esther Condota da Assuero*, I inform her, features a portrait of a white greyhound in the right foreground.

"I didn't know you were pals with Veronese!" I say, tousling her behind the ears.

She stares at me with her limpid brown eyes. At that moment I can't say I've seen any art more beautiful.

* * *

As sublime as Florence is indoors, it can be distressing outdoors, where trash fouls the otherwise picturesque streets. (To be fair, there may not be more litter in Firenze than in any other major European city, but when you've spent half a day surrounded by immortal creations, the collision with ugly reminders of man's less pleasing side can be jarring.) Ella, of course, adores rubbish indiscriminately strewn on the sidewalks. Each hastily discarded sandwich wrapper and half-eaten ice-cream cone is an opportunity for her to grab a few illicit sniffs (and, if her dad's not looking, a very naughty free meal).

I guess it's possible that the municipal workers who are supposed to pick up trash are on strike. It seems, while we're in Italy, that every day at least one tragically oppressed *gruppo* is having a work stoppage. Museum guards, bus drivers, trash collectors—someone's always not showing up for their job. One morning some workers involved in trains—I couldn't determine if it was engineers or ticket takers—called a national rail strike. For five hours. And politely announced their walkout forty-eight hours in advance so that the rest of Italy wouldn't be too terribly inconvenienced.

Ella and I are having a leisurely stroll through the cobblestone-and-jetsam streets, on our way to do something I know she really likes: getting a haircut and a shave. More precisely, she likes lying in the barbershop while *I* get a haircut and a shave.

She herself never needs haircuts because she sheds constantly, no matter how often I brush her. Back home in Los Angeles, Ella relishes our every-three-weeks jog to the barber in West Hollywood, where she's treated like one of the boys, an old customer welcome to lounge around and discuss politics, read the latest *Playboy,* and refrain from drinking the blue stuff in the comb jar.

The West Hollywood barber who cuts my hair, Franco, is a voluble American citizen originally from Iran who considers himself half Italian. (He lived in Bologna for ten years and started his family there.) Franco speaks Farsi and Italian fluently, and English slightly less so, and though my dog and I have been patronizing his shop for nine years, he still calls Ella "Allah."

"Mikey! How are you? Good morning, Allah. How are you?" he asks whenever we show up. Despite years of repetition, Franco still gets a kick out of Ella shaking his hand before she curls up at the foot of the barber's chair. And should a new customer wander in, Franco makes a big point of introducing him to "Allah," stressing that she is "much cleaner than most dogs." Franco has told me at least thirty times how he really doesn't like dogs, but that "Allah" is different. "So clean!" he emphasizes. "Like a person."

During each visit, Franco also likes to repeat his favorite Socratic inquiry with me. "If someone, he give you one million dollars, you don't sell her?"

"Never," I say for the hundredth time.

"Not even for a million?!"

"Nope."

"She's like family. Like child. Someone, he give me one million for my daughter, I say 'No!' Same thing for you?"

"Yep. She's like family."

"You don't sell her for nothing?!"

While Franco clips and pontificates—he's a strongly opinionated barber, especially about Middle Eastern affairs and soccer—Ella looks up from the floor, supervising my coiffure. I don't know if she understands what Franco is doing to me, but I think she's satisfied that it's nothing bad. When Franco removes the bib from around my shoulders, Ella has learned that it means it's time to go. She gives a last handshake to Franco—"Good-bye, Allah! Thank you for coming, Allah!"—and jogs back home.

To Ella this all qualifies as a big adventure, a morning of intense amusement. After so many years of regular visits, she associates Franco's barbershop with a pleasurable pack experience, a chance to hang around in a nice group, where everyone knows her name (sort of) and everyone likes her.

So when we find a tiny, two-chair barbershop in Florence, near the cathedral, not far from the lucky boar, Ella feels secure and familiar enough with the process to offer her paw to the startled shopkeeper and then arrange herself at the foot of his chair. The barber, Luigi, a gentle soul in his late fifties, doesn't speak a word of English, but then, technically, neither does Ella. They get along famously.

After communicating what I want—it's not difficult given the state of my beard and curls—I ask Luigi where I should put

Ella. He indicates that where she's lying is fine. He'll work around her.

Every time Luigi needs to switch from one side of my head to the other, he gingerly steps around the reclining dog at his feet, sometimes straddling her precariously when he reaches a tricky spot. Ella never moves. And Luigi acts like it's the most natural thing in the world to have a big white mutt sprawled on the floor of his little barbershop.

I ask Luigi all sorts of dumb touristy questions—"How long is the train to Perugia?"; "Do any other customers bring their dogs to the barber?"—to which he claims he doesn't know the answers. I half suspect he just doesn't want to be bothered while he works. Luigi moves around my head with alarming alacrity, his scissors beating like a hummingbird's wings. In a less experienced, less Italian barber's hands I would be concerned. But he seems like an old pro. And he doesn't mind tiptoeing around my dog as he clips. So I shut up and let him attend to business.

When Luigi's finished making me look somewhat presentable, he peels the bib off my shoulders. Ella hops up to go.

But wait! Luigi intends to apply a battery of pomades and sprays to my hair and a host of lotions and fragrances to my face. I tell Ella to go lie down and stay out of the man's way. Luigi, seeing my hand signals, indicates it's okay. He can manage. And so, while Luigi kneads and slaps and tickles his customer's scalp, Ella Konik stands between the legs of an Italian barber, "helping" him groom her dad by knocking herself against the inside of Luigi's thighs.

Luigi doesn't seem to mind the odd choreography—in fact,

I'd have to say he seems to *enjoy* it—so I indulge Ella's proclivity for running between the legs of total strangers. After all, we *are* in one of her favorite places, a barbershop. This one just happens to be in Firenze.

On the way back to Hotel Joya we encounter Dante's church. (This is one of the very cool things about being in Europe. You occasionally have the opportunity to randomly encounter, among a host of other awe-inspiring sites, Dante's church.) It's a tiny, unprepossessing building that you wouldn't ever guess was Dante's church, except there's a small sign out front of it that says "Dante's Church."

I peek inside while Ella waits at the door. There's no one here. Not an attendant, not other tourists: no one.

I approach the altar, where a solitary candle flickers, illuminating a small sixteenth-century painting of Jesus Christ on the cross. He looks inexplicably serene, despite the nails through his palms and the thorns puncturing his brow. I sit on a pew and look around the chapel. Was it here, perhaps on this very spot, where Dante Alighieri first had his visions of Hell? Was this the place where his Inferno grew from inchoate sparks? According to a small plaque on the wall, a certain Beatrice Portinari worshipped here too. Did he fantasize about her, even as his priest warned against the temptations of sin? Maybe this was where the seed of genius germinated. While Latin homilies echoed in the chapel, perhaps a young poet heard a rhyming epic in his head.

Recorded organ music plays softly through hidden speakers. Bach, I think. Hypnotized by the contrapuntal harmonies—and by the hard-to-digest idea that maybe I'm sitting in the spot, the *very spot,* where Dante imagined the first lines of a work literature students to this day are made to suffer through—I almost miss the unmistakable sound of toenails upon a stone floor.

Ella slinks up the center aisle of Dante's church. She has her neck down, ears back, and tail tucked: the body language of a doggie who knows she's just been a naughty girl—yet has a slim chance of getting away with it because she's so cute.

"Ella," I hiss, "you're not supposed to be inside a church."

She forces herself between my legs, wagging her tail. "Do you want to get both of us sent to Hell?"

Chastened, Ella tries to put her paws in my lap. "Hey! No carousing in Dante's church."

She hops off me and lies on the floor, resting her muzzle on her demurely crossed front legs. While I take a few more minutes to let the writer's spirit seep into my brain, Ella stays prostrate, assuming a posture that, if I didn't know better, I would assume was her attempt at prayer. Within seconds she's asleep.

I look at my pup, on the floor of Dante's church, and I giggle. She's not even Catholic!

On our way out of the church, I kneel down to kiss my reflective mutt. "Ella," I remind her again, "you're in a church. *What are you doing in a church?*" She tucks herself against my side and offers her butt for scratching.

I escort the furry apostate out into the afternoon light, in search of memories.

Every time we pause for a commemorative photo during our perambulation around Florence, I face the same problem. Whether I'm after a snapshot of Ella in front of a pretty fountain, or an imposing statue, or a storefront with a cat in the window, the result is moderate bedlam. Just as I get her posed like a self-conscious couture model, a horde of fellow tourists swoops in to shoot their own keepsakes of the nice white doggie sitting there so cutely. Thus, when I get the film developed, I discover that an inordinate number of my souvenir photos turn out to be excellent portraits of German, British, and Japanese rear ends.

Depending on the looseness of your definition, I suppose it all qualifies as "art." The Renaissance oil paintings, the marble sculptures, the snapshots—they're all attempts (some more successful than others) to show what the world looked like at a moment, in an era, during a bygone time. And if you think like a Dadaist, a connoisseur of "found objects" and aesthetic "events," then maybe everything in Florence, Italy, could be considered artful.

Luigi's haircut: art. A perfectly cooked plate of pasta: art. A white dog dodging a speeding Vespa . . .

I know if Ella could speak (in English, I mean), she would say that her favorite art is the performance variety. Not angry women smearing themselves in chocolate and shouting quotations from Gertrude Stein. Not two smelly college students chaining themselves together with twine for nine months. She likes art that *performs*.

In Florence, a startling number of enterprising street entertainers paint themselves gold or silver or copper green and pretend they're statues. I don't know if these "living monuments" are fledgling mimes or Buddhists in training or just really desperate for tourist handouts, but they've cultivated a remarkable talent for standing still—still as stone or bronze or whatever they're supposed to be made of. When a passerby drops a coin into the collection box, the "statue" comes to life, bowing or waving or executing an elaborate commedia dell'arte dance step. Then they go back to being a statue again until someone gives them a quarter. (Hey, everyone's got to make a living.) The living monuments of Florence, I notice, can stand, unblinking, for what seems like an impossible amount of time. And more than a few passersby are startled to eventually realize that the gold-plated sculpture they've been admiring is, in fact, a twenty-four-year-old art student named Eugenio.

My artistically sheltered dog would fall into the category of easily alarmed tourist. When, not far from Dante's church, we first encounter a living statue, spray-painted white to look like an angel, wings and all, Ella pays no attention to the static figure. But then, perceiving something I cannot—a tiny movement? an odor?—her body stiffens and the hair on her back goes up. She's alerting. She's protecting. She's *working*.

"What is it, Ella?" I ask her.

She begins to growl.

"What?" I know what, but it's fun asking her anyway.

For the first time in several weeks—since, in fact, we've been in Europe—Ella emits a full-throated bark. The statue doesn't move. Ella barks again, louder and more rapidly. The statue holds his pose: no money, no show.

With each bark, Ella leans toward the motionless figure and then quickly retreats. She's rocking like a Hasid at the Wailing Wall.

The noise of her voice echoes off Florence's stone buildings. I'm scared my mutt, spooked by art she doesn't understand, is going to get in trouble. So I tell her, "It's okay, Ella. It's okay," as soothingly as I can through my chuckles. Never taking her eyes off the frozen angel, she dials down from code red shouting to guttural, mildly concerned grumbling.

Then a towheaded child tosses a coin into the statue's box, inspiring a sudden "flight" to the heavens.

Ella goes berserk, barking like a pit bull on a chain.

The angel begins yelling back at Ella in Italian, making rather unangelic gestures with his glittering fingers.

I try to apologize, but I'm laughing too hard. The leash goes on around Ella's vibrating neck, and off we go in search of less shocking amusements.

For the balance of our time in Florence, Ella doesn't see a single Leonardo, Donatello, or Michelangelo. But she does see dozens of living monuments. Every time she's confronted by a motionless King Tut, Whistler's Mother, or Lady Liberty, her senses go on high alert, and she seems more provoked and stimulated—more *alive*—than she's ever been. And every time it happens, I stifle my guffaws, wrap my arms around her rigid muscles, and remind my aesthetically confused dog that this is what art is *supposed* to do, no matter how many legs you've got.

VIN

Sandrine revisits the Teatro Morlacchi
with a diva in training

Chapter 9

On the way to Rome—a phrase that has such a nice ring to it—we make a detour in Perugia, hopping off the train for a day of impromptu exploration. Built on a towering hilltop, Perugia looks like the pastoral fantasy some frustrated American, stuck in a job he hates, will flee to and then memorialize in a best-selling book called something like *Always Umbria: A Year in Perugia.* Medieval fortresses rub up against vineyards and olive groves. The stark un-American-ness of the place delights travelers from the United States seeking someplace that clearly isn't their own.

Already overdosed on *otherness,* I've made a point of stopping in Perugia with Ella because Sandrine loves the town. She summered here often with her family and spent a memorable fortnight performing with her Berklee College of Music classmates at the climax of the annual Umbria Jazz Festival. As soon as we get off the train, stow our luggage in lockers, and determine that Ella is allowed on the city bus, our first stop is the Teatro Morlacchi, where nearly a decade ago Sandrine played jazz guitar (one of five instruments she's mastered) to a packed house of music lovers. We snap commemorative photos and then we repair to the Café Morlacchi, across the street, where the silhouette of Miles Davis graces the front window and where, in her youth, Sandrine fled in panic after her combo's set. (Gripped by stage fright, she thought she was horrible; the faculty gave her the Most Promising Student award.)

"It's like déjà vu," Sandrine says, settling into a corner table. Just as it was on the night of her debut, the bar is filled with hopeful young musicians, clouds of blue cigarette smoke, and the sounds of bebop. The big difference this time is that on the floor there's a big white mutt named in honor of America's First Lady of Song.

All around Perugia we see stages everywhere, publicity posters everywhere, the word JAZZ everywhere—which is sort of odd, since Perugia is the kind of haunted Catholic city where you would expect to see the word REPENT plastered on the stone walls. A small Italian town replete with sun-washed cathedrals doesn't exactly suggest the cool hipness embodied by cats like Diz and Bird. But the fact is, for ten days in July, Perugia is the Jazz Capital of Europe. Our brief pop-in was decided upon at the spur of the moment, on a whim. But the lords of fate have looked after us well: We've arrived on the afternoon before the music starts. Last-minute bandstands and light canopies and speaker towers are being erected as we storm into town. I'm inspired to sing the Gershwin tune "But Not for Me," with nonsense lyrics meant to tease the nonsinging member of our band:

They're writing songs of love/But not for fleas
A smelly dog's above/But not for fleas

With bones to lead the way
I've learned to sit and stay
Though I prefer to play
With steak and cheese

Ella wags her tail in appreciation, happy to be sung to, no matter how objectionable the song. She's the perfect audience: Everything sounds good to her.

For the briefest of moments, Ella strays from my heel to investigate an interesting scent wafting out of a butcher shop. I quickly retrieve her and begin to make a mock speech on the sidewalk about how mortally ashamed I am of her scandalous behavior. But I don't have the will. I'm feeling too happy.

The truth is, today I'm proud to be an American (with an American dog) in Perugia. I come from the country that invented jazz, the land that produced Louis and Duke, Fats and Count, Billie and Sarah—and, yes, Ella. Many of them the descendants of slaves, the offspring of families brought to America in chains, these great artists were all citizens of a country that righted one of its essential wrongs, a country that listened to the sons and daughters of the disenfranchised express their newly won freedoms and ideals in a musical form that was all about freedoms and ideals.

Ella—the canine Ella—wears her American flag scarf, which an Italian shopkeeper who sells me film calls a *fazzolétto,* a handkerchief. I feel Ms. Ella is even more beloved here and now than she usually is, even more *bellissima* and even more *amorosa*. Because she's a *cane di jazz*.

I've tried numerous times to explain to my otherwise very

smart pup where her name came from. But no matter how many Ella Fitzgerald albums I put on the stereo, no matter how many times I say, "That's the lady that gave you your name! Her! That's your godmother!" Ella stares at me quizzically, perplexed at my animated shouting. To her, everything sounds like scat singing.

* * *

The concept (and enduring wisdom) of the siesta, a highly civilized interregnum during the hottest part of the day, becomes transparently clear to me in Perugia, where the midday sun sizzles the streets so mercilessly that Ella can't walk on them without singeing her pads. Most of the shops in Umbria close between one and four P.M., and then, post-siesta, stay open until seven-thirty or eight.

But not everyone in Perugia, I discover, is in bed listening to Mario Del Monaco on vinyl. The *osterìe* and *fiaschetterìe* and bars do a rollicking business while the sun shines. Generously marbled salami and chilled local wine taste especially good when you're anywhere but out in the heat.

Having never lived in Italy—and I can think of worse fates to befall an innocent lad—I haven't yet cultivated the admirable Perugian talent for drinking Chianti all afternoon and then managing to stay awake past six P.M. No, with a few *bìbite* of the good juice in me, I feel like my Ella, capable of instant narcolepsy. So after lunch, while much of the Perugian population continues to imbibe, my fellow napper and I find a grassy park beside a fifteenth-century church. We locate a shady patch beneath a towering fir tree. And then we look at the sky and do nothing. (Actually, Ella visits an Italian rottweiler puppy named Emma, drinks from a muddy puddle, and *then* does nothing.) For an hour or so, we celebrate what the Italians call *dólce far niente,* which I translate as "the sweetness of doing nothing."

This is very difficult for me, ridiculous as that sounds. It's an utterly new and, well, foreign way of spending my time. I'm accustomed to measuring my usefulness on earth by what I've accomplished, or learned, or made, as though having the industriousness of an ant is the road to nirvana. It's a huge challenge for me to acknowledge that sometimes inertia isn't so bad, that it's acceptable to be a body at rest.

The concept of *dólce far niente,* of course, couldn't be easier for Ella, who ought to have the motto tattooed on her butt. "You're my role model," I tell her. "For one afternoon at least."

We lie on the grass near a young Italian man who has the universal accoutrements of the bohemian disaffected: dreadlocks, an apostle's beard, and the emaciated physique of a heroin addict. As I study his counterculture visage, wondering what he does with his life and curious what he would think of mine, Reggae Jesus falls asleep. I turn my attention to Ella but, predictably, she's already deep into the second act of a dream I would guess involves salami. Following their sterling example, I drift off into a light slumber, half aware that I really ought to be doing something constructive.

When I awaken an hour later, Jesus has risen. Later in the afternoon, Ella and I discover him in Perugia's main square twirling a flaming baton for the amusement of the tourists, who toss him a few stray coins. *Dólce far niente,* indeed.

I look at Reggae Jesus. I look at Ella. They both seem happy enough, living simply but contentedly. Maybe I could be that way too. Maybe I could scrape out a living singing arias in stone piazzas, or by charging a few cents to take a photo with my glamorous jazz dog.

Maybe an obsession with *doing* isn't good for the soul. (Maybe obsessions in general aren't good.) Maybe, like Ella, I should learn to be fulfilled by a life spent dreaming—and occasionally getting a chunk of dried meat.

"What's the secret?" I ask my dog, who seems fascinated by the fire show her nap colleague is performing. "Doing or not doing? Balancing or obsessing?"

Ella walks between my legs and presents her hindquarters. The answer, apparently, is getting one's tushie scratched at regular intervals.

* * *

What Italy in general and Perugia in particular teaches its visitors—besides the astounding yumminess of things soaked in olive oil and garlic—is the merit of oldness. In America, everything is new. New and improved. The latest. Brand-new! Cars, houses, restaurants, dances, fashions—new is better. Anything not new is decrepit, and worse, probably boring.

I live in an eighty-seven-year-old home with an eighty-seven-year-old piano and a soon-to-be-seventy-seven-year-old dog. Both the house and the piano are considered ancient by Los Angeles standards. (The dog no longer gets calls for the ingenue roles, but then neither does Sharon Stone.) American culture, especially as exemplified by Hollywood, celebrates youth and despises age. Oldness frightens us because it's an outcome we can't escape, no matter how many new possessions and playthings we surround ourselves with.

In Italy, however, if something has the word *vècchio* (old) describing it, we tourists know it's probably worth seeing.

I watch my Ella walk up and down Perugia's staircases with her big tongue hanging out of her mouth. I watch her rise slowly and with obvious effort when I declare it's time to do and not to dream. I watch her pant in the Umbrian heat.

She never complains and she seldom falls behind. But my Ella is getting older.

We both are.

There are several churches and museums and other opportunities for cultural betterment in Perugia, not to mention dozens of places to listen to the world's best jazz musicians making magic.

But looking at my Ella, the swingingest, hippest, coolest jazz lady on four legs, I decide we're going to spend the rest of the day in Perugia sitting on a park bench, smelling the air and tasting the light, doing nothing together.

The best way to beat the heat in the Piazza Navona in Rome

The Roman Colosseum

Chapter 10

One of the clever nicknames assigned to Rome by travel writers bereft of ideas and reduced to copying from publicity brochures is "the Eternal City." That description seems to turn up in every story about Rome I've ever read—as ubiquitously as the phrase "Big Apple" in articles about New York. *The Eternal City.* It has a nice ring to it. And, frankly, Rome seems to have a less tenuous connection to eternity than Manhattan does to apples.

When we arrive in Italy's capital in late July, the phrase dances in my head. *Eternal City, Eternal City,* as though it were a catchy muffler-repair jingle that's insidiously burrowed into my brain. *Eternal City.* I don't know about the future part of that sobriquet. (At the rate we produce weapons of mass destruction, I'm not sure *any* of our civilization's great population centers will be around eternally.) But after my first look around the city, the past part seems fair enough. Rome feels like it's been around forever. I catch myself repeating the marketing slogan like a mantra. It's what I think every time I see another two-thousand-year-old dome or an even older senate building standing placidly and permanently as modern motor scooters and taxis rumble past.

I know from reading Stephen Hawking that all of Rome's seemingly "ancient" landmarks are mere eye blinks on the incomprehensibly long continuum of Time. But, man, compared to America, this place is *old*. Back home we have the Forum Shops at Caesars Palace, in Las Vegas, where souvenir hunters can buy all manner of consumer detritus *and* play the slots. Here they have the Roman Forum, where deteriorating but still proud edifices offer incontrovertible proof that all the history we were made to read in high school actually occurred. (And shaped the world we inhabit today.) If the Forum on this eastern side of the ocean seems somehow more inscrutable (how did this all happen, Mr. Gibbons?) than the one in the Mojave Desert, it also feels more real, more alive—despite the notable absence of NikeTown stores and mechanized gambling devices.

As in Perugia, I'm learning that the Culture of Youth isn't nearly as impressive to me as the profundity of oldness. Rome is hip and sexy and edgy. But it's also stolid and wise and permanent. It's old but not decrepit. Rome is old and noble.

Relatively speaking, so too is Ella Konik. She's an aging dowager with the spirit of a child, an enthusiastic sensualist trapped in the body of a declining spinster. Yet here she is, nonetheless, the Eternal Doggie, faithfully tramping along beside her dad, oblivious to the history that exists (and slowly erodes) around her.

What Ella likes most in Rome, I'm learning, is for a mild fuss to be made over her. Like most American women, she's a sucker for the attention of Italian men, even the patently insincere ones whose flattery is merely a ruse to get girls (hairy and otherwise) to look their way. Ella likes when we visit a place like the Spanish Steps, which her soul mate, Audrey Hepburn, descended so glamorously in *Roman Holiday.* Freshly brushed and combed, with a smart kerchief around her throat, Ella is all Hepburnian glamour as she reprises Audrey's sashay down the stairs, and the local lads whistle appreciatively at the elegant lady in their midst. (The fad for men this season is oversize smoked sunglasses, the kind I associate with homosexual drama teachers of the 1970s. When the Roman boys peer at Ella promenading down the Spanish Steps, their glasses have the effect of making their eyes look as though they're bugging out, like in a comic strip: *"Hubba-hubba! Wow-wow-wee!"*) Ella, like most proper and cultivated gals, summarily ignores their wolfish advances. She focuses her attention where good girls with a highly developed sense of smell ought to: alternately on Daddy and the aromatic street.

We're determined to visit all the usual tourist sites—particularly those that Ms. Audrey turned into mere backdrops for her unconsummated love affair with Gregory Peck. I've somehow got it in my head that my dog, were she capable of wearing dark sunglasses and perfectly tailored dresses, might draw favorable comparisons to movie starlets of yore. What good such associations do I cannot say. Ella's chances for international celebrity have long since passed, thanks to my having done absolutely nothing to generate a career for her. She did one fashion shoot in a Beverly Hills park with a bunch of other dogs when she was a young lass, and her smiling face has appeared in a few of the magazines I've written for when the photographer didn't want to pay for a proper model. But Ella's never had an agent or a manager, just legions of fans, including a dad who, I am slowly realizing as I type, sounds like a complete lunatic.

Now that we're in Europe together, I figure Ella ought to have a Roman holiday of her own. Something out of the movies. And if I'm the only one firing off snapshots of her exploits, the dog won't mind in the slightest. Ella doesn't know who Audrey Hepburn is. She doesn't care about clever romantic comedies, or, for that matter, unclever ones. Her taste in movies runs toward G-rated family pictures with four-legged protagonists, like *Air Bud, Beethoven,* and *Babe 2: Pig in the City.*

Nonetheless, when we arrive at the famed Fontana di Trevi, I sense that Ella feels some sort of psychic kinship with other attractive ladies who have been here previously. Like, say, Anita Ekberg.

While dozens of visitors (including me) take souvenir photos in front of the immense waterworks, Ella, performing a credible homage to *La Dolce Vita,* makes one vaulting leap and plunges into the fountain.

It's a hot day and, truth be told, I didn't exactly discourage her from investigating the liquid landmark. But I swear, Ella seems somehow drawn, as if by International Movie Star magnets, to the famous splashing water (and the fortune in coins contained therein). There's an enormous crowd around the Trevi—which is normal for a summer day—and a buzz of excited shouting passes through the crowd. I note an abundance of finger-pointing and camera-aiming, the kind of animated gesturing that typically accompanies the arrival of a celebrity at her movie opening. Ella, like one of the actresses she is unconsciously emulating, pretends not to notice the commotion she's caused. (She's too busy taking bites of the water as she cavorts in the spray.) Were I a highly paid Hollywood flack, I would stand aside and watch the spectacle unfold, content with another job well done: There's my client in the eye of the media storm.

But I don't have time to admire my public relations handiwork. One of the members of the large congregation at the Trevi Fountain this morning is an Italian policeman, irritable perhaps that he's been made to wear a funny hat in front of all the foreign tourists. The policeman blows his whistle as officiously as a whistle can be blown. You can almost hear the outrage in its shrill tone.

I reckon it's time to cut short my starlet's public outing and hustle her back into the safety of her limousine—or, failing that, back on her leash and onto a side street.

It's like a scene from a suspenseful action thriller: Our heroine (a very wet American dog) tries to extricate herself from the pool; the bad guy (the cop) works his way through the thick crowd unintentionally impeding his progress. To hasten Ella away from what I imagine could be an unpleasant brush with the law, I unceremoniously scoop her out of the fountain, clip on her collar, and drag her by the neck to the nearest alleyway, all the while leaving an incriminating trail of wet footprints in her wake. (Such a fate never befell Ms. Ekberg, but then she had Fellini on her side, not just a monolingual tourist with some funny ideas about his mongrel.) I speed-walk Ella to safety, all the while pretending to deliver stern remonstrations, as though I'm shocked—*shocked*—that my dog would actually swim in the

Trevi Fountain. My mock dismay probably doesn't fool anyone. I'm chortling too much at the sight of a soaking wet Ella scampering through the streets of Rome, her saturated tail sending demure parabolas of spray from side to side as she wags.

Later in the day, Ella immerses herself in another of Rome's best-known fountains, the one at the Piazza Navona. But this time, instead of getting scolded by the irate *carabinièri,* she makes the evening news in a brief montage illustrating the sweltering heat. (When the clip comes on in our hotel room, I think at first that I'm hallucinating, still feeling the effects of too many glasses of lunchtime red wine. But when Sandrine screams, "Ella's on the TV!" I know my stage-father fantasy has been realized: My pup has finally been discovered.) Being part Lab, Ella naturally likes the water, even if it's too shallow to swim in. So while I look at postcards from a vendor's nearby cart, Ella stands motionless in the fountain, like a weary saleslady soaking her feet in Epsom salts after a hard day at the mall.

A man named Dino, who says he's a sculptor—and who is apparently also a musician, based on the guitar he has slung over his shoulder—asks me in halting English a series of questions that I can't immediately decipher. He doesn't seem offended by the sight of Ella in the Navona fountain, but he doesn't seem amused either. Dino stares intently at my dog as he talks with me. He seems almost hypnotized.

Finally I figure out what Dino wants: a pose—for a photograph, I assume.

"No," the sculptor corrects me. "I make her."

"Oh," I say, not comprehending his intentions fully, but sensing that they're harmless, whatever they might be. Dino strikes me as a gentle soul with the heart of a poet—and an aversion to soap and razors. If he wants to "make" Ella, hey, by all means.

Per Dino's almost intelligible instructions, I get Ella out of the fountain and onto the flat stones surrounding it. He directs me to arrange her in a reclining pose, with her front legs stretched outward in front of her muzzle and her rear ones tucked into a neat package, like two backward commas.

Ella complies, of course, cooperating for the millionth time with one of Dad's inscrutable projects that she vaguely understands involves her staying still.

I giggle softly as Dino the sculptor-musician meditates upon my mutt's supine form. He says he wants to "internalize" her image. It will only take a minute.

"Sure," I say, trying to show Dino my appreciation of the visual arts. "Take your time." Ella cocks an eyebrow at me, looking for a sign that she's allowed to get up. I tell her, "You're modeling now, young lady. Just stay there and look beautiful." She cocks her eyebrow again and takes a deep, annoyed breath.

Dino isn't moving. He's concentrating.

I feel like I might have a laughing fit. But I catch myself. Who am I to say that one day a lovely marble rendering of my *cane* won't show up in the permanent collection of the Vatican Museum, along with all the other masterpieces the Church has hoarded throughout the centuries?

"Sì," Dino pronounces solemnly as he wakes from his trance. *"Sì."* He takes my arm. *"Grazie, signore."*

I tell him *prego* and inform Ella that she can get up and shake Dino's hand—the same hand that might well be wielding an expressive hammer or chisel while she's back in America, being a regular neighborhood dog. He extends his fingers for a shake. But Ella hops back into the fountain to cool her belly, baked hot from the stones.

"Temperamental talent. What're you gonna do?" I joke with Dino.

He nods solemnly and shuffles away, mumbling Italian phrases I don't recognize.

* * *

Our hotel is located just down the block from the Via Veneto, made famous—notorious?—in *La Dolce Vita,* a movie that's still fun to watch, even if, like me, you don't understand all of it. When Ella and I have a stroll there late one afternoon, I'm pretending (extremely unsuccessfully) that I'm Marcello Mastroianni and Ella's pretending (rather successfully) to ignore the heavy Italian accent I'm employing while imploring my *bambina* to give me *baci.* No one offers us a ride on their Vespa or in the back of their convertible. No one invites us to a weird party at some freaky castle on the outskirts of town. (In fact, I'm discovering that people—Italian or otherwise—tend not to talk at all to American fellows shouting nonsense phrases at a white dog.) But we still have a Felliniesque moment on the Via Veneto.

A local cat—there are thousands, maybe tens of thousands, roaming Rome—expresses his dismay at Ella's congenial attempt to make friends. Ella expresses her affection by trying to stick her nose in the cat's butt. The cat, a large gray tabby, hisses petulantly and makes a halfhearted lazy swat with his paw.

Trained well by Sammy, her brother back home, Ella understands that this feline gesture means Ms. Otis regrets she's unable to lunch this day, and that the smart thing for a canine to do is beat a hasty retreat. Ella pins her ears to her skull, tucks her tail between her haunches, and backpedals away from the menacing rain-cloud of fur.

But instead of leaving matters at that, the gray tabby stalks Ella for another fifty meters, hissing all the way. Ella looks over her shoulder, concerned, and walks faster. The cat continues to follow. We speed up again. So does the cat.

"What did you say to that cat? Some sarcastic comment about Prime Minister Berlusconi?" I ask Ella. "He's really offended!"

Now we're almost sprinting down the Via Veneto, and I'm not feeling very Mastroianni-like at all. The cat seems to lose interest, but not before sending us on our way with an Italianate gesture of his paw: "Geddadah here! *Cane pazzo!*"

Our Roman travails, unfortunately, aren't limited to sociopathic felines. During our July visit, the city gets hotter and hotter, so hot that even surreptitious dashes into off-limit fountains can't keep man or pup cool for long. I at least can use the oppressive sun as a feeble excuse to consume about fourteen times as much gelati as anyone not planning to become a sumo wrestler ought to. Ella, however, just broils in her standard wardrobe of white fur coat and bare feet.

One afternoon at the Colosseum, I'm attempting to get my hirsute gladiator beyond the ticket takers, none of whom seems particularly eager to have a (*molto educata, molto tranquillo*) dog at their tourist attraction. I make a feeble joke (in English) about Ella being really eager to see the site since she's the descendant of Christian-eating lions—which, of course, makes no sense whatsover, because she hails from an entirely different species. The guards understandably fail to see the humor in my remark. Request denied.

As I'm explaining to Ella how she'll just have to wait until we're home and watch *Gladiator* on video, I notice that she's doing a funny little dance, bouncing from side to side, front to back. She's also panting heavily and her tongue is the size of a cricket bat, but it's the dance that concerns me.

"What's wrong, baby?" I ask her.

She dances more strenuously and lets out a mild yelp.

Then I realize the stone pavement around the Colosseum has become so hot in the Roman sun that it's burning her paws. I bend down to touch the ground—possibly the same ground over which a sacrificial slave/entertainer once strode to meet his death—and it singes my fingers. I immediately lift Ella off the sizzling pavement and carry her through the crowd of tourists to the nearest patch of grass I can locate—which appears to be nearly a quarter-mile away. Like most stadiums, the Colosseum doesn't have many trees or lawns around its perimeter, just plenty of wide-open spaces for enterprising locals to dress up in breastplates and swords and sell souvenir dreck. Huffing like an unarmed combatant facing down a hungry beast, I carry Ella in both arms, one beneath her thighs, one beneath her chest. To the astonished onlookers, she must look like a mortally wounded colleague whom I'm transporting to her final resting place.

When I finally arrive at the grass and set down my furry

load, I've just about decided bringing my dog to Europe in the middle of summer was a really stupid idea. Ella, apparently, disagrees. She's hopping and wagging and play-biting, thrilled with the new game she thinks we've just made up—the one where I risk a myocardial infarction to spare her petite paws from the heat. "Ella," I tell her, kneeling down on the grass, struggling to catch my breath, "we're in Europe. In Rome. At the frickin' Colosseum. And I've got to carry you around like I'm Russell Crowe and you're some guy who just got his arms chopped off?"

Ella has an uncanny sense of the best times to give me a kiss. Like when I'm pissy. She knows how to make it impossible for me to stay annoyed with her.

She licks me across the nose, which must taste pretty good to her at this point, since it's drenched in perspiration.

"Don't try to sweet-talk me, you hairy beast," I warn her.

She kisses me again.

"I'm not carrying you anymore," I vow. "You're too heavy. And too hairy. And too smelly. And you're not a movie star, no matter how many Italian boys whistle at you." Since I say this all in a tone of voice that suggests we're about to play a really fun game involving a squeaky toy, Ella translates my diatribe as *You're the best dog in the world and it's an honor to lug you around Rome*—an interpretation that may, in fact, have a tiny bit of merit to it.

I examine Ella's paws. They don't seem to be burnt too badly. But her nails, I notice for the first time, are ground down to the pink, and some of them are cracked and splintered. This happens, I suppose, when you walk dozens of miles without socks and shoes. I've been a bad chaperone: I should have considered the difference between the dirt paths of our neighborhood canyon and the stone surfaces of European cities.

"Ella! Why didn't you tell me about your feet? Are you all right?"

She answers me with another kiss.

I look at my eleven-year-old mutt. I look at the Colosseum looming above us. And I realize that one of us resting on the lawn is more of a warrior than I previously realized.

It's way too hot to make the thirty-minute walk back to our hotel, especially given the state of Ella's pedicure. So I attempt to hail a cab.

This hasn't been a problem thus far. In every city we've visited, whenever we wanted to take a taxi I just made the standard waving motions, waited for a cab to pull over, and trundled into the back with my mutt. In Rome, however, the first two parts of the process seem to work properly, but the last part—the actually getting into the automobile part—doesn't happen. I signal; the cabbies pull over; and then, when they see Ella, they drive on past. Then, to add insult to injury, they inevitably pick up someone else (someone without a dog) fifty meters down the block.

After several weeks of traveling through Europe with Ella by train, tram, bus, subway, and, yes, taxicab, I feel righteous indignation welling in my breast. The nerve!

Leaving my dog in her small patch of shade not far from the Colosseum, I stomp over to a formal taxi stand a short walk away but still within her sight, where drivers congregate to pick up fares. She sits patiently in a little square of darkness beneath a tree while I venture out into the blazing sunlight. Her ears are standing up and her eyes are opened wide, on full alert, waiting to see if I'm going to summon her or if she's been "abandoned" yet again.

I call back to Ella, "Just wait there, baby." And then I start asking taxi drivers to take me (and, oh yeah, that nice white dog standing over there in the shade) back to our hotel on the Piazza Barberini. Four, five, six drivers—they all decline. None will take a dog, no matter how *educata,* in their car.

I explain in broken Italian to one obstinate taxi driver after another that a cabbie took us from the train station to our hotel when we arrived, so I know it's certainly possible and legal, and I promise if my dog rides in the back of their car she won't cause any harm. So what's the problem?

"No, signore. Mi dispiace," they all say. *"No cani."*

I finally catch on that this has all been an elaborate negotiating tactic. "Fine," I say. "I'll give you double."

I see a flicker of calculation run across the brow of one enterprising driver. And then he, too, declines.

As each cabbie drives away (toting a dogless customer), I grow more irate and even resort to Italian swearwords—or what I think are Italian swearwords—to express my displeasure. This just makes the drivers talk faster and wave their hands about more vigorously.

So furious I could scream, I slump back to Ella in defeat. She seems happy to see me, despite my failure to provide her with transportation back to our hotel. "I'd carry you, young lady," I tell her, "but you're too heavy. Not to mention hairy." That's Ella's cue to start kissing me, and she doesn't miss a beat.

"What are we going to do?" I ask her. I gaze vacantly at the Colosseum in the distance. This is too weird. I'm stranded in Rome beside the Colosseum because my dog's feet have gotten burned by hot pavement.

She lies down in my lap, panting.

We can get on a series of random buses and hope that one of them passes our hotel—the odds of which are slightly better than Nicole Kidman phoning me up for a dinner date. Or we can just lie in the shade until the sun sets, watching fellow tourists stream in and out of the stadium, and when the streets of Rome begin to cool, we can resume our walking. (The wisdom of the siesta concept seems even clearer to me at this moment.) While I mull our options, stewing on our patch of grass, several new cabs appear at the taxi stand. But like their predecessors, none wants our business.

After twenty minutes of fulminating, during which time I try to compose in Italian the phrase *But she's better behaved, cleaner, and far more responsive than the average child,* a smartly appointed man in a suit approaches our tree and starts talking to me in thickly accented English.

"You looking for a taxi? Yes?"

"Yes," I assure him, obsessed by the notion that this man is wearing a suit jacket and not perspiring in the slightest. I mop the moisture from my brow. "No one will take us."

"I take you," he says, nodding. "Where you go?"

I tell him.

"Double price," he informs me. "Twenty euro in my cab." He indicates a big purple car-van hybrid parked at the taxi stand. It looks extremely air-conditioned.

I'd pay fifty at this point. But I sense the stranger expects to be bargained with, wants to be mildly challenged. So I sigh deeply, smile winningly, and shake my head. "Come on, it's usually a five-euro ride. I'll give you ten."

The stranger thinks for a moment. "Fifteen. Okay?"

"Okay," I say, grinning. "Fine. Let's go!"

As soon as we conclude our brief negotiation, the man extends his hand. "My name is Guido," he says.

"*Mi chiamo Michele.* And this is Ella. She's really a very good dog, actually. Nothing to worry about at all, I promise."

"I know," Guido says. *"Bellissima."* He opens the door for us. I sit in the back and direct Ella to lie down at my feet, in the space behind the driver's seat.

"Is no problem," Guido says. "She can go on the chair." He starts the car and pulls away from the curb. "Let me tell you something. Me? I am a big dog lover. A *big* dog lover. I see nobody takes you in the taxi. I feel bad, because me? I am *big* dog lover."

"Well, I'm glad to hear that, Guido," I reply. "At least someone in Rome is."

"I am big dog lover," Guido reminds me. "But in Italy we have big problem. *Big* problem. Not so many dogs here. People don't know the dogs. Don't know how to train them, educate them. Our culture, it is not a dog culture, you see? So many bad dogs. Not the dog's problem. People problem. But . . ." He shrugs, taking both hands off the steering wheel. "So I see this happen to you and I think, 'No, this not right. Ella, she is very beautiful. *Bellissima.* I take them in my taxi.' Because I'm big dog lover."

As Guido drives, he frequently turns to look at Ella and tell her how *bellissima* she is, and four times he nearly plows into oncoming traffic. As we get nearer to our destination, I notice Guido is driving more slowly. He wants to hear stories about how smart Ella is, about the tricks she knows, about her education—as though she held advanced degrees from several of America's better institutions of higher learning. I tell Guido how Ella has learned to do her "junk food" trick in Italian, and how she walks around Rome without a leash, stopping and sitting at every street corner until we look both ways to cross. "She's really a very good dog," I report. "But I guess you're the only cabdriver who cares about that."

"I love the dogs. I want to have two or three," Guido announces. "Does she make babies?"

"No," I tell him. "She's a virgin and is going to die that way. She was fixed at three months. She's a mutt, you know."

"But *bellissima*."

"Yes. Very." (Ella sleeps through all of this flattery, having heard it all a million times before.)

"Aaaah." Guido sighs heavily. He pulls the cab to the side of the street, in front of our hotel on the Via del Tritone. "Here we are," he says ruefully.

I sense that Guido wishes we could continue driving for another fifteen minutes. "Ella," I say, waking her from her slumber. "*Bacio*. Give Guido a kiss. *Bacio*."

Guido closes his eyes and sticks out his chin. Ella complies with a slurp across his face. "Ah, *bellissima!*" he exclaims.

I pull money from my pocket and proffer the agreed-upon fare. Guido gently pushes my hand back and waggles his finger at me. "No," he declares. "No, no."

I protest. "No. Come on. I said I would pay you fifteen."

"Please. You go. *Buon giorno*."

I start to say something, but Guido makes the finger-waggle at me again. So I express my appreciation and exit his cab with my dog. On the backseat I notice a few stray white hairs Ella has shed from her flank. For a second I consider brushing them away. But then I see the look in Guido's eyes, and I leave them there for him to discover later.

* * *

Notwithstanding Rome's "big problem" with dogs that our taxi-driving savior described, Ella is welcomed in every Roman restaurant we visit. After a few days of dining out, I grow accustomed to the following sequence acted out by the proprietors of Rome's trattorias: a brief look of skepticism; begrudging acquiescence; close surveillance transitioning into a satisfied smile; complimentary doggie treats; and, by evening's end, a long and intimate conversation over dessert about how he, the proprietor, knew all along that Ella would be a perfect guest. Ella's ability to somehow charm a populace that, if the taxi drivers are any indication, has a pervasive prejudice against dogs, confirms to me her burgeoning star power. Maybe, I begin to consider, it's not Mozart who inhabits Ella's fur but Audrey Hepburn herself.

One night, at an indulgent *osterìa* on the Via Margutta, a charming lane filled with art galleries and antiques dealers, Ella and I re-create the most memorable moment from *Lady and the Tramp*. (Ella takes the part of Lady. I'm the other guy.) When no one but Sandrine is looking, I find the longest strand of linguini on my plate, put one end in my mouth, and dangle the other end down to the floor, where Ella is lying beneath the table. We're supposed to slowly slurp the noodle together until our lips meet. But one of us—the alleged lady—starts snapping at the quivering pasta like a largemouth bass going after a worm. In seconds, her clacking incisors are inches from my nose.

Shortly thereafter, the owner of the restaurant comes over to visit. Sandrine and I tell him what a nice place he has, and how much we like the cute little lane on which his restaurant is situated. I tell him we found the street—and subsequently the *osterìa*—because a local shopkeeper noticed our thirsty dog and told us there was a nice drinking fountain around the corner.

"We would have never found you if it hadn't been for our thirsty dog leading us to the restaurant," I tell him.

"Thank you," he says ceremoniously to Ella.

"You know," the restaurateur says to me and Sandrine, "many people come here to Via Margutta because of the movie."

At least that's what I think he's saying. *The movie?* I really don't know what he means. *The movie.* It's one of those moments that often arise during foreign travel, when you're not sure if you're missing something because of the language difference or the cultural difference, or if you just misheard. *They come here for the movie.* Did he spy me and Ella doing our rendition of *Lady and the Tramp*? Or does he mean to say something else altogether?

By the time we depart the Osterìa Via Margutta, plastered on Barolo and singing Verdi arias in the resonant alley, I've convinced myself that people from the world over visit Via Margutta because it has something to do with an animated Disney movie. And then I promptly forget about it, fixated instead on the idea that Ella has really good taste in restaurants, and that restaurants that welcome her on their floor have really good taste in dogs.

"You're such a star," I tell my mutt. "She's such a star!" I repeat to Sandrine, who politely reminds me that I'm behaving like a lunatic. And that my voice is echoing off the walls in a way that the neighbors probably don't appreciate.

"All right," I whisper. "But she really is."

I consider it compelling evidence of my dog's blossoming celebrity status when, the next day, Ella and I are wandering around the Piazza Barberini, searching for an Internet café, and she single-handedly (quadra-pawedly?) inspires dereliction of duty in a well-trained member of the service industry. A hotel doorman on the north side of the square stands at attention on the red carpet in front of his hotel's entrance. I can tell he's fascinated with Ella, but, like the guards at Buckingham Palace, he's bound to his post, unflappable and focused. We pass his station once, and then again on our way home to our own hotel, on the south side of the square. He starts to creep away from his front door, nonchalantly inching toward the street. Then I see a look of pain flash across the doorman's face.

I make silent eye contact with him, seeking reassurance that everything is okay, that he doesn't need help. The doorman smiles broadly at me. I wave back. Then the doorman looks around, as though checking for traffic on his sidewalk, and strides purposefully out toward me and Ella, his hand extended.

"Buona séra!" he exclaims to Ella, ignoring me. *"Buona séra, mi amore!"* He gets down on one knee and hugs her like a quilted blanket.

"Hello," I say to the preoccupied man. "That's Ella. She likes to kiss Italian men. But, hey, who doesn't?"

The doorman rises from his embrace. His name is Enrico, he tells me, and although he's supposed to stay at the door, and although he has five dogs of his own, he couldn't keep his eyes—or his hands—off of Ms. Whitey. Enrico also has three cats at home, and all eight of his animals get along beautifully, he reports, except when the dogs try to eat the cat food—then the cats get a little mean.

"I thought people in Rome had a big problem with dogs," I comment as Enrico caresses Ella's back.

It's not true, he insists. "Only taxi drivers."

I recount our travails at the Colosseum, and Enrico tells me about how he walks five dogs at once (very carefully, it seems). I tell him all the places Ella has been. He asks me if everyone loves her as much as he does. I ask him if he's seen the movie *Vacanza Romana*. And he never stops petting the glamorous dog who wandered into his life.

Enrico looks brokenhearted when a quartet of guests approach his door. He dashes away to open it and bid the visitors good evening. Then he disappears inside the hotel. I tell Ella what a good puppy she is, and we start to go.

We get a few meters down the sidewalk before I hear Enrico shouting, *"Signore, signore!"*

He's clutching a point-and-shoot camera. *"Per favore, signore,"* he implores.

I take several photos for Enrico, most of which involve him embracing Ella from various angles. He thanks me profusely, kisses Ella on both cheeks, and returns to his station, grinning like a lottery winner.

We never see him again.

In all our rambling around Rome in search of seldom-viewed Bernini angels and Signorelli frescoes, whether I'm at the Sistine Chapel (where Ella waits outside and many of the human tourist shuffling through the queue to see Michelangelo's ceiling behave worse than untrained dogs) or in the courtyard of a neighborhood church, I get the sense that my mutt is making a lasting impression on the locals that I never could. Five years from now, the Romans who once met me, Ella, and Sandrine will probably not remember the long-legged Belgian beauty or the perspiring American guy trying to pass as quasi-Italian (mostly on the strength of his authentic Italian haircut and shave). But the white dog—they'll remember her.

I imagine Enrico or Dino or Guido seeing Ella's face in a photograph, or a marble sculpture, or on a book cover, and thinking, "I kissed that dog. She looked at me and she smiled! Her. That beautiful white mutt. That's her!" They'll tell stories about their celebrity encounter—just as I tell stories about running into my neighbor Sheryl Crow up the street, or visiting with Steve Martin and his golden retriever Arthur at the dog park, or sitting next to Denzel Washington (or Ron Jeremy) at a restaurant. And when the Romans remember their brief moment of communion with Ella Guinevere Konik, I imagine, like me, they'll be glad to have known her.

* * *

At every city we visit, Ella has her "spot," a reliable place where, in the mornings, she can be hustled out of the hotel and given a chance to relieve herself. In Rome, the only place I can find near our central district lodgings is a scruffy tract of grass around the corner from the Roman outlet of Planet Hollywood, which, inexplicably, actually has a few customers every night. (I have a dark and evil impulse to encourage Ella to do her business at Planet Hollywood's front step as a kind of social commentary, but the good angel on my shoulder, the one who looks like Bernini made him, urges me to behave like a responsible dog owner and walk past without incident.) Ella finds her pee spot just inside the gates of an imposing building undergoing some structural renovation, a building that, according to a sign out front, has something to do with the Ministry of Culture. This being Italy, where there's more high culture than in a carton of yogurt on a transoceanic airplane, the gates seem to be open round the clock, or at least whenever Ella needs to go. Day and night, we visit Ella's spot.

It's not until three days later, when I schedule a midday visit to the National Gallery of Art, that I realize Ella has been relieving herself all this time in the chiaroscuro shadow of Caravaggio: inside the front gates of the National Gallery of Art.

To get to the National Gallery, I followed the brief directions provided by the hotel concierge—directions that led me directly to Ella's pee spot. The strange thing is, when I realize Ella's pee spot is in fact the National Gallery, I feel somehow that I've been to this building before. And I don't mean with Ella in tow looking for a place to squat. I'm certain I've never been *inside* the National Gallery before, but I'm equally certain I've seen this building, as though it were an integral part of a past life.

It's not until we return home and rent a copy of *Roman Holiday* that my déjà vu becomes clear.

Rome's National Gallery of Art—Ella's pee spot—is the "embassy" of the unnamed country from which Audrey Hepburn hails, and from which the naughty princess escapes at the start of her scandalous escapades with newspaperman Peck.

Who, in the movie, lives at *6 Via Margutta.*

For the next three days, I insist on calling Ella "my little Audrey Hepburn." And she doesn't seem to mind at all.

On the red carpet, Cannes

At the Hôtel de Ville in St. Tropez

Chapter 11

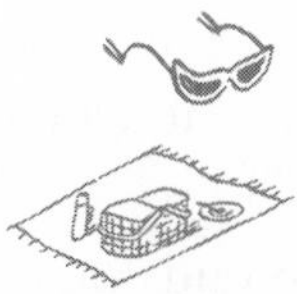

While I fill out paperwork for a car rental at the Nice train station, Ella waits in the lobby, mesmerized by a *jeune fille* holding a flaky croissant. The little girl, five or six years old, sits cross-legged in front of my mutt and hums a song as she chews her pastry. There seems to be an invisible thread connecting Ella's muzzle to the girl's fingers, pulling the dog's head in every direction. Soon the little girl recognizes the magic power she possesses. She experiments drawing figure-eights and crosses in the air, and Ella's nose traces the outline of whatever the girl commands. I don't detect sadism in the girl's imaginary paintings; she seems to be fascinated with the aesthetic possibilities her new friend has brought her.

Ella continues to follow the movements of the girl's left hand as though it contained a raw lamb chop. After a few minutes of torturous play, the girl's parents emerge from the Avis office, and she politely bids *le chien "adieu."* Then, when her parents aren't looking, she turns back to her playmate and gives Ella the last piece of her pastry. Welcome to France, Ella!

Ah, France, land of people who allegedly adore Jerry Lewis

and Mickey Rourke, yet still produce piles of plotless movies the average American finds unwatchable. France, where wine and cheese are approached with as much seriousness as sports and shopping are in the United States. Where the populace in general really and truly loves its dogs.

Dogs in France are treated unlike dogs anywhere else in the world. In France, dogs are adopted members of the family, entitled to as much affection and respect as one would give to a son or daughter. Dogs here are not meant to be hidden away in shame like a dirty secret. They're a part of public life, a welcome addition to the skein of social interaction that weaves us all together.

France is more tolerant of and encouraging toward Man's Best Friend than any country on the planet. For an American mutt accustomed to being left outside (or left home altogether) when Dad goes to a restaurant or a shop or a beach, France is the earthly version of Doggie Heaven.

At our hotel in Cannes, two blocks from La Croisette, where movie stars and European royalty parade for the paparazzi (and willingly pay nineteen dollars for a cocktail), Ella strolls into the lobby *sans* leash. The staff at check-in coo and kiss and proffer to Ella the kind of sweet nothings (in French) that every American guy wishes he could have whispered in his ear. For the duration of Ella's stay in Cannes, the hotel staff address my mutt as Mademoiselle Ella Blanche. I'm just plain old Monsieur.

On the Croisette, with grand hotels looming on one side and the shimmering sea speckled with jillion-dollar yachts sparkling on the other, Ella doesn't merely walk. She promenades. It's as though she were expecting to be discovered by a European movie producer. Perhaps after her adventures in Rome she already considers herself a star of the first magnitude. Nearly everyone else we encounter on our stroll seems to be of that opinion. (And I can't say I disagree.) When we arrive at the Festival Hall, at the far end of the Croisette, where the Frenchies hand out the awards for movies that are inevitably reviled in America, there's a ceremonial red carpet out front. It's not far from the gallery of handprints, like the one around the corner from our Hollywood home. Hundreds of tourists pause here to snap a photo of their spouse or sibling standing on the place of honor—the very spot where George Clooney and Bobby DeNiro and all sorts of handsome French men whose names we can't pronounce also stood, posing for their symbiotic partners in the fame industry, the slick celebrity magazines. During a brief moment of whimsy standing on the red carpet at Cannes, we middle-class, anonymous, and homely tourists can all be rich, famous, and beautiful too.

When I position Ella on the carpet for what I imagine to be her fabulous cover shot, wearing sunglasses, a floppy hat, and a beach towel around her neck, a crowd of photographers swarms around my mutt, possibly having mistaken her for Julia Roberts. After I get my own series of souvenir snapshots, the throng compels me to leave the fashion model just where she is for another five minutes. Amateur photographers from Portugal, Holland, Greece, Israel, England, and, of course, Japan capture her visage on film. And just like that, without having to endure casting couches, thieving managers, or a decade of purgatory on a daytime soap, Ella Konik vaults from relatively unknown Hollywood working girl to international celebrity status.

Joking aside, my humble hound continues to have a muselike effect on the strangers we encounter in Cannes—just as she has everywhere else we've visited. Every third person who meets Ella, it seems, feels compelled to share with us his own dog story, tales of profound devotion and inconsolable grief at the loss of a dear friend. Ella is both a catalyst to remembrance and a receptor of pent-up affection, a dog who gets people talking and petting simultaneously. Hotel lobbies, wine bars, ice-cream stands—Ella is an ambassador for human intimacy, bringing together disparate people who might never share two words with each other, let alone the contents of their heart.

One evening before dinner, at that magic dusky hour when the air has cooled and the lights have come on but the sun hasn't yet dipped into the sea, we're having a glass of *vin rouge* at the foot of le Cannet, the narrow walking street lined with restaurants that climbs upward toward the medieval castle that overlooks the Cannes harbor. We're at one of those peculiarly French places where the tables are about the size of a frying pan, and all the chairs nearly touch each other, so that you must learn to quickly make your neighbor your pal. Tonight we're next to a family of three on holiday. For a happy half hour, the Hoffmans (from Switzerland) regale us with their tales. And while they don't rival Offenbach's, I'm glad to listen, because, clearly, the Hoffmans have fallen in love with the white beast sitting beside them. While Dad Hoffman queries me on the cultural differences between our two countries—"Why is there so much violence on the television and no sex?" he wonders intelligently—Dad only once removes his hands from Ella's fur, to hand Mom a pen.

Mom Hoffman, who bounces between French and English, also pets my contented mutt, and I notice her caresses becoming unconsciously more vigorous as she tells the sad story of saying good-bye to Willy, a beloved family pet who was part of their clan from the time their teenage daughter was born until just last year. The Hoffmans talk and pet, pet and talk. And Ella stands and listens until they're done, like a big soft set of worry beads.

Given so much affection and attention and *acceptance,* Ella, I reckon would be content to relocate to the South of France, where she could subsist on scraps of Brie and baguette. (I probably would be too.) If you're not careful—and I'm not—being in France with your dog can give you the misimpression that your hairy mutt is, in fact, entitled to all the rights and courtesies enjoyed by human beings. Our first night in Cannes, we plan on dining at a pizza joint Sandrine used to frequent as a child, when her family spent holidays in Provence. She's eager to return there with me and Ella and see if the *pizza moules* (pizza with mussels) is as delectable as she remembers it. When we arrive, however, the host—who, I hasten to add, is not French, but of a nationality I will refrain from specifying—tells us we cannot eat inside his restaurant with *le chien*.

I'm thinking maybe I didn't hear him right. But I can tell by the vexed look on Sandrine's face that my translation was accurate. "I wonder why?" I say, puzzled. "Well, in any case, we can just sit outside, on the terrace."

Mais, non! Not there either.

Only one day in France and I've already developed an attitude—a nasty French one, the kind of snooty pomposity Americans like to lampoon and belittle but of which they are secretly frightened. In less than twenty-four hours I've learned all the stock gestures of French derision: the snide little *puh,* blown through circular lips; the tired shrug; the roll of the eyes; the softly muttered *quel idiot.* Someone gives me the slightest bit of hassle regarding my sweet puppy and I turn into Charles Aznavour on crystal meth. Before I even know what I'm doing, I implore the proprietor of the pizza restaurant to be fruitful and multiply, though not with that precise locution. And then, like a complete ass, I make a big show of how perfectly Ella heels as we storm out of his shabby dough joint.

"Maybe it isn't as nice as I remember," Sandrine says helpfully.

I begin to recite a list of places Ella has dined with us in Europe, starting in Belgium and working my way around to Italy. But before I even get to Germany, Sandrine stops me. "It's all right, Michael. Don't take it personally. That guy just had a problem with dogs. He wasn't French. Everyone else still loves Ella."

Sandrine's right. After so much affection and inclusiveness, I take the odd rejection of Ella personally, as though my daughter or wife were being told she wasn't good enough to be seated and served. Ella, of course, doesn't feel the sting of canine prejudice. She exists in the blissful state of believing everyone on the planet, including cruddy pizza place owners, loves and adores her. If we suddenly leave a restaurant, she doesn't believe she's unwanted; she assumes we leave because Daddy wants to take her for a walk. "You're right," I say. "No big deal."

After I've sufficiently composed myself—for a few moments I feel myself trembling with rage—we concoct a game plan to exorcise the unpleasant taint of the pizza snub. I propose we find a nice place—a *really* nice place—and have those *moules* Sandrine has been craving. And lobster and oysters and crab claws, and all the other chilled *fruits de mers* we can handle. And a bottle of champagne.

And Ella can have a piece of bread.

We locate a seafood restaurant on the water, a place called La Marée, where Sandrine and I have visited during previous trips to Cannes, albeit without the mutt. As we approach the front door, I feel a hitch in my step, a hesitancy. All of a sudden I'm like the kid who did a belly flop from the high board. I'm scared to jump back in the pool.

What if no one wants Ella in their restaurant anymore? What if, suddenly, everyone in France has eliminated his egalitarian attitude in the last three hours, while I was busy drinking wine?

Sensing how addled my mind has become from the Pizza Incident—despite my protests to the contrary, I'm still not over it—Sandrine approaches the hostess of La Marée by herself, while I wait in the doorway with Ella, whom I ask to sit as elegantly as she possibly can. We two hold still, expectant and anxious. (Well, I'm expectant and anxious. Ella is oblivious to the unfolding drama.) I see Sandrine chatting amiably with the lady of the house, with much nodding and laughing passing between them. This looks promising.

When Sandrine turns to face me, I can tell by the smile on her face that the conversation went well.

The women return to us, beaming. Sandrine motions with her hand that Ella and I should come into the restaurant. As we step in, Mme. Hostess clutches at her chest and lets her jaw fall. (She looks like she's singing *Manon*.) Then Mme. Hostess starts chattering in rapid-fire French, gesturing at Ella, turning to Sandrine, talking at me. Given my poor grasp of the Gallic tongue, the exact content of her exclamations I cannot say. But I'm pretty sure she's smitten.

Then, in the middle of La Marée restaurant, on the waterfront in Cannes, Mme. Hostess puts down the menus she's carrying and smothers Ella Konik in hugs and kisses. Sandrine and I stand aside and watch.

"She says *of course* Ella is welcome in her restaurant," Sandrine reports to me. "She loves dogs."

"You sure you don't want to go back to the pizza place?" I ask, feeling vindicated and relieved.

"No, let's drink some champagne."

And so we do, celebrating good sense, good cheer, and, above all, the goodness of strangers being brought together by the simple glue of a furry white mutt. After we're seated and Ella is positioned beside our table with her own bowl of water, we offer a glass of the bubbly to our hostess. But she politely declines. She just wants another wet dog kiss.

* * *

Brigitte Bardot, the former cinematic sex kitten and present animal-rights activist, is a longtime resident of St. Tropez. She, like Elton John and Mick Jagger and countless other people whose music I don't listen to, owns a magnificent estate, La Madrague, overlooking the Mediterranean Sea. And it is there we are headed on a spectacular summer day, in search of the one

French lady I'm hoping can eloquently summarize all that is right about the European outlook on dogs.

When I first got the idea of traveling to Europe with Ella, I wrote Mme. Bardot, in care of her foundation (la Fondation Brigitte Bardot), which is known throughout the world for taking passionate and sometimes unpopular stances on issues involving seals, whales, and poultry. I had hoped Mme. Bardot would meet me (and Ella) in St. Tropez, where we could discuss her ideas for making America more accepting of its canine residents. I had been to St. Tropez once previously on a day visit, the highlights of which (as far as I can remember) were drinking far too much wine in the midday sun, posing for a silly photo on the steps of the Hôtel de Ville with a gendarme, and purchasing a cheesy watercolor for my cheesy watercolor collection. Despite that brief adult experience, my strongest association with St.-Tropez goes back to my childhood, when an American suntan lotion company ran constant commercials on AM radio, repeating the phrase "Bain de Soleil: For the St. Tropez Tan," until it was permanently tattooed onto my consciousness. As a dreamy kid, I always associated St. Tropez with fabulously bronze beauties—until, of course, we all learned that tanning causes melanoma and turns unprotected skin into something like saddle leather.

Today, with Ella in the rental car in the backseat, I'm hopeful my visit to St. Tropez will garner more than precancerous lesions. We're seeking a face-to-face interview with Mme. Bardot, an *unscheduled* face-to-face interview. Guerrilla journalism, if you will.

I tried the usual avenues. First I contacted Mme. Bardot's

foundation and told the functionary who fielded my call the nature of the book I was writing and my interest in having Mme. Bardot comment on dogs in general and canine life in Europe in particular. The assistant asked that I put my request in writing.

Which I did.

Then my "case"—this was the euphemistic term the French-speaking foundation people coined—was brought before another higher-ranking functionary, who told me that should Mme. Bardot's schedule not allow an in-person interview, I would be granted a phone interview. The higher-ranking assistant asked that I put my request for a possible phone interview in writing.

Which I did.

A short time later I was contacted by yet another functionary, this one a gentleman who characterized himself as Mme. Bardot's executive assistant. He asked that I put my questions in writing.

Which I did (begrudgingly).

Then, several weeks before my interview—which I was under the impression had been scheduled and which the Bardot people were under the impression had never been *officially* scheduled—*another* functionary, this one apparently as high as one could go on the food chain without actually speaking with Madame herself—asked if I would send the foundation a manuscript of the book in which I was proposing to include Mme. Bardot's interview.

Which I did not do, seeing as the book was not yet written.

The highest-ranking of the functionaries then explained to me that interviewing Mme. Bardot would be impossible at this time.

(But that they would look forward to seeing the book.) I reiterated to the foundation people that I was not writing a tome celebrating *101 Fabulous Uses for Baby Seal Fur,* but a sweet little story about traveling around Europe with my American dog.

"Surely you understand," the functionary said cryptically.

I assured her I did not. And that was the last of my telephone calls to la Fondation Brigitte Bardot.

But then I figured if Michael Moore can ambush the head of General Motors for a documentary film, I could knock on the door of Brigitte Bardot's estate in St. Tropez and see if she'd like to have a cup of tea with me and my mutt. Indeed, I convinced myself that Brigitte Bardot probably was not even made aware of my interview request, and that if she *had* been, she would have been delighted to chat with me and Ella.

Plus, it's a really pretty drive between Cannes and St. Tropez.

The onboard navigator in my rental car features a startlingly stentorian male voice speaking in French—*Tournez à droite!*—who orders me around the South of France, in search of an aging sex symbol turned animal rights gadfly. The navigator, whom Sandrine and I name "Jerome," knows a lot about small Provençal highways, but not very much about Brigitte Bardot's whereabouts. When I type "La Madrague" or "Brigitte Bardot's Place" in the computer, Jerome informs me that these locations are "unknown." (He can, however, recommend both a fast *and* a slow route through seaside towns so unrelentingly charming you could scream.) So I have him lead me to downtown St. Tropez instead, where Jerome can nap in the car while Ella and I continue our search on foot.

When we arrive in the Land of the Perfect Tan, Ella seems

immediately at ease strolling through the narrow streets. Flanked by pastel hues on the sun-baked buildings, my dog proves the fashion maxim that everything goes with white. Like the town itself, Ella is simultaneously glamorous and laid back, as though she knows she belongs among the jet set, cavorting with the locals and projecting the kind of blithe assurance and social confidence her dad could never muster. Observing Ella exploring St. Tropez off her leash, receiving more unabashed attention than the sixty-foot yachts moored in the harbor, it seems to me that my humble American mutt has become completely accustomed to the Good Life. Whether getting illicit handfuls of bread from beneath the lunch table, or invitations to visit the interiors of boutiques featuring clothing only an anorexic teenager could possibly wear, Ella immerses herself into St.-Tropez culture with the passion of a hedonist employing all of her senses. She seems happy here. Maybe, I think, it's because she knows her potential new best friend Brigitte Bardot is near.

I now have myself almost thoroughly convinced that Mme. Bardot will actually be *pleased* to have me and Ella drop in unannounced. I imagine her chastising the incompetent underlings who almost prevented her from making the acquaintance of such a lovable American dog. How tragic, she'll declare, that an historic rendezvous was derailed by bureaucratic officiousness. *Vive Ella! Bisou! Bisou!* Then Mme. Bardot will invite Ella to play in the special doggie park she's had constructed in the back forty hectares of La Madrague. And while the dog romps in the grassy wonderland, Brigitte and I can talk about canines in French restaurants, and, once we've gotten to know each other a little, Roger Vadim.

The only problem, I discover after some rudimentary investigation, is that Brigitte Bardot's compound is entirely inaccessible from public roads. A nice man at the tourist information booth describes a mansion surrounded by private driveways and gates and security personnel, none of which, he suggests, indicates a warm welcome to visiting Americans, with or without dog in hand.

The Information Man, however, suggests that if I'm really committed to seeing Mme. Bardot's digs, he's got a clever idea. La Madrague, he says, can be viewed (from afar) during a scenic boat tour of the celebrity villas, the South of France equivalent of the star jitneys that crisscross my Hollywood neighborhood.

To get my interview, Ella and I would have to jump overboard and swim ashore, a proposition that has way too many complications, not the least of which is that I'm prone to the kind of wicked seasickness that makes me beg for euthanasia. Plus, I can't see showing up at Mme. Bardot's place dripping wet, with seaweed and hermit crabs clinging to my shirt, and Ella tracking sand all over the nice Oriental rugs.

So, instead of consummating our journey to St. Tropez with a happy introduction between two international beauty queens, we find a cute place by the water to have lunch and enjoy (vicariously) the boats skimming across the whitecapped waves. Ella lolls in the shade, waiting for handouts. Sandrine and I eat salade niçoise and drink Côtes de Provence, and we muse about which rooms of my house back home could be repainted St. Tropez orange and Brigitte Bardot brown.

After lunch, I take Ella to the seashore and facetiously suggest she swim out to La Madrague and report back to me when she knows something. With a moderately graceful running crash into the water, she complies. Like everyone else frolicking in the salty bath, Ella seems to enjoy the Mediterranean Sea's unusual warmth, which feels like amniotic fluid bathing tired old joints. Unlike everyone else, Ella gleans infinite joy in retrieving driftwood from the gentle surf and subsequently burying it in the wet sand on the beach. After all the burning cobblestones and constant perambulations Ella has endured for the past month, she must feel utterly content to be in the soothing sea, chasing a stick. I daresay that stick is probably more interesting to my well-traveled mutt than lying on the floor of a mansion owned by an old movie star.

"Ella, you're in the Mediterranean," I remind her. "Would you please tell me what you're doing in the Mediterranean?"

Ella throws her stick a few feet and swims over to get it where it floats. She paddles back to shore, drops the stick at my feet, and performs a full-body shake. Her hair sticks out in a million wet spikes.

"You're playing in the Mediterranean, you know," I tell her. "In St. Tropez."

Ella barks at me. I throw her stick back into the sea and watch her swim.

* * *

Back in Cannes, courtesy of Jerome's expert directions—*Tournez à gauche!*—I resolve to provide Ella with as much beach time as I can possibly force myself to tolerate. I'm not a big beach lover. The sand annoys me, and I don't like being exposed to the summer sun for long, with or without Bain de Soleil. But the girls in our caravan love *la plage.* Especially the hairy one. Plus, making the scene at the beach is de rigueur in Cannes, a rite of social passage among a certain class of European society types and affluent foreign tourists. For many of the Americans, the topless bathing that occurs on French beaches is slightly scandalous and naughty and exciting. For Ella, who goes through life in a state of blissful nudity, exposed breasts—not to mention thighs, jowls, and tail—are as natural as peeing in public.

In Cannes, most of the prime waterfront sand is owned by the fancy hotels along La Croisette. The hotels divide their precious plots of beach with color-coordinated lounge chairs and parasols, under which privileged clients sip costly cocktails and avoid actually going in the water. Not only are dogs not allowed on these private beaches, plebeian tourists lodging at a commoners' hotel off the Croisette aren't welcome either. But at both ends of the Croisette, like two civic bookends, a couple of public beaches provide the same sun, sand, and surf the rich folks enjoy, albeit without the parasols or the twelve-dollar glasses of wine.

Dogs are not allowed on these public *plages* either. Immediately adjacent to the beaches, however, a cluster of giant sea rocks pokes through the salt water. These smooth boulders, I discover, are perfectly proportioned and shaped to accommodate towels, sunbathers, and an American mutt.

Since the boulders are directly beside the public beach, they make a fine entry point for visiting swimmers and their water-obsessed Lab-greyhound mix. The beach itself may be *interdit,* but the sea is certainly not.

Ella and I swim for what seems like hours in the tepid water, not stopping until my skin has been broiled into a vibrant shade of pink. We swim and splash and play, surrounded by frolicking French vacationers, spectacular sultanic yachts at anchor (some with helicopters tied to the aft deck), and countless crabs, urchins, and mussels that cling in the crevices. It's nirvana.

Then Ella makes the acquaintance of Guillaume, Kevin, and Pierre, three impossibly cute French lads of ten or eleven, all of whom seem to have a serious (but healthy) obsession with dogs. Now life for my pup enters a realm one stage beyond nirvana. It becomes truly *magnifique*.

After determining that Ella is *très gentille* and ridiculously amenable to their caresses, the boys wonder if Monsieur (me) would allow them to play in the water with the nice doggie.

"Mais, oui," I accede.

The boys produce an orange-and-black plastic soccer ball, and the five of us—four guys and a mutt—splash into the sea together. (One of us is already barking in excitement.) I don't know if Ella's aging cardiovascular system can handle it, but I know her retriever instinct makes her believe she can chase the ball the entire day, and probably most of the night too. I have to remind her to come ashore every fifteen minutes or so to have a rest break.

We five play a crude game of football in which Ella vainly attempts to get her jaws around the slippery orb. The ball bounces crazily every time she bats it with her flailing mouth, like an orca toying with a baby sea lion. When one of the boys is holding the ball, the others scream for him to pass it to them. "Pierre! Pierre!" And when I've got the ball, they all scream, "Monsieur! Monsieur!"

This goes on for I don't know how long. The hound, of course, never tires of playing water polo. And the boys find a second wind just as their interest seems to be flagging. What reenergizes them is discovering I'm an American. (They assumed I was from England, because I spoke English.) The boys quiz me about the popular culture my country exports to the rest of the world, and they seem particularly impressed that I "know" Eminem and Snoop Doggy Dogg. (I try to communicate that I am familiar with these two hip-hop characters, but my limited French gives Guillaume, Kevin, and Pierre the mistaken idea that I'm actually personal friends with the two rhyming gentlemen—which, much as it pains me to admit, I am not.) The boys seem so excited to be playing in the sea with someone who "knows" the heroes of their favorite music videos that I tacitly encourage their misapprehension by telling them that Mr. Dogg comes from Long Beach. "That's only about forty minutes from my house!" I report.

Much excited French murmuring ensues, and we continue playing with Ella until my shoulders are too scorched to go on. When I indicate to the boys that the pup and I must go to shore, I can't tell who's more disappointed, the crestfallen trio of *garçons* or the saturated *chien*.

The lads implore me to let Ella stay in the water with them while I watch from the rocks. *"S'il vous plaît, Monsieur. S'il vous plaît!"*

Ella smiles at me, and I can't say no.

While the four of them shout and paddle (and bark) in the sea, with the French Riviera in the background, I lie on a warm boulder, like a walrus sunning himself after a bloodless bout of chest-thumping. I watch the boys and my dog at play, and I marvel at how sweet life can be when the simple act of chasing a ball in the water can reap so much uncomplicated joy.

What brings me such simple joy—and what simultaneously proves what a simpleton I can be—is having my mutt, my American mutt who never gets the respect she deserves back home, treated like a proper lady in the finer precincts of Europe. The morning after our swimming adventure with Guillaume, Kevin, and Pierre, I take Ella to her Cannes "spot," which happens to be a plot of *herbes* on the Croisette, across from the swanky Hôtel Martinez. (The locals pronounce it "mah-tee-NAYZ," which somehow sounds so much more sophisticated than the North American version, popular among Major League Baseball pitchers.) When Ella does her business on the finely mown grass fronting a swatch of priceless private beach, I produce a plastic sandwich bag from my pocket and remove the refuse.

As I turn for a rubbish bin, a dapper older gentleman clad in a pink shirt and brilliant white slacks that match his neatly trimmed mustache and hair calls out to me. *"Pardon, Monsieur."*

At first I think he's asking me a question.

"Oui?" I reply, praying he hasn't mistaken me for someone who can conduct a remedial conversation in French.

Then the gentleman repeats himself. *"Bravo, Monsieur! Bravo!"* He applauds demurely and nods appreciatively toward me and my bag of dog poo.

"Ah!," I say, finally comprehending. *"Ah, oui. Merci, Monsieur. Merci!"*

If I were wearing a top hat, I would feel compelled to doff it.

Instead, we exchange knowing smiles, and I fairly dance off La Croisette, thrilled to have not offended a Frenchman. For the rest of the day I look at Ella and repeat the phrase *"Bravo, Monsieur"* with annoying frequency, and every time I do I feel insanely happy.

* * *

The Carlton Hotel is supposedly the swankiest of the swank institutions lining the Cannes waterfront, where rooms cost six hundred dollars (and up) a night and gentlemen are expected to wear suit jackets in the casino. The Konik family, sadly, is not in residence at the Carlton this particular week, having been successfully discouraged by that chillingly effective filter known as The Price.

That her dad concerns himself with prosaic irritants like, say, mortgage payments, shouldn't, however, prevent Ella from having The Carlton Experience while she's in Cannes. A sweet European lady I know likes to use the lobby bathrooms in luxury hotels she's not staying at as a way of enjoying the property vicariously. Ella, I suppose, could pee on the grass out front, but it probably wouldn't have the same satisfaction for her as using a gold-plated toilet. So, instead, I doll up Ms. E in her finest shawl, make sure she's got all the sand out of her paws, and take her to The Carlton Hotel's lobby watering hole, the Bar des Célébrités.

Sitting beneath larger-than-life photographs of Sean Connery, Andie MacDowell, and Anjelica Huston, Sandrine and I drink kir royales and eat marinated olives while Ella reclines on the frequently vacuumed carpet, trying vainly to go unrecognized by her legions of fans. We lounge on the Carlton's plush velvet chairs, where so many members of secular royalty have sat before us, sipping and nibbling and consummating three-picture deals. Few of these stars, I reckon, have had a white mutt wearing a leopard-print scarf lolling at their feet and subtly soliciting food donations.

While we three bask in air-conditioned comfort, I find myself involuntarily looking over my shoulder. (And not because I'm searching for vacationing movie stars.) Even after a month in Europe, my lifetime of American conditioning triggers a paranoia reflex. I still half expect someone in a uniform—armed with a clipboard or a walkie-talkie, perhaps—to march out from behind the handsome mahogany bar and demand that the dog be removed from inside the premises at once!

But this is France. The only people who approach us in the Bar des Célébrités are a stately man dressed in traditional African garb (an exiled despot, maybe?) and a gang of four giggling children. The African man points at Ella, says something in French, and laughs at what I assume was a clever joke he cracked, possibly involving the irony of Ella's leopard scarf. (I could be completely mistaken about this; for all I know, he might have been talking about the marinated olives.) The children, however, approach our table much more cautiously, as though they were seeking an autograph. They inch forward, smile self-consciously, and muster the courage to perhaps ask me if I'm Tom Cruise. (I could be completely mistaken about this; for all I know they've confused me with Ben Affleck.)

"Can we pet your dog?" the eldest of the children, a girl, asks in perfect, lightly accented English.

"Of course! Her name is Ella, and she loves to make new friends," I tell the lass.

Upon hearing her name, Ella lifts up her head to do the meet-and-greet, just as she's done a thousand times before at nursing homes, battered women's shelters, and a growing number of European metropolises. When Ella realizes that it's children who want to stroke her fur, she becomes animated and excitable, as though youthfulness were infectious. (And maybe it is.) The children immediately recognize in the happy dog a kindred spirit, and everyone gets along famously.

"Ella likes you!" I say, watching my mutt kiss four new faces. "Maybe you should be formally introduced." I say to my seasoned performer, "Ella, please shake hands and say hello. Shake, Ella!" She dutifully offers her right paw to the eldest girl.

"Hello, Ella. My name is Charlotte," the girl says. "This is my brother, Alexander." (She pronounces his name with a soft, British *A: Ahlexahnder*.) "And this is my best friend and Alexander's best friend," she says, indicating the two other children. "We're all best friends."

"Are you all English?" I ask. "You speak so well."

"No. We live in Scotland," Charlotte says.

"And sometimes Italy," Alexander adds.

"You don't sound Scottish," I say gently. "I mean, I don't hear the accent."

"We speak Italian and French also," Charlotte reports, nodding confidently.

"And you're on vacation now? With your family?" I wonder.

"Yes. And then we have to go back to Scotland," Charlotte says. "That's where we live now."

I look at Sandrine. She shrugs and says, "It sounds like you travel a lot."

"Yes," Alexander says. "Our father is Caniggia."

"Oh," Sandrine says, perplexed.

"*Claudio* Caniggia," Charlotte says proudly.

"Caniggia? The football player Caniggia? From Argentina?" My obsessive World Cup television viewing seems to have paid off.

"Yes!" the children all say in chorus.

"He's an international star," I tell Sandrine. "Very famous player from Argentina. World Cup and everything."

"Ah. A football star," Sandrine says, nodding.

"Now he plays for the Glasgow Rangers," Charlotte explains. "So we live in Scotland. We have four dogs there. They couldn't come with us to France. We miss them a lot."

"Aww," Sandrine and I say in tandem.

"Yes. We all have a dog. Mine is Jack," Alexander says. "He's a German shepherd. We miss our dogs, you know."

"Yes. It's very sad to leave them at home," I say. "We took Ella all the way from America where we live, because we didn't want to be without her."

The children nod and return their attention to snuggling with Ella, whose ears tend to perk up every time someone mentions the word "ball." What a life, I think, to be the offspring of a rich and famous athlete, to have Eloise-like holidays at The Carlton Hotel. To play with an American dog in the lobby bar. And to be so nice and well mannered in spite of the extraordinary privileges.

And what a life, I think, to be an animal that everyone wants to pet, to hug, to love. To be the source of so much pleasure, just because you're furry and soft and sweet. (And to be so nice and well mannered in spite of all the extraordinary attention.)

The children tell us about their dogs and their schools and their favorite games, and they give Ella about a thousand kisses before Mama Caniggia shows up in the lobby and calls them away for supper.

I look at my dog sprawled on the floor, emotionally spent from another intense exchange of affection. And I can't imagine any other circumstances under which I might meet the family of one of Argentina's great football stars. In Cannes. At the Bar des Célébrités. Inside The Carlton Hotel.

"Bravo, mademoiselle!" I say, softly applauding Ella. "Bravo!"

At the Grand Casino in Monte Carlo

Chapter 12

The gorgeous car ride up the coast from Cannes to Monaco does not take very long—approximately an hour, depending on how many times you stop to take snapshots of the Lifestyles of the Rich and Famous real estate along the Mediterranean. But when you're a dog who's been gorging herself on handouts from French waiters you've managed to charm, you need to find a place (other than the backseat of Dad's rental car) to relieve yourself. Gawking at cliff-top mansions that are owned, I presume, by former dictators and charter members of OPEC is highly amusing for humans. Doggies, however, are far more interested in fragrant spots to pee.

So when we get to Monaco, we postpone our visit to Al and Gracie's palace in favor of finding a canine toilet. Because of parking considerations—and Jerome's utter inability to navigate along the Formula One Grand Prix race route, no matter how strenuously I imagine myself to be Jackie Stewart—Ella's first opportunity in Monaco for excretory fun happens to be in the finely manicured sculpture garden directly in front of the famous Monte Carlo casino.

I look around self-consciously, realizing what she is about to do here will be the outdoors equivalent of taking a dump on the lobby carpet of Alain Ducasse's restaurant. Everywhere I turn I see Rolls-Royces and Ferraris and Lamborghinis (and the expensive-looking passengers who emerge from such vehicles, looking like so many airbrushed advertisements come to life). There's costly art everywhere. An enormous Calder spider stares down a bulbous Jean Arp woman; nattily uniformed attendants open doors and make bows; thousands (millions?) of dollars' worth of exquisitely tailored silk and wool fashion statements parade past, clinging to the shoulders and waists of the .00001 percent of people in the world who actually buy haute couture creations directly from the Paris ateliers.

And in the midst of it all, my American mutt has her tail in the air and her nose in the grass. Having no conception of money or social class, Ella isn't intimidated by either of those spectral forces. Billionaires and paupers, workingmen and royalty—they're all the same to her. *You can keep your Versace and your Bentleys,* she seems to say. *Just give me a plush lawn beneath my feet and enough unhurried time to sniff every square inch of it. Now that's living!*

As Ella squats, a (very well-dressed) policeman appears from behind a neatly trimmed hedge and starts to yell at me in French. Clearly horrified, and vigorously wagging an angry index finger, he shouts *"Non! Non!"* and charges toward my offending beast, who blithely continues to answer nature's call.

I immediately hold up one of my special collection bags high above my head, like a soccer referee presenting Claudio Caniggia a red card for rough play.

The policeman stops in midsentence, flummoxed. It appears that he's never seen a plastic bag before.

When I put it to good use on Ella's contribution to Monaco's civic beautification, the policeman's face softens, eventually breaking into a big smile.

We exchange courtly nods and bid one another good day.

Monaco, in fact, is the only principality I've seen that has a "Dogs Allowed to Poo" sign posted at strategic locations throughout the baron-friendly environs. Instead of the usual image of a dog surrounded by a red circle with a prohibitive line running through it, Monaco has green circular signs that depict a squatting dog with a demure pile of feces beneath his tail. Wherever these signs are posted—and the garden in front of the casino is *not,* I must admit, one of the exalted spots—you find highly fertilized patches of grass that don't seem to get a lot of attention from Monaco's otherwise assiduous municipal grounds crew.

Aside from exclusive doggie relief stations, catering to visiting dogs isn't Monaco's chief concern. (Catering to the whims of some of the world's wealthiest tax dodgers is more like it.) Yet I wanted to bring Ella here, anyway. I'm hoping to fulfill an admittedly weird but utterly harmless fantasy of mine: I want to play blackjack with my faithful hound at my feet.

Now, granted, this doesn't seem like a particularly outrageous (or even fun) fantasy for a moderately debauched American man to be harboring. But having written a couple of books about gambling, I've spent way too much time in smoky dens of depravity, watching the cards and dice and reels flash by in an interminable parade of randomness. Stuck at a felt-covered casino table, numbed by the crushing boredom of unwavering odds repeating their dance of chance, I've often daydreamed about my numerically oblivious friend Ella. How much nicer it would be, I've often imagined, to have her curled up beneath the table, thinking about squirrels. How reassuring it would be to give her furry back a comforting stroke in the midst of an oppressive losing streak. How life-affirming it would be to have my happy mutt counterbalancing the hordes of degenerate losers dying a slow (but inevitable) death.

Alas, Atlantic City and Las Vegas (not to mention Reno and Biloxi) are loath to allow four-legged lucky charms inside their temples of excess. Until this day, the closest Ella has ever come to entering a casino was a few summers back, when she waited out front of the MGM Grand (in the car) while I ran in to cash a sports bet.

Today, however, she's in Monte Carlo—not the one on the Vegas Strip, but the real one, in Monaco, where, fortified with enough money, anything is possible.

I'd been to the Casino Monte Carlo once before, and I was impressed by the preposterous faux glamour of it all. The tuxedoes, the pearls, the eighteenth-century paintings on the ceiling—all of it meant to distract the well-groomed livestock from their impending slaughter at the hands of roulette croupiers and baccarat dealers. Gentlemen who owned plumbing supply businesses in Frankfurt could pretend for an evening that they were James Bond. Ladies whose closest brush with celluloid immortality was a visit to the Cineplex could pretend for an evening that they were Grace Kelly—or, even better, could hold out the hope that Grace Kelly herself might pay a royal visit. All the noble tasks that casinos were supposed to accomplish happened here. The jejune ordinariness of everyday life was washed away in a world of sublime style and subtle danger.

I did not, however, notice any duchesses toting yippy lapdogs adorned with diamond-studded collars. Nor, for that matter, did I see any Rhodesian ridgebacks or Saint Bernards. The Casino Monte Carlo, last I visited, was bereft of dogs.

But what the hell. I'm with Ella. We're in Europe. In Monaco. It's worth a gamble.

My mutt and I descend through the sculpture garden, whose official name, I note with some amusement, is actually La Parade des Animaux. I perform a final inspection: No eye goo on the muzzle; no mud on the paws; coat gleaming white; scarf hanging just so around the neck. *Parfait*.

We waltz past an ornamental fountain—No swimming today, Ella!—and through a fleet of luxury automobiles. Then up a few carpeted stairs, flanked by stern doormen who don't seem particularly seduced by the sight of such a cute pup in their midst. And we're at the Casino Monte Carlo's baroque entrance.

I immediately notice a sign beside the gilded doorway. The word "Prohibited" stands out. Beneath it I see about a dozen symbols, including cameras, cell phones, and portable tape players. There's one symbol, in the upper left-hand corner, that makes me feel like the air's been knocked from my lungs: a dog.

Dogs prohibited.

The dog on the sign looks like a Jack Russell terrier, or maybe a Scottie.

"You're a very lucky animal," I say to Ella. "The casino doesn't allow little terriers. But luckily you're not a terrier. You're a mutt. A big mutt. It's only terriers they don't want."

Ella begins to pant jovially. I tell her, "I see nothing here prohibiting hairy white mongrels." She pants some more.

Already knowing what the answer will be, I approach the nearest doorman, a middle-aged gentleman outfitted like a Central American general, teeming with epaulets and chest badges. I make Ella sit beside me. The doorman eyes me warily.

Mustering my very best French—which isn't even as good as George W. Bush's very best English—I ask the splendidly costumed keeper of the door if I may enter with my dog, who, he will note, is not a terrier.

He replies in English, "No, sir, it is not allowed."

"Well, let me ask you this," I say, switching to my native tongue. "What if I told you I was a very high roller?"

The doorman looks at me quizzically.

"A *very* high roller," I repeat.

"I'm sorry?"

"What if I told you I'm a very big customer? That I make very large bets—then what?"

The doorman, confused, fetches an assistant doorman who, perhaps, is more current with the American gambling lingo. This new fellow is slightly younger, possibly hipper to the ways of Vegas, where money lubricates every potentially difficult transaction, turning ninety-minute waits and "Sold Out" signs into frictionless satisfaction. "I'm sorry, sir. What is the problem?" the younger doorman asks me.

"Oh, not a problem at all," I say genially. "I was just asking your colleague here what the casino policy toward dogs might be, especially when they're in the company of a high roller."

"Eye roller?" He smiles bashfully.

"Like, for instance, say I bet like, I don't know, ten thousand dollars—or euros—ten thousand per hand. Could I bring my dog with me then?"

The doormen look at me, deciding perhaps if a guy dressed in khaki pants and toting around a dog of indeterminate origin could possibly bet that kind of money. They murmur together in French. Then the younger of the doormen says to me, "I'm sorry, sir. The policy is no dogs."

"Even for the sultan of Brunei?" I ask.

"I'm sorry?"

"So, what I'm asking is, if someone came to the Casino Monte Carlo wanting to bet, like, one hundred thousand on baccarat, and he happened to have his dog with him, you're telling me you wouldn't let him in?"

"No dogs, sir. I'm very sorry," the young man says patiently.

"Not even really nice ones?" I ask, giving up.

"No, sir, I'm sorry. No dogs in the casino. But I must say, sir, he is a very nice dog."

"Yes, she is," I agree. "And she likes to gamble. Very high roller, this dog."

"Yes, it is a pity." The doorman shrugs.

"Very big player. Bets millions on chemin de fer." I return the shrug.

"Ah, yes," the doorman says, understanding my drift. "She is eye roller!" He laughs Gallically and reaches down to pet the VIP gambler on his doorstep. "Ah, she is very nice. But I'm sorry, sir, no—"

"Dogs allowed. Yes, I understand." I shake hands with both doormen and bid them good day.

"Sorry, Ella," I say to my high-rolling puppy. "We'll have to roll the bones someplace else." She looks at me blankly. "That was a gambling joke, sort of," I tell her.

We skip down the carpeted steps of the Casino Monte Carlo and head for the parking garage. But before we go, I pose Ella for a photograph beside a navy blue Bentley convertible parked directly in front of the casino's ornate facade. (They're both very good-looking models, though the white one is more animated and has a better smile.) While I get my camera focused, about forty-nine other snap-shooting tourists swarm in for their commemorative picture of Monaco.

The two doormen come down the stairs from their post to investigate the commotion. I figure they're going to shoo us away, what with the official "no dogs" policy and all.

"Sir," the younger of the two says to me, "would you please? A photo with the eye roller?"

POST

An American dog
at the Eiffel Tower

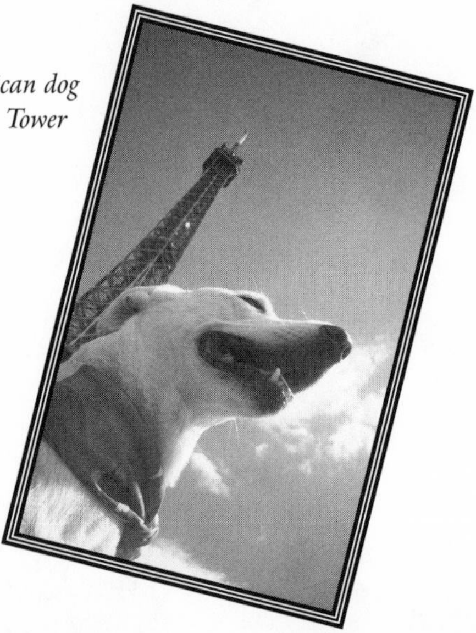

In the lobby of the Hôtel Meurice, Paris

Chapter 13

Paris, France, is the city I've always thought Ella would love best, and it's the city where I've always thought I'd most love to see her being herself. As corporate pundits like to say, the possibilities for *synergy* seemed ripe. The symbiosis was obvious to me. Here was the World's Most Beautiful City playing host to the World's Most Beautiful Dog (according to a highly partisan search committee consisting solely of me). I could almost picture the headlines in French *Vogue*: "Elegant Paris Meets Elegant Ella—a Harmonious Marriage of Character and Style." *(Photos by Avedon.)*

On many prior trips to Paris, I often imagined what it would be like to have Ella at my side, strolling on cobblestoned streets lined with aromatic *boulangeries* and *charcuteries,* pausing for a glass of Bordeaux at an outdoor café beneath a Gothic steeple, looking in shop windows and, if the urge should hit us, stepping inside to browse, confident that no one would ask for the dog to be left outside. I had enjoyed Paris immensely without Ella—what's not to like?—but I also knew I would enjoy Paris even more with her. Witnessing how Parisians assimilated dogs into their daily life, I believed that of all the great cities on this planet, Paris was the one where Ella would probably feel most welcomed. Most *at home*. Despite the prodigious geographical distance between the familiar comforts of her Hollywood garden and the fresh fragrances of the Tuileries, I suspected Paris would feel closer to Ella's perfect spiritual haven than almost anyplace I could take her in the United States.

She's been about as good and loving a pet as I could have dared to dream, and, yes, I've wanted to give her back a minuscule fraction of the pleasure and peace she's brought into my life. But it would be disingenuous—okay, a bald-faced lie—to say that I wanted to bring Ella to Paris (and the rest of Europe) solely to reward her for all the charitable work and boundless love she's given to humankind in general and me in particular. I wanted Ella in Paris because it would be fun for *both* of us. I like to be with her. She likes to be with me. We both like freshly baked baguettes and pan-seared foie gras drizzled with port-wine reduction. It's a satisfying deal all around.

I'm careful, however, not to treat my eleven-year-old Lab-greyhound mix as though she were my child, or, for that matter, any other human being. I don't believe dogs are entitled to the same pleasures and comforts as people, and the stories one hears about dotty old ladies feeding their Pomeranians caviar and transporting their shih tzus to the beauty salon in chauffeur-driven limousines make me embarrassed to be a dog lover.

So I should emphasize that when I check in to the justifiably celebrated Hôtel Meurice, on the rue de Rivoli, Ella's comfort is an important bonus, but not my priority. Pampering Sandrine and myself is the main point. After nearly a month of almost constant moving, dashing in and out of modest hotels around Europe, I'm treating our pack to the kind of ridiculous luxury that is best appreciated by those who are not accustomed to it. For a long weekend of hedonistic bliss, we'll be swaddled in down and cotton and silk, lodged in a grand palace of a room in which the bathwater is always hot, the air-conditioning always works, and the service staff leaves plates of kumquats and plums on the bedside table.

To Ella, of course, none of these superfluities makes any difference. She'll end up sleeping on her green travel mat, no matter the quality of the paintings on the wall or the thread count of the bedsheets. But for the humans in our entourage, the Hôtel Meurice represents an oasis of comfort in a desert of travel indignities. *And* we get to have our dog with us.

As foul as I find the concept of spoiled pets (like those who are provided for by an inherited annuity), I must admit that Ella Guinevere looks smashing in the Meurice's gold-plated marble lobby. I'm struck by the usual cognitive dissonance—*What is my dog doing in the lobby of a luxurious Paris hotel?*—but I quickly become accustomed to the sight of Ella amid such grandiose splendor. To say she "fits right in" seems at first like a hackneyed cliché. But, in fact, there are two gold greyhound statues in the Meurice lobby—the two pups are the corporate emblem of the hotel's parent company, the Dorchester Group—and Ella stands directly between them for a series of photos with members of the hotel staff, who, with typical Frenchness, are already showering my mutt with kisses and compliments. The two greyhounds, the concierge tells me, were abandoned puppies that masons building the hotel in the 1800s rescued on the construction site. The Meurice, he tells me proudly, has always been very kind toward dogs.

That would be an understatement. When we first enter our room, in a quiet corner of the third floor, I see a silver tray on the carpet. Upon this silver tray is one porcelain bowl filled with water and another brimming with boiled rice, diced carrots, julienne of haricots verts, and nuggets of ground lamb. If I hadn't just had breakfast, *I* would eat it.

"Welcome to Paris," I say to my ecstatic dog.

She inhales half of the gourmet repast and collapses on her mat, a very happy puppy.

I look at my old friend, resting on her side, with all four paws pointing in the same direction. She seems content in a way I've personally never known. It's an elemental contentment that goes beyond happiness or pleasure. Ella's contentment is the kind that comes from living in the present, from being immune to future worries and amnesiac about past travails. I look at her napping on the floor of a deluxe room at the Hôtel Meurice, and I think in some ways I'd like to be more like my dog.

One of the many lessons Ella has taught me on our journey through Europe together is that Class—the collective Anglo-American obsession that dare not speak its name on the western shores of the Atlantic—is, in fact, a figment of our human imagination, akin to the suspension of disbelief that we willingly engage in when we go to the theater. In the case of Class, we willingly suspend our *belief*—in egalitarianism, namely. Americans, despite our alleged disavowal of our British heritage, still distinguish between upper- and lower-class pursuits. Opera, for example, is generally considered an extravagance meant for the moneyed. Professional wrestling, conversely, is for the masses. Lower-class people stay at motels where the bathroom cups are made of plastic and the remote control is screwed into the bedside table. The "better" class of person stays at places like the Meurice.

Since I normally don't patronize a hotel like the Meurice—and, not being of the right class, I don't usually socialize with people who do—I'm conscious of not belonging, of being a middle-class guy who's overstepped his bounds.

Ella, however, reminds me that comfort with oneself is the key to comfort in your environment, no matter how grand (or squalid) it is. She's utterly oblivious to the price of a room at Hôtel Meurice, and she doesn't know (or care) that the furniture is made of rosewood, or that terrycloth robes and cotton slippers adorn the bathroom. She doesn't grasp that six of the channels on the satellite television originate in the Middle East, or that these channels are meant to keep the Meurice's more typical guest apprised of what's going on back home near his oil fields.

All she knows is that she's with her pack, in a safe nest that has a soft place to lay her head after a delicious repast. When we pass expensively attired hotel guests in the hallway, while her daddy wonders if he should say "good afternoon" in French or English, Ella speaks with a friendly wag of her tail, the one universal language that she (and everyone else) knows. When we loiter in the ornate lobby, while her owner worries about if he's dressed properly, she reclines (in the nude) on the cool marble beneath the grand piano, unintentionally more regal than if Michelle Pfeiffer were crooning on top of it. The idea that she might be violating some obscure code of etiquette never crosses Ella's mind. Reclining quietly beneath the piano is what she does whether she's home or abroad. It's only natural. She's perfectly well behaved while remaining utterly unaware of this thing we call "manners." Ella Konik in the Hôtel Meurice is the same dog she is in a highway motel, the same dog in Paris as she is in Hollywood. Ella is Ella. And I'm discovering for the thousandth time what a fine thing that is.

* * *

When we three arrive at Le Grand Véfour, the renowned restaurant at the Palais-Royal, down the street from the Louvre, I have a momentary panic attack. Despite weeks of evidence to the contrary, I'm still vaguely frightened that some mean authority figure is going to have me and my mutt deported for having the temerity to patronize a restaurant together. Dozens of positive European experiences notwithstanding, I remain haunted by a lifetime of American dining, which has always been resolutely canine-free. (I refer to the company I've kept, not the content of mysterious entrées.) So I must silently remind myself that Europeans, particularly the French, aren't nearly as neurotic as my countrymen are about bringing dogs into eating places.

But Le Grand Véfour, owned by the Taittinger family of champagne notoriety, is not any old eating place. It's one of those temples of gastronomy over which food-fetish magazines swoon, one of fewer than two dozen establishments in all of France awarded the vaunted *trois étoiles* by the Guide Michelin. A legion of French statesmen and writers and artists—Hugo, Colette, Sartre—have eaten here, and each name is inscribed in brass on the back of the diner's favorite banquette. The dining room, lined with lead mirrors and lighted by crystal chandeliers, has been called one of the most beautiful in the world. There are so many original masterworks upon the walls and ceilings that the menu provides a viewers' guide. The chef, Guy Martin, is himself a cooking celebrity, with a series of best-selling recipe books to his credit, not to mention an almost endless parade of hungry and curious eaters queuing at his door for a taste of his latest culinary creation. Getting a reservation here normally requires two months' advance notice or an extremely well connected concierge.

I employed both techniques and managed to snare a lunch booking—for two people and one *très gentil chien*.

When I wrote and inquired of Le Grand Véfour if they welcomed dogs in their haute cuisine wonderland, their e-mail reply was succinct and explicit: *"Oui. Avec plaisir."*

With pleasure!

With pleasure, I remind myself, approaching the restaurant's door. *My dog is not merely welcome she's welcomed with pleasure.*

Still, I can feel my heart racing. This is one of the finest restaurants in the world—and I'm about to walk in, to have lunch, with my hairy white American mutt. What if Le Grand Véfour management thought I was bringing not a seventy-three-pound Lab mix but a little lapdog named Fifi? What if in my e-mail I misspelled the French word for "dog" and gave them the mistaken impression that I was inexplicably hoping to bring along a miniature oak tree? What if Le Grand Véfour I'd been writing to was actually Le *Grande* Véfour, a down-market entrecôte joint trading off the good name of its famous neighbor?

What if this has all been a terrible and humiliating mistake?

"Ah, Monsieur Konik," the maître d' says when I approach his podium, precisely at twelve-thirty P.M. "*Bonjour.* And zees must be your dog?"

"Yes. *Elle s'appelle Ella,*" I say expectantly, nodding at my seated mutt. Prior to opening Le Grand Véfour's front door, I adjusted Ella's leopard-print scarf, brushed away a few stray hairs, and fairly begged her to behave better than she's ever behaved in her life. "Please, Ella," I implored her. "I need you to be a good girl for me. This is really important. No begging. And, please, please, don't have any accidents. Not that you ever do, but I'm just saying. Please be a good girl."

She looked at me solicitously and attempted to lick my chin. Ella, I think, can sense when I'm nervous, and she's somehow figured out how to calm me by simply staying calm herself. I clicked on her leash—a sign to her that we were about to do something serious—and took a deep breath. *"Avec plaisir,"* I said. *"Avec plaisir."*

The maître d', a youthful man named Christian, admires Ella's "outfit." Indicating her shawl, he says, "It ees Hermès?" I laugh nervously at what I assume is a joke.

Then he says, "Ella, she ees much bigger zen we expected." I laugh nervously at what I fear isn't a joke.

Christian the maître d' asks us to wait in the foyer, and then he disappears into the dining room to "make arrangements" for our party of three. I envision him and his colleagues spreading sheets of newspaper around an isolated table.

While we wait, several other members of the restaurant staff, all of them attired in tuxedos and bow ties, peek around the corner, presumably to get a glimpse of the boorish American fellow who has had the gall to bring his wild beast into their culinary sanctum. I'm about ready to run to the nearest crêpes stand and file our visit to Le Grand Véfour under Really Bad Ideas That I'll Never Have Again.

Then the maître d' returns and says, "Sank you for waiting. Zis way, please!" I grasp Ella's leash firmly in my left hand and say a silent prayer to the Lords of Canine Deportment. Sandrine, clad in a smashing pantsuit, follows Christian the maître d', and Ella and I follow her through the dining room to our table, which is neither in a distant corner nor surrounded by prophylactic newsprint, but almost in the middle of the restaurant, beside a mirrored wall. The sparkling room is full of other diners engaged in conversation and wine-sipping, and I try valiantly to not notice what I imagine to be their horrified stares. Ella, of course, does not grasp the gravity of the moment. She strolls through Le Grand Véfour nonchalantly, almost regally, aware only that there are numerous delicious aromas (aromas she must summarily ignore) wafting from every direction. Sensing my anxiety, she heels perfectly and looks straight ahead, breaking concentration only once, when an enthusiastic party of older ladies makes repeated kissy sounds at her.

Ella wags her tail enthusiastically at the ladies who lunch. Under my breath I hiss *"Heel,"* vetoing the prospect of any impromptu introductions.

I just want to get to our seats without incident, without making too much of a spectacle of ourselves. This isn't some beer hall in Prague, I realize; there aren't four other pooches on the wooden floor, as in Vienna. This is Le Grand Véfour, where people pay hundreds of dollars to be mesmerized by the concoctions upon their plates. Oenophiles savoring the structure and nose of their Pichon Longueville '89 aren't interested in some strange animal wearing a scarf; they want serenity with their Sauternes.

And yet . . . I see smiles. I see affirmative head-nodding. I hear approving murmurs.

And I see a waiter pulling out a chair for Sandrine while his colleague pulls one out for me. The maître d' motions toward our seats. "Mademoiselle? Monsieur?"

I want to ask him where he would like Ella to be stowed. Underneath the hems of the tablecloth, perhaps? But I'm far too nervous to compose such a sentence in French. So I ask Sandrine to translate. Before she can answer, Christian the maître d', comprehending my English question, says, "And for Ella? Here?" He points to a spot on the carpet beside my chair.

"She won't be in the way?" I ask, directing Ella to her place on the floor.

"No, Monsieur, not at all. We welcome you weeze pleasure."

"Avec plaisir," I say stupidly.

"Oui. Avec plaisir." The maître d' makes a tiny bow and turns to go. But before he leaves, he kneels down beside the white crescent at his feet and pats her head affectionately. *"Bon appétit!"*

A platoon of waiters descends upon our table. One bears butter and fresh bread, another has menus, and a third proffers the encyclopedic wine list. The first waiter—the bread-and-butter man—asks me if he can get anything for Ella. "Perhaps some pâté?" he suggests.

I look at Sandrine, who smiles and shrugs. "Maybe just some water," I say.

"Yes, of course," the waiter says, seeming mildly disappointed.

After the servers have departed, I exhale heavily in relief. And then I giggle.

"We're in the Grand Véfour!" I whisper to Sandrine.

"With Ella!" she whispers back. "I can't believe it!"

"They seem to like her," I whisper.

"Of course. Everyone likes her!" Sandrine whispers in reply.

I nod. "True." I lean toward Sandrine. "Why are we whispering?"

She whispers back, "I don't know."

"We should just talk normally," I suggest, still whispering.

"Sure."

"In French!" I declare, a little louder.

"Really?"

"Sure. That way Ella won't know what we're saying about her." I look down at my mutt. She has her front paws crossed, and she rests her muzzle upon her forelegs. "God, she is so good."

"En Français, Michel! En Français," Sandrine corrects me.

"Oh, right. *Mon dieu, le chien est très bien!*"

She really is. I look at Ella Guinevere Konik reclined on the floor of Le Grand Véfour, and I feel wildly sentimental. Guests who are just arriving for lunch don't even know she's here. And the ones who do seem to be marveling at her peaceful disposition. (Of course, given my meager French vocabulary, they might well be politely calling for her to be drawn and quartered.) Ella is so calm, so utterly unobtrusive, she seems to me like one of the Watteau-esque paintings on the wall, another sublime decoration that pleases the eye and warms the soul. I watch her slowly falling asleep as waiters bustle past with trays of delicious morsels, and I feel vindicated.

Or at least not completely crazy. Her presence at Le Grand Véfour is the ultimate refutation of all the spurious dogs-should-be-excluded-from-restaurants arguments I've heard. Indeed, at the moment I feel like nothing could be more pleasant, more natural. More *right*. I consider telling Sandrine all this, but I can't figure out how to say so in French. So I merely gesture toward our slumbering companion and nod contentedly.

Sandrine nods back, and I know she understands what my heart is trying to say.

We order the tasting menu and a bottle of (Taittinger) champagne, and I propose a toast to Ella, who has a way of making dreams come true without even trying.

A cascade of courses falls upon our table: lobster, turbot, lamb, pork—all accompanied by pungent glazes and puddles of fragrant oils. As each new sensational dish arrives, Ella opens her eyes to observe the parade of delicacies, and she thumps her tail twice when I say her name and remind her what a good puppy she is. Yet she never stirs from her assigned spot.

A smartly attired couple with their two young daughters at the table across from us comment (in English) how well behaved my dog is. I thank them and smile, as though I have lunch every afternoon in gourmet Parisian restaurants with an American mutt at my feet. Turning to Sandrine, I say, "I wish we could do this every afternoon."

Then I look at the last bite of *filet de porc* on my plate, a morsel of tender meat the consistency of hardened butter. Would it be a sin, I wonder, to "waste" such sublime food on a dog?

I ponder Ella's face, serene and untroubled there on the carpet of Le Grand Véfour. I say to her, "I'm very proud of you, Ella. You're a *really* good dog. Possibly even *great*—although that could be the champagne talking." And I quietly slip her the last of the pork.

Since she barely bothers to chew the thumb-size portion, the hints of fruit and spice don't seem to make much of an impression on her. But in that one hasty bite, I'd guess Ella becomes a devout Guy Martin fan, just like everyone else in the room.

Long, languid meals in France are like novels by Proust, associative and rambling affairs in which time stands still or runs in reverse. Half drunk, I notice a few of the hundred or so people in the restaurant getting up to leave. I also notice one of the waiters—Jean-Marc, he says, is his name—returning to our table with uncommon frequency, watching over our meal as though he were a personal bodyguard. Is he subtly urging us to finish? I wonder. I can't tell if we've been at Le Grand Véfour for an hour, or three. (And with a belly full of yummy things and a now-empty bottle of champagne in the bucket, I'm not too concerned with clocks and watches.) I do realize, however, that our reverie must be drawing near its conclusion, because here comes Jean-Marc with the penultimate course. He's pushing out the cheese cart!

Besides the *amuse-bouche,* the entrée, the *plat,* the dessert, the petits fours, and all the beverages that go with them, the cheese is my favorite part of the French gourmand experience. At a classical place like Le Grand Véfour, lovers of *fromage* can choose from several dozen varieties, creamy or hard, pasteurized or not, innocuous or stinky. I like them all. But whenever the cheese cart rolls up to my table, I immediately ask if there is any Epoisses to be had. It's an unpasteurized goat cheese from Burgundy known both for its strong odor and its powerful taste, which reminds some people of cooked earth. Because of strict import laws, getting Epoisses in America is difficult. (Purveyors have to smuggle it in between shipments of Camembert and Muenster.) I know one shop in Los Angeles where it's sporadically available—but only if the owner knows you well and you say the right code words.

When I ask Jean-Marc if he has any Epoisses, he shakes his head gravely and says he thinks they're all out. But perhaps I would enjoy a little of this and a smidgen of that?

Of course I would.

As Jean-Marc slices, he tells us that he has two passions in life: cheese and dogs. (My kind of guy.) His mother, he reports, oversees the French equivalent of the Humane Society in Provence, and, he says humbly, he therefore has extensive experience with *les chiens*.

I tell Jean-Marc that Ella was in fact a rescue dog. He looks amazed. "It's true," I say. "I found her in a park near my house."

"And may I say, sir, zat your dog is quite exceptional?"

"Merci," I reply. "And may I say, Jean-Marc, so is your cheese selection?"

"Ah, thank you. We work very hard for it." I see a twinkle in

Jean-Marc's eye. "Pardon me, sir, for a moment." He disappears into the kitchen, leaving his cheese cart parked beside our table, dangerously close to filching range, where I could spear a taste of every curdled chunk with a well-aimed fork.

Ella looks up at the smelly conveyance parked above her. She sniffs three times quickly and sighs.

Jean-Marc returns with a small plate upon which sits a runny wedge of cheese leaking from an orange-yellow rind: Epoisses.

"I was able to find a leetle beet in a special place," Jean-Marc says devilishly.

I taste a small piece on the end of my knife and shudder with pleasure. *"Superbe, mon ami,"* I say. "I think maybe you should have some with us."

Jean-Marc holds up his hand and shakes his head, smiling. "Please. Enjoy." Then he leans down and pets Ella on the back of her neck and glides away.

We savor our Epoisses, letting it melt on our tongue like caramel candy. Shortly thereafter, Jean-Marc returns, this time with a bottle of Sauterne and a colleague. He pours two glasses of the nectar, compliments of the house. "Because what goes better wiss Epoisses, no?" Then he asks me to confirm for his fellow waiter that Ella is, in fact, a dog that I found in a park, not the product of a champion breeder.

I say yes, it's true. "But, as I think you can see" (by now I've long since abandoned any attempts at paragraph-length French), "she's a very good dog, despite her lack of noble lineage."

"Very nice," Jean-Marc comments. "A perfect guest, yes?"

"And a very discerning gourmet," I say. I can't help myself.

Even though we're at Le Grand Véfour, sipping obscenely expensive wine and savoring viscous mouthfuls of rare Epoisses, I've got to show the waiters Ella's "junk food" trick. "Here. Let me show you something," I say. "Come on, Ella. Get up, please."

"Oh, Michael, please," Sandrine implores me quietly. "Is this necessary?"

But I'm too drunk on dog-love to listen. "Ella," I say, offering a piece of bread to her, "this is . . ." Dare I say "junk food" in Le Grand Véfour?

Sandrine recognizes my dilemma and explains to the waiters that I only mean it as a trick, a doggie amusement.

"This is junk food, Ella," I say guiltily.

"Mauvais pour la santé," Sandrine translates. "It's very silly."

Ella refuses to eat the (anything but junky) bread. I look at the waiters with wide, faux-amazed eyes. Then I tell Ella that "Guy Martin made the bread. It's healthy food," and she takes it from my fingers.

"Incroyable!" Jean-Marc exclaims.

"Quelle magique!" his colleague interjects.

They babble together in French, rapidly describing to each other what the dog just did, making sure the other understands the significance of what he has just witnessed.

"It's just a little trick," I say, striving vainly for modesty. "Now go to bed, Ella." She immediately lies down on her tableside spot, placing her muzzle on her paws. "All the way, young lady," I remind her. She stretches out on her side and rests her head on the carpet.

Jean-Marc shakes his head vigorously and marches away. He promptly returns with a complimentary dessert and two other members of the staff, and he insists I show them the "junk food" trick.

A minute later, two other waiters, also bearing a plate of sweets, look in on our happy table.

Then Christian the maître d' and a man in white emerge from the kitchen. Possibly Guy Martin himself—though I'm too embarrassed to ask.

Sensing a mild commotion, several other diners on their way out of Le Grand Véfour stop to see what all the fuss is about. Most of them, I gather, didn't know they had been lunching in the company of a dog for the last two (or three, or more) hours. They, too, want to see the performance, and, naturally, we oblige. By the time she's satisfied her eager audience, Ella has had a seven-course meal of her own, albeit one composed of the same ingredient served repeatedly (with a garnish of corny showbiz patter).

Our lunch has turned into an informal party, with Ella providing the free entertainment. The waiters, while as polished and respectful as ever, have dropped their air of formality. Sandrine is joking with them in French. And I'm inviting everyone to shake hands and introduce themselves to the *mutt magnifique.* We're within the hallowed walls of Le Grand Véfour. But somehow the boundaries between customer and server, client and artisan, have been blurred. We're all just a bunch of happy drunks—well, at least I am—reveling in our mutual love of dogs.

After I've paid the bill and posed for photos with "the boys," only one other party remains in the restaurant, two French lovebirds staring dreamily in each other's eyes. I look at my white dog and start to say something. But she looks back at me in a way that makes me know words aren't necessary. I remove Ella's leash, kiss her on her hairy cheek, and totter out of Le Grand Véfour into the late-afternoon Paris sunshine.

* * *

Here's the problem with lunching at Le Grand Véfour in the company of your American dog: You get the idea that she will henceforth be welcome everywhere you dream of taking her. You don't bother calling to ask if maybe possibly it wouldn't be too much of a problem if perhaps your dog could come along? You just show up, confident that if dogs can enter the refined chambers of one of Paris's legendary restaurants, they surely will be welcomed everyplace else—even the places that don't serve foie gras ravioli topped with truffle shavings.

One morning at the Meurice, I'm lying in bed, reading a guidebook. In a moment of insanity, I suggest to Sandrine that we bring Ella to the Louvre. "You know, to look at paintings."

"You're kidding, right?"

I start to say no. Then I regain my senses. But still. She *did* have lunch at Le Grand Véfour.

Which leads me to believe that anything—well, almost anything—is possible. At least in Paris, otherwise known as Doggie Paradise.

I thumb through the guidebook, looking at lists of restaurants. Then I recall Christian the maître d' wondering about Ella's scarf. "Let's buy Ella a scarf," I blurt out. "At Hermès!"

"You want to buy an Hermès scarf for Ella?" Sandrine asks.

"Yes," I say, intoxicated by the idea. "Oh, and one for you, of course."

"Of course," Sandrine says dryly. "Are you sure? They're very expensive."

"I just think it would be so cute. Ella in Hermès."

"Do they allow dogs in their boutique?" Sandrine asks reasonably.

I hadn't even considered that they might not.

"Maybe you should call," Sandrine suggests.

Instead, I insist that we just show up unannounced. It's only around the corner, and the worst they could say is no. "And how could they say no to a lady as elegant as this one?" I wonder out loud. On cue, Ella emits a prodigious belch.

"Ella! You swine!" I tease her. She hops onto the bed and tries to lick me. "They don't let piglets into Hermès. Only elegant ladies. Especially ones who eat at three-star restaurants and stay at the Meurice." I say this all in a preposterously high squeaky voice that gets her all excited.

Ella performs her choreography of playfulness, the series of moves she makes when she's happy. First she "takes a bow" (another of her better tricks), stretching her front legs outward and dipping her head. Then she does her Stallion Dance, running in place like a circus horse. Then she chases her tail.

The tail-chasing typically ends with barking, and we can't have that in the Meurice. So I calm her with my regular voice overlaid with soothing FM disc jockey tones. Very Barry White. Once Ella settles down, I look her in the eye and ask as conversationally as possible, "I'm just curious. Is there anyone here who would like to go for a walk?"

Her eyes widen.

"Oh, I see. Would *you* like to go for a walk?"

The maniacal dancing starts again, and I figure we best exit the hotel before someone calls the police.

What does one wear to shop at Hermès? I wonder. I mean, if one is a dog? (Sandrine and I put on clothes that cocktail party planners would call "smart casual," but *our* look, I figure, isn't the problem today.) Ella could do her minimalist thing, a naked dog in search of something to wear. Or maybe one of her brightly colored shawls—which the fashion police might recognize as white-trash bandannas tied into cravats. Too downmarket for one of the finer boutiques in Paris, I decide. "Here, Ella," I say, clipping on her red collar decorated with jalapeño peppers. "Your look today is 'Hot.' As in hot dog. You're a hottie. Get it?"

Ella does another avant-garde dance and we depart for Hermès.

On the brief walk from our hotel to the boutique, we pass the flagship ateliers of dozens of designers whose names even a fashion-ignorer like me recognizes. Versace, Gucci, Chanel, Yves Saint Laurent. I peer through their shop windows. Inside each place I see more or less the same scene: beautiful salespeople, a stable of very thin men and women whose chief accessory this season appears to be cigarettes, obsessively folding and smoothing the merchandise. There doesn't seem to be much to sell—which isn't a problem, I suppose, when you can get people to pay you $16,000 for a piece of cloth the size of a napkin. At one place, which may be going for a survivalist kind of theme, I count exactly seven pieces of clothing for sale.

Whenever we pause in front of one of these fancy joints, the staff eyes us through the glass warily, almost aggressively, like caged tigers at the zoo. I can't tell if it's because they're silently scoffing at my suit jacket, the lapels of which might be three-quarters of an inch too wide (or is it too narrow?) to be au courant, or if they don't appreciate Ella's tendency to shed white hairs on tropical-weight black rayon. Maybe the red jalapeño collar was a big style mistake. Whatever the reason for their haughty coolness, I don't feel as though we're exactly being beckoned into their rarefied quarters.

So on we amble down the rue St-Honoré, which, to Ella's dismay, contains a dearth of grass. "It's all going to be worth the trip," I promise her. "You're going to look *très élégante* when I'm through with you. Just fabulous!" My mutt pauses to scratch an itch on her right flank. As she flicks at the spot with her rear paw, she pulls her lips back and tight, like a beauty pageant contestant flashing her teeth at the judges. "Itchy smile!" I say to her, which is what I always say when Ella gets this expression on her face (which happens only when she's scratching an itch). "Itchy smile! Itchy smile!"

A shopgirl inside a fancy dress store casts a look of utter boredom and malaise in our direction and busies herself with some important folding.

"Come on, Miss Elegant," I say to Ella. "Let's go. And remember. No itchy smiles in Hermès."

When we arrive at the doorway of the famous boutique, I don't feel the heart palpitations that accompanied our arrival at Le Grand Véfour. I feel now as though we're hardened veterans of the chi-chi social scene, with carte blanche to come and go as we please. I could be gravely mistaken, I realize, but Paris, it seems to me, has flung open its arms to Ella Guinevere Konik, welcoming her (with pleasure) into a world of congenial accessibility. And she, of course, is happy to waltz right in and make herself comfortable.

I click on Ella's leash, straighten her collar, and brush away a few stray hairs from her butt. Then we walk inside Hermès.

The first thing I notice is several large, earpiece-wearing security guards, all of whom wear nicely tailored blazers and look as though they could be models for both the fashion and collection agency industries. They eye us carefully as we enter. I suspect for a moment that we are about to be politely escorted from the premises. But no. One of them nods at me. Another smiles. And another unclasps his hands from behind his back and steps forward to give Ella a pat on her head.

I get the idea that they let dogs shop at Hermès after all.

It's midmorning on a weekend day, and the shop is crowded with customers who seem to belong to one of two distinct species: tourist ladies looking for a preposterously expensive piece of silk to take back home to Boca Raton/Short Hills/Palm Springs, or local ladies of a certain age looking for a preposterously expensive piece of silk to wrap around their bonnet/neck/just-out-of-the-salon coiffure. Ella, I must admit, fits in particularly well with the latter group. Like them she is unhurried, unbothered, languid. (Having no idea whatsoever where she is probably helps in this regard.) Like the local ladies, she feels no pressure to buy for the sake of buying, and no amount of idle flattery from clever sales associates will convince her that she simply *must* have that orange-yellow-turquoise floral number.

We browse. I fondle lengths of silk. Ella stands at my side, flirting from a distance with the security guards. We move on to the next display case. I pick up things and put them down. Ella yawns. We browse some more. I feel like someone at an art museum in search of the Monets who gets lost in the de Kooning section, someone who has no idea what he's looking at or what it's supposed to mean.

So I do what all men do in such situations: I let the woman decide.

"Could you pick something out?" I ask Sandrine. "I have no idea. Maybe something pink. Or with flowers? I don't know. And what's with these scrunchy things? They're like accordions. How are you supposed to wear this?"

While Sandrine goes off in search of something appropriate for an American mutt (and a tall Belgian), I aimlessly pick through a pile of scarves. I ask my dog which item she fancies. But instead of answering she lies down on the brightly polished floor, fatigued, apparently, from so much beauty being thrust upon her at once.

I drop her leash and let her rest while I continue to pick through the fabric. Everything in Hermès—the goods, the display cases, the staff—is pretty, in the conventional sense. But it's the customers who really catch my eye. The Ladies of a Certain Age seem to wear more makeup than I'm accustomed to seeing on anyone who isn't about to be photographed under klieg lights. They also dress as though they were on their way to a bar mitzvah, or a gala wedding, in the style of Queen Elizabeth, with hats and gloves and soft colors that appear in the sky at dusk. Curled up among so many grand dames, Ella seems to me to be like Eliza Doolittle (before Higgins gets his hands on her) surrounded by so many society matrons streaming out of the opera.

Yet none of these Ladies of a Certain Age seems offended or nonplussed by the presence of a simple mutt in one of their favorite shopping haunts. Indeed, many of them pause to admire her, waiting so quietly there on the floor. Ella, as is her inclusive nature, does not differentiate between Ladies of a Certain Age and plain old ladies. Everyone at Hermès is a potential friend, and she greets each of her visitors with a cordial tap of the tail, a raising of the ears, and a widening of the eyes. It's her way of saying "Hello, good looking! Wanna play?" After more than nine years of disarming strangers with unforced charm, Ella's gotten the routine down pat. And even shoppers who aren't in the habit of mingling with American mutts in Hermès stop to say *"bonjour."*

Sandrine returns with an armful of shawl candidates, most of them in the pink family of colors, which, according to Ella's personal shopper, will highlight her femininity. Under the supervision of a smiling saleslady who, despite her grinning mien, does not strike me as particularly amused, Ella "tries on" a little pink-and-lavender number. (Which is to say she submits to Sandrine tying a scarf around her neck.) I think the dog looks lovely—but what do I know? The saleslady and Sandrine confer with each other in French while Ella and I stand by dumbly. Both women shake their heads, and Sandrine replaces the deficient item with something putatively better, or more appropriate, or whatever it is a fancy silk scarf is supposed to be when it's wrapped around the throat of a hairy Lab mix. Again the women agree the new accessory is not quite right.

I look at Ella sitting in the Hermès shop, being outfitted in a succession of sublime scarves, each one of which costs as much as an entire year's supply of dog food. It's very cute and all, but suddenly I feel as though buying fancy gifts for a dog—even if she *is* the best doggie in the world—isn't the right thing to do. In fact, the longer I look at Ella among the Tourist Ladies and the Ladies of a Certain Age, the more convinced I am that it's the wrong thing to do.

"I'm sorry," I say to Sandrine and the saleslady. "I think maybe this isn't right."

The saleslady emits a barely perceptible sigh and tells me she'll find some other items to consider.

I tell her not to bother. Not for the dog, anyway. For the lady—the human lady—yes, please, by all means. But not for the dog. She's not getting a $350 silk scarf.

The saleslady looks mildly peeved (but then, even when she smiles she does). Sandrine, however, looks relieved. "No, it's silly, isn't it?" she says, removing a brilliant floral print from around Ella's shoulders. "A little too much."

"That's what I'm thinking. I mean, it feels obscene in a way. And you know what? I don't think Ella really cares if her scarf is from Hermès or Kmart." I shrug. "You know what I mean?"

Sandrine nods. And she tells me she doesn't want an Hermès scarf either.

I protest. "No! I want to get *you* one. It's just, you know, for the dog, it seems . . ." But Sandrine shakes her head. She's made up her mind.

"I could explain," she says, petting Ella's back, "but you understand, don't you? It's very sweet of you, *mon chéri,* but not necessary. No."

Ella doesn't seem to care, either way. She's infinitely less interested in *things* than she is in *people*. (Although things she can eat do tend to capture her imagination.)

I apologize to the saleslady, who's off to the next customer before I can finish expressing my regrets. With a nod toward the security guards, I begin to lead Ella out of the store. When we get to end of the aisle, not far from the front door, a Lady of a Certain Age, wearing a pink Chanel suit with a matching pink bonnet, stands in our path, gasping.

"Oooh," she moans, clutching her chest. "Oh! She is precious!" the woman says in Continental English, with an accent I can't quite place. "Precious!"

I ask Ella to sit and shake hands, to introduce herself like a proper dame. She complies, extending her right paw toward the Lady in Pink.

"Well, hello, darling," she says. "My name is Pilar. What is yours?"

"This is Ella," I say.

"Ella! Oh, you are precious!" Pilar shakes hands with her new friend, and I see the brilliant smile on her face begin to fade and slowly turn downward, almost into a frown. Her blue eyes become misty, and her bottom lip starts to tremble.

"Are you all right, Madame?" I ask her.

Pilar composes herself. "Yes. I'm sorry. This is just the first time that I have petted a dog, such a nice dog, in quite some time. Not since Freddy."

Freddy, Pilar explains, was her beagle and best friend, a mischievous little fellow who Pilar and her husband raised in their native Portugal. Everywhere they went, Freddy accompanied them, including to Paris, where they kept a small apartment. At age twelve, Freddy became very sick—Pilar does not say with what—and she was forced to say good-bye to him. This is her first trip to Paris since Freddy passed on, six months ago. "I'm sorry," she says, arranging her face into a forced smile. "I miss him terribly."

"I understand," I say. And I really do. Freddy was a good friend, a member of the family. Truly precious. Nothing more need be said.

"Ah, but I see Ella here today in Hermès. What a beautiful lady. Do you think I could kiss her?" Pilar asks hopefully.

"Of course! Ella loves to kiss."

Pilar bends down toward Ella's head. *"Bisous,"* I instruct my dog. "Kisses!"

Ella enthusiastically licks Pilar's chin. The contact of her tongue upon the lady's skin seems to ignite something deep inside that pink Chanel suit. There, in the middle of Hermès, Pilar begins to sob. Little rivulets of tears run through her carefully applied makeup, and she dabs at her eyes with the back of her petite hand.

I try to comfort her, wrapping my arms around her shoulders in a light embrace. Then Ella does what she can to ease this stranger-friend's pain, leaning against Pilar's legs in an improvised hug. "I know," I say quietly to a fellow dog lover. "I know."

"I just miss him so much," Pilar says, sniffling. "He was such a good boy."

I look down at Ella, pressing her flank against Pilar's pink skirt. My dog looks up at me, searching for a sign of confirmation, an indication that she's doing the right thing. I nod at her silently, and Ella understands what I'm trying to tell her. She knows then everything I feel about her, and I'd like to think it gladdens her heart as profoundly as her goodness gladdens mine.

Pilar catches her breath, sighs heavily and laughs. "Oh, what a mess I've made. So silly. I'm sorry."

"No, please. Not at all." I hug Pilar once more and tell her that I am proud to have met her.

"And Ella?" Pilar says, addressing the mutt against her legs. "Will you say farewell to me?" Pilar bends over and plants a long, sincere kiss on Ella's forehead, right between her brown eyes.

We leave Hermès this morning without an expensive scarf or an extravagant bauble. (Later in the afternoon we'll find a cheap Hermès knockoff at a sidewalk vendor and pay less than one twentieth of the original price. And Ella will look just as adorable.) But though we have nothing material to show for our visit, we depart Hermès with something far more valuable than a pretty bolt of cloth. Ella walks out of the famous boutique and into the brilliant Parisian summer light with a bright red lipstick imprint of two elderly lips on her white fur, a fleeting but powerful reminder that no matter what a dog wears around her neck, she is always loved.

* * *

Each morning I sit with Ella in the Tuileries gardens, across the street from the Meurice, and I wonder how we'll ever be able to return to the United States. While I sit on a wooden bench and write, Ella lounges on the grass, looking like one of the bronze historical statues that speckle the grand grounds. Officially speaking, she's not really supposed to be in the Tuileries off a leash; and she's definitely not supposed to be lying on the grass. But each morning we find a quiet little corner of the gardens near a row of hedges, away from most of the foot traffic, and nobody seems to mind. French mothers walk their children to play dates, and young lovers embrace beneath trees. A municipal gardener prunes begonias and waters impatiens, and teenage boys kick around a soccer ball. Cars honk their horns on the rue de Rivoli, and people shout oaths and opinions in the still morning air. And my dog and I enjoy what seems like utter serenity.

When the sun gets higher and the air begins to warm, we go together for a light breakfast at a nearby café, where they serve croissants and madeleines, and steaming cups of café au lait. If it's late enough—close to ten A.M.—we have breakfast at Angelina, the celebrated teahouse next door to our hotel. My dog wears her fake Hermès shawl, a pink, white, and magenta floral pattern, and as the greeter locates an available spot, Ella and I wait in the doorway, one of us looking appropriately elegant. On a signal from the hostess, we go to our table, pausing briefly to gawk at the display case of yummy napoleons and tortes. When I sit in one of the cushy chairs, Ella takes her spot beneath the table and waits for me to order, holding out the not altogether unreasonable hope that I'll share a bit of my breakfast with her.

We eat pastries and drink hot chocolate. (Well, I drink hot chocolate; Ella gets water.) The hot chocolate at Angelina is exactly that: a pitcher full of melted dark chocolate, accompanied by dollops of whipped cream. Unlike the American version, which invariably consists of powder and water, the French rendition must be taken promptly, before the chocolate hardens and you end up with a pitcher full of Hershey Kisses. On days when I'm feeling particularly abstemious, I order a salad or fruit to go with my brown nectar. But most mornings, I give in to my addiction and spend a listless hour sipping liquid candy, nibbling on cakes, and listening to the music of the French language being spoken by the denizens of the café.

When I'm finished and Ella has gotten the last of the buttery crumbs, we stroll out of Angelina onto the rue de Rivoli. As we exit, I enjoy hearing fellow American tourists whispering to one another about the "French guy" and his "French doggie with the shawl" breakfasting together. "That is so cool!" some of the people say. "The way they bring their dogs everywhere with them. I wish I could bring Bubbles to Starbucks."

I feel as though Ella and I are part of the local color, a couple of the mildly eccentric "characters"—like the *aquarelliste* in his beret and the old man in the park who lets pigeons alight upon him as he distributes bread crumbs—that help make a visit to Paris so memorable. We're indubitably tourists, English-speaking strangers who view Paris as an enormous source of amusement, not merely a place to live and work and play. Yet it's here in the epicenter of alleged Gallic snobbery that my dog and I feel most welcomed, most assimilated into the French way of life. We could live out our days happily here, I think, if not for a billion practical obstacles (like language, career, family) that make America a better place to call home.

Strolling (*sans* leash) on a gorgeous Left Bank lane, where we're welcomed in every shop we visit, every bistro we eat lunch, every gallery we peruse, I imagine how sweet life would be back home in California if I could fully share in the last few years of Ella's life. How much richer our lives would be, never having to "abandon" her when I need to do a People thing. When we jump into an underground métro car or an overground taxicab, when we loiter on the Île St-Louis, wondering who owns all the beautiful apartments, when we cross the Champs-Élyseés, with the Arc de Triomphe looming over our shoulders—each time I imagine what it would be like to do something impulsive and stupid and utterly wonderful, and just chuck it all and move to Paris with my mutt.

Expatriate American artists have been coming to Paris for decades, where they make legendary music and books and pictures, and drink a lot of wine. I wouldn't be the first, although I might be the first to do it for the sake of his lifelong canine friend.

The latest notable journalist to uproot his American family and start a new life in Paris—and then write winningly about the experience—is the brilliant *New Yorker* contributor Adam Gopnik. This former art critic and master essayist, whose beautiful and affecting memoir of his five-year French sojourn, *Paris to the Moon,* makes chucking it all seem like an exceptionally good idea, is one of my favorite writers. Adam Gopnik is a clear-eyed analyst who nevertheless remains funny, enlightening, and endearingly human. He has a knack for gracefully synthesizing bunches of smart ideas and anecdotes into one delectable literary dish, like a hearty bouillabaisse that cooks all day on your stove, tempting you to abandon your work and take little tastes. I look forward to each of his new dispatches in *The New Yorker* like some people used to look forward to the latest episode of *Friends*.

One afternoon, the girls (one of whom is also a big Gopnik fan) and I perform an informal walking homage to *Paris to the Moon,* visiting several of the places mentioned throughout his book: bistros and parks and streets that recur like Wagnerian leitmotifs. To Ella, it's all just more aimless wandering—which in her view isn't necessarily such a bad thing, as aimless wandering affords numerous opportunities to squeeze out a few drops of pee in a wide variety of *arrondissements*. To me, our Jour du Gopnik is a simple way to reconnect with a work of art—and a writer—I adore. Based on the book's huge sales figures, I'm confident I'm probably not the only American fellow traipsing around Paris in search of landmarks and restaurants memorialized in sublime prose. But I may be the only one doing it with an all-white Lab mix wearing a fake Hermès shawl and lodging at the Meurice.

Our first stop is the Pont Royal bridge, which according to Mr. Gopnik affords the loveliest view in all of Paris. The vista down the Seine is indeed wondrous. But I would suggest that it looks even better when you're viewing it through the lens of a point-and-shoot camera and there's a smiling hound sitting in the foreground, trying her best to be a good model by staring directly at the finger-snapping photographer instead of the far more interesting barges and tourist boats passing on the river below.

We cross over the river to the Left Bank and walk to the 7th arrondissement, where Gopnik and his family lived during their time in Paris. I feel a bit silly insisting that we find #16 rue du Pre-aux-Clercs, the apartment building where Monsieur Gopnik wrote the bulk of *Paris to the Moon.* Have I become like the people who ride tour buses through Bel-Air, eager to get a peek at Barbra Streisand's front lawn or Johnny Carson's driveway? What's next? The bakery on the rue du Bac? Gopnik's favorite butcher?

I can see now how people who start out merely liking *Star Trek* gradually morph into Trekkies. You want to solidify your connection to an artist or a work of art (or a pop culture phenomenon that speaks deeply to obsessive people who attend conventions in costume) by doing something other than rereading (or watching reruns of) the object of your affection. Loving a book—or a movie or a 1970s television show—means your love will always be unrequited. Going to the place where your love interest was created, however, feels like one of the few ways a real fan can refresh his vows of devotion and experience anew the joy and pleasure he felt when he first discovered his favorite book/movie/pop song. This spatial communion—if it can be called that—between creator and reader makes nonfiction feel even more "real" than it supposedly already is. Plus, it's fun to see if the "real" thing—the street, the building, the sidewalk—is how you imagined it to be, or if the eye and mind of your beloved author had somehow painted a word-picture of an "unreal" place you didn't envision.

Mr. Gopnik didn't lie. The charming, seductive, peculiar Left Bank neighborhood he described in his book is just as charming, seductive, and peculiar in person, albeit even more so with an inquisitive mutt at my side sniffing every centimeter of fragrant 7th arrondissement pavement. I've made my oblivious hound into an involuntary literary groupie. What we're both doing this day, I realize, is more or less the same thing: She's tracking down past visitors by smell; I'm searching for a vanished author by investigating pungent memories. Walking along the sunny Boulevard St. Germain, I decide there are worse fates to befall a dog (and her dad) in Paris.

Stately stone buildings on tree-lined streets near the Seine are nice, and recollections of amusing Gopnikian anecdotes (returning the fax machine; joining a gym; ordering a holiday turkey) are fun. But in Ella's view of the world, of course, nothing beats a walk in the park, where grass, glorious grass, grows in abundance. And where packs of potential petters congregate with picnic baskets and ball games, some of which could mistakenly fall into the wrong paws. So she's thrilled to discover our next stop on the Gopnik Tour is at the Luxembourg Gardens.

Many of the most heartfelt moments in *Paris to the Moon* take place here, where the author's son, Luke, attends puppet shows and rides the carousel and says one terribly cute thing after another. I myself had seen the puppet show theater and the carousel on previous trips to Paris, before reading Gopnik's memoir. Since reading his book and returning to the Luxembourg Gardens, these quaint attractions have grown in my mind from the theater and the carousel to the *Theater* and the *Carousel,* places that I want to revisit and see the way Gopnik might have seen them.

On the way through the park to the carousel, I keep Ella on a tight leash, since the grounds are patrolled by a small army of uniformed municipal guards. I'm not sure if they're fully accredited policemen, but they appear to have the authority to hand out citations, and there are signs all over the place explaining where one can and cannot bring one's *chien*. Indeed, along the outer ring of the Luxembourg Gardens, near the fences that separate the arbor from the streets, dogs are allowed. But the interior portion is *interdit.* To get from one legal portion of the Luxembourg Gardens to another legal portion requires either a mile-long detour around the exterior of the park or navigation of a sort of no-dog's-land in the middle.

I can almost make out the carousel across the way, perhaps five minutes' walking directly across the prohibited zone, or nearly half an hour by the long way. I opt for the direct route, figuring I can act like a dumb American tourist who doesn't really understand French—which shouldn't be too much of a stretch—if I get detained by one of the rangers in a baby blue shirt.

Smiling brightly (as if that would make any difference to a French park policeman), I stroll across the Luxembourg Gardens toward Luke Gopnik's carousel, where he and the other neighborhood children attempted to lance wooden rings with a stick as Luke's dad sat on a nearby bench, composing a best-selling book. Approximately halfway across the danger zone, I see a squadron of park policeman guys loitering near the egress toward which my forbidden dog and I are headed. Instead of risking a confrontation, we blend into a large crowd of weekend revelers congregated around a giant fountain, the centerpiece of the gardens. I figure we'll wait here, inconspicuously biding our time until The Man—or, in this case The Men—move on.

It would have been a good plan if not for the radio-controlled boats.

There's an armada of them skimming across the fountain, piloted by laughing children (and a handful of nautical-minded adults), who delight in crashing their miniature galleons into someone else's frigate. Ella eyes the boats suspiciously as they glide across the fountain pool, like so many ducks on a pond.

Then she barks at them. Ferociously.

What feels like a thousand French heads turn toward the offending sound. A dog! In the forbidden zone!

"Ella! No!" I hiss. "Stop it."

As much as it pains me to report, Ella is *not* listening to me at this point. Her hackles are raised, producing a spinal Mohawk that would be the envy of any self-respecting punk rocker. A deep growl worthy of Samuel Ramey rumbles in her chest, erupting finally into full-throated dog-shouting.

The commotion attracts the attention of the authorities, who advance on the hairy perp with the kind of alacrity one normally sees from congressmen accepting an invitation to pick up a large campaign donation. We're busted.

Two policemen approach us, quickly ascertain that I'm not a native French speaker, and tell me in patient and precise English that my dog is not allowed to harass the boats in this part of the gardens. My feeble plea of ignorance seems to go well, and my insistence that my trespassing hound is usually an extraordinarily well-behaved and calm animal earns some sympathy points. But Ella does not help our case when I let go of her leash to retrieve my passport from my pocket (thus proving I'm a stupid American). She dashes around the exterior of the fountain, chasing the sailing vessels as though she were herding sheep.

The authorities raise their eyebrows at me and smile. After some intracop murmuring, they let me (and my scofflaw mutt) go with a warning. I make a queer little bow and say *merci* about sixty-four times and hustle away from the crime scene.

She keeps peeking over her shoulder at the boats as we dash away. "Don't look at that!" I instruct her. "They're not what you think."

It occurs to me that maybe they *are* what Ella thinks they are. Maybe she's quite certain that the radio-controlled boats in the Luxembourg Gardens fountain aren't ducks but are, in fact, radio-controlled boats. Maybe she just doesn't like radio-controlled boats. If I were Adam Gopnik, I would be able to explain what all these semiotics mean (and how they show us the true essence of Paris). But I'm just a guy with a naughty dog who's relieved to have escaped the wrath of the French penal system.

We visit the Guignol Puppet Theater (no dogs allowed inside) and the carousel (where children are spearing wooden rings, just as Mr. Gopnik described), and after I've sat for a while and sufficiently connected with the spirit of one of my favorite writers, we depart the Luxembourg Gardens. Along the legal path.

Our final stop on the Gopnik Trail is the author's favorite

restaurant, the Brasserie Balzar, which he thinks might be the greatest eating spot in the world for a million different reasons, none of them concerning the food. This is the modest neighborhood place where Gopnik and a gang of regular patrons staged an "occupation" to protest the Balzar's acquisition by a heartless conglomerate that, the regulars feared, might change their beloved brasserie into something incrementally less charming and welcoming and familiar. When Sandrine and Ella and I arrive, I'm uncertain for a moment if we're at the right Brasserie Balzar. It looks so much smaller than I pictured it.

But, no, it must be. The warmth with which we three are greeted; the perfect balance of attentiveness and casualness with which the maître d' arranges a spot on the floor for our beast; the old-fashioned (or whatever the opposite of *nouvelle cuisine* is) menu, featuring trout in foil and lamb chops with white beans—it's just as Gopnik promised.

Every time a waiter brings a dish or refills our wineglasses with good cheap house Bordeaux, I'm tempted to ask him if he's mentioned in *Paris to the Moon*—and more to the point, does he know Monsieur G.?

Just before dessert—a classic crème caramel—I can no longer contain my curiosity. With significant coaching from my French tutor, I summon the maître d'. *"Pardon?"* I query him. *"Avez-vous entendu parler du livre* Paris à la Lune?"

"Yes, of course," he says in French, his face creasing in a happy smile. "How could we not?"

I ask the man, who seems to be about fifty, and who wears a handsome jacket and slacks, if he is mentioned in the book. He shakes his head ruefully and says he is not.

Then, at the risk of sounding like a weird French waiter-stalker, I ask if any of the other staff working this fine evening is mentioned. The maître d' looks around the brasserie. He doesn't think so, but he'll ask around.

"It's okay," I tell him. "Please, don't bother. I was just curious."

He nods assuredly.

I explain. "It's such a great book, and the way Mr. Gopnik described the waiters—'the boys,' as they call themselves . . . well, I've just been looking forward to this evening for some time."

The maître d' confesses that he has not actually read *Paris to the Moon,* but that many others employed at the Brasserie Balzar have, and they say it's a marvelous book. And while he is not personally mentioned in the text, he does in fact remember meeting the author on more than one occasion, and he can report that M. Gopnik is a very nice fellow. "Whenever he comes back to Paris, he eats here," our host reveals.

I imagine Adam Gopnik showing up unannounced at the Balzar with a few friends. He has undoubtedly brought the restaurant a measure of fame and admiration that the reputation of the dining experience alone could never muster. Surely when the author returns he's treated like a conquering hero, with much fuss made over him, like Bogey or Sinatra walking into the Stork Club back in the days of fedoras. Indeed, I imagine at the Brasserie Balzar there's more ado made over the arrival of Gopnik than over a rather sizable greyhound-Lab mix.

We drink the last of our wine, donate a few morsels of bread to the canine needy, and formally introduce Ella Konik to the staff of the Brasserie Balzar. I tell them that I too am an American author, and that I'm writing a book that features the great city of Paris. I tell them that unless some evil editor works her nefarious magic on my manuscript, their restaurant will be mentioned all over again. The staff nods and murmurs and smiles.

"But unlike the Gopnik book," I say, "the one I'm writing is about traveling through Europe with my dog."

I can tell by the nervous laughter and the blank looks that I've either expressed myself incorrectly in French or the concept of my book doesn't register with the service staff of Brasserie Balzar. "Did I say that right?" I ask Sandrine. She nods.

Then I get it. What exactly is so damned interesting about a dog in Paris—or anyplace else in Europe? Of course the waiters are perplexed. Because bringing a dog into the Brasserie Balzar (or the Luxembourg Gardens, or upon the Pont Royal) is as common a Parisian occurrence as one of their politicians having an affair. (And in France nobody bothers writing books about that either.) What does one say about the utterly natural, the usual, the effortless? Dogs in Paris (American or otherwise) are handled with simplicity and grace—like an Adam Gopnik sentence that makes you understand afresh what you've been looking at your whole life.

We lurch out of the Brasserie Balzar into a cool summer night. Ella walks at my side, sniffing the sidewalk and wagging her tail. A full moon illuminates the Left Bank, and for a moment I imagine a gossamer stairway, brilliant and white, like Ella's fur, connecting Paris to the heavens.

* * *

Though there are about 32,000 reasons why a dog, no matter how docile, would not be allowed to visit an amusement park in the United States, for the sake of brevity I will only enumerate a few of them:

- The dog might bite someone wielding an oversize plush squirrel. And there would be a lawsuit.
- The dog might be trampled in a mad stampede of humans attempting to be first in line at the Tilt-A-Whirl. And there would be a lawsuit.
- The dog might be so irresistibly cute and snapshot-worthy that customers who would normally acquire all sorts of branded crap featuring mice and rabbits would forget to buy their children overpriced plastic souvenirs. (And there would be a lawsuit.)

Which is all to say that Ella Guinevere Konik's prospects at attending a carnival in America would be as substantial and enduring as a wisp of cotton candy in a heavy rainstorm.

So when I awake one morning to find that overnight the portion of the Tuileries gardens directly across from the rue de Rivoli has been transformed into a full-scale American-style county fair, I decide my dog and I must take advantage of what could be a once-in-a-lifetime opportunity. I cancel dinner plans at another fancy museum of gastronomy. Ella can eat in restaurants anytime she's in Europe. But when else will she be able to forage deep-fried confections off the dirt while hundreds of screaming and seminauseated Frenchmen ride the roller coaster?

When the sun begins to set on another brilliant Paris day, the sky turns pink and the millions of shimmering lights that give the city its nickname sparkle like so many nocturnal jewels. The air cools, and the unmistakable scent of incredibly unhealthy yet utterly irresistible comestibles wafts from the Tuileries. Dressed in a light sweater and old jeans—which, in the Meurice, feels like the sartorial equivalent of nakedness—I escort the girls out of the calm stateliness of our hotel into the chaotic energy of the fairground. By this hour, most residents of the Meurice are probably on their way to Tour d'Argent or Lucas-Carton, where their bottle of '66 Haut-Brion awaits. I reckon we're probably the only guests of the hotel who are spending their evening eating sugar-coated dough and trying vainly to win huge stuffed-animal prizes (that would be impossible to transport home anyway). And we're doing it with a *real* animal at the ready, who's observing the whole psychedelic scene with what must be mild concern and confusion.

An amusement park provides a panoply of stimuli—visual, aural, olfactory—that piques our human senses: the familiar pipe organ music and hectoring barkers; the screaming and whooshing and crashing and laughing that accompanies the rides; the aroma of grilled meat and burnt sugar; the flashing lights and lurid decorations. Imagine what an amusement park must feel like to a dog. As though she's eaten a hallucinogenic mushroom, maybe? Ella, smart as she is, can't possibly understand the reasons and explanations for this sensory overload, this feast of sights and sounds and smells.

But she doesn't seem the least bit frightened. The park is

filled with thousands of people, mostly families and young couples, the kind of teeming crowd that would send Emily Dickinson trembling to her notepad. To Ella it's paradise. She loves to be in large packs—particularly when members of the clan frequently drop bits of what they're eating in her general vicinity.

Nonetheless, I keep her on a short leash. I'm concerned a gunshot from one of the arcade games or the explosive rumble of the water flume ride will startle her. Each time there's a wild noise or frantic commotion, however, Ella observes it coolly, cocking her head slightly and raising her ears like two military radar dishes. She's alert but unalarmed, as though attending nighttime fairs in the capital of France were something she's been doing ever since puppyhood. When she determines that all the noise is just human beings being silly, Ella wags her tail happily and tries to walk in between my legs.

Despite the presence of a very real, very alive animal wiggling against my thighs, I'm compelled, nonetheless, to try to win a very plush, very unalive animal from one of the larcenous carnival games tempting me to throw darts at balloons and softballs at milk cans. Never mind that a spongy turtle (wearing a fabric sombrero) can probably be bought for ninety-nine cents at any decent variety store. The idea at a carnival is to spend approximately twenty times as much on unsuccessful but mirthful attempts to "win" the worthless trinket.

Ella eyes the cheap prizes lustily. These are exactly the kind of fluffy toys she loves to ritualistically "kill" and then eviscerate, leaving the backyard littered with fibrous stuffing.

"This is crazy," I announce. A guy out on a first date trying to impress his doll with his ability to knock over six cans with two beanbags is one thing. But doing it for a dog?

Sandrine reminds me we're at *la foire*. And that I should play along.

I accede. But if I'm fully to get into the spirit of things, I suggest we should probably go on one of the discombobulating rides. Of course, given my motion sickness, these pernicious things would surely cause me to, um, do something really unpleasant. (I was in an amusement park in Indonesia once, where a poor lass who had the same malady as I was stuck on the ride that swings passengers in ever-widening and quickening circles around a pole. The symmetry of her vomit contrails was beautiful in a way, but that, I fear, did not allay her embarrassment at coating the crowd beneath her in spew.) Generally, I try to avoid any ride at the fair that involves centrifugal force, sharp changes of direction, or turning in one direction. Which disqualifies just about everything but the miniature car track—and I'm too big to squeeze into tiny Peugeots designed for three-year-olds.

"What about the Train Fantôme?" Sandrine suggests, pointing to an attraction across the way. "The scary train!"

"Ah, the haunted house," I say, noting the skeletons and devils and witches peeking out of fake windows painted onto a plywood facade. "I could probably do that."

I propose that Sandrine go first while I wait with the dog. And then we'll switch.

"No. That's not fun. We have to go together," she insists. "Le Train Fantôme! Le Train Fantôme!"

Momentarily forgetting that we're in France, where almost

anything dog-related is possible, I ignorantly suggest that there's absolutely no chance whatsoever that Ella will be allowed on the scary train. Then, before the words are completely out of my mouth, I suppose that maybe what I'm thinking isn't entirely accurate. I mean, Ella did have lunch at Le Grand Véfour . . .

There's no line for Le Train Fantôme. Most of the people at the fair tonight seem to be attracted to a horrible ride in the shape of a Viking ship that rocks back and forth in ever-larger arcs. It's basically a child's tree swing amplified a thousand times and taken to a violent and nauseating extreme. (Which, based on the excited screams emanating from the bowels of the pendulous ship, people really appreciate for some inscrutable reason.) The heavy-lidded man at the Train Fantôme ticket booth has his hair cut short, in the current French fashion, and reads a comic book, in the current American fashion. He looks up from his reverie when I approach, surprised, it seems, to have a customer. *"Oui?"* he says as I smile winningly and perhaps a bit too persistently.

"Excuse me," I say in terrible French. "I would like to buy two tickets. But I would also like to take my dog. Is it possible?"

He peers over my shoulder. Ella is sitting demurely, projecting the kind of angelic innocence that melts the hearts of surly Train Fantôme ticket takers.

The man in the glass booth shrugs and nods, tired and resigned as Jean Reno in a Hollywood action movie. *"Oui,"* he says flatly.

"She can? It's possible? I mean, the dog? Yes?" I stammer.

"Avec vous, oui?" he says, his weariness growing.

"Oh, yes, of course!" I assure him. "Two adults, and, um, one dog." I hastily give him money for three tickets, before he changes his mind. He pushes some of it back toward me.

"Le chien ne paye pas," he says, shaking his head. And with a flick of his wrist, he waves us in.

We pile into the first of the empty wagons waiting mournfully at the entrance of the haunted house. They seem underused and lonely, passed over in favor of more pyrotechnic attractions. Ella hops up onto the seat and sandwiches herself between her two companions. I put one arm around her back and one across her chest, hugging her lightly, in case the scary train lives up to its name.

She stares ahead, mildly curious.

The guy in the booth nods at us. We wave back. And then there's a little jolt and our wagon begins to roll into the haunted house.

It's dark and spooky, and there are faux cobwebs and bones and ghouls everywhere, and it's scary in the way that Halloween is scary, which is to say not really, although sometimes a flash of light or movement makes you startled and giggly at the same time. Our wagon trundles on its track, crashing open creaky wooden doors and nearly colliding with mirrored walls. Ghosts pop out of corners and snakes hiss and dead bodies fall from the ceiling—and I only scream once, when a demon reaches out from behind a curtain and grabs my shoulder.

And all the time Ella looks straight ahead, alert and curious but definitely less scared than me. I hold her progressively tighter and I check to see if she's panicking, but every time I look, Ella appears intrigued and piqued—*entertained*—by the unfathomable spectacle racing past.

I read somewhere that of all animals, dogs understand human facial gestures and hand signals and body language in general better than any other beast, including our distant cousin the chimpanzee. Something in a canine's DNA makes dogs adapt to human behavior, to the human mind. Dogs, in a sense, have been made and molded in our own image—though they're generally hairier and enjoy atonal symphonies slightly less. All the incredible stories one hears about dogs and their seemingly incomprehensible ability to read minds and communicate emotions and find their way home after being hopelessly lost don't seem so hard to accept when one realizes that, if the scientific reports are to be believed, dogs know us human beings better than we sometimes know ourselves.

Ella rides Le Train Fantôme, phlegmatically notes all the banging and yelling and spooking, and ascertains (correctly) that there's nothing that warrants alarm. She's rolling along on yet another new means of transportation, in yet another (exceedingly) strange place, witnessing yet more unfamiliar sights and sounds and smells. But, like all the other times, from Brussels to Brigitte Bardot's place, she's with her dad—a member of her pack she understands perfectly. She's not sure exactly what's going on; there's too much fresh data bombarding her eyes and ears and nose. But she knows it's nothing bad. Not so long as Dad keeps his arms around her shoulders and his cheek against her neck.

When our wagon returns to the front of the scary house, the ticket taker nods at us and returns to his comic book. Ella hops down from the rolling bench and performs a few happy pirouettes on the dusty ground. "Ella, you just visited a haunted house," I remind her. "You're not supposed to be so jolly."

She sits down and put her ears back, but the tip of her tail is still wiggling behind her. "Why are you such a good dog?" I ask her. "Why is this dog so good?" I ask Sandrine.

Ella stands out of her sit and walks through my legs, whipping me with her tail. Then when she's facing the same direction as I, she stops and sits again, and she looks straight up and backward at my face, exposing her neck, which I scratch vigorously. This causes her to thump one of her hind legs and make her itchy smile, which I find most charming.

We leave the low pleasures of the *foire* for the high comforts of the Meurice. But before we depart the Tuileries, I pause at one of the stupid carnival games. This one involves pulling a series of strings (*ficelles,* they call them) and discovering which tawdry prize you've "won." With the last of the euros in my pocket, I get a little stuffed rabbit for Ella to destroy with her incisors. She carries it across the rue de Rivoli to the hotel while the speakers on the Ferris wheel play "La Vie en Rose." I make up French-sounding nonsense lyrics, and Ella graciously pretends to be such a contented mutt in Paris that she doesn't even notice.

* * *

Ella Konik, like most dogs, is far more interested in *entrecôte* and *frites* (and anything else that might drop off someone's plate onto a bistro floor) than she is in famous tourist attractions. She is oblivious to Nôtre-Dame Cathedral, the Arc de Triomphe, and every other noteworthy Parisian landmark you can't eat. Ella does, however, seem to like the Eiffel Tower. It's not the engineering achievement or iconic grandeur that fascinates her, but a small pond in the park beside the edifice. The murky water hole has a few ducks in it that flash annoyed French glances at Ella, as though they were busy reading *Le Figaro* and had Gauloises quivering from their beaks. *Les canards* eye my mutt as though they were evaluating her poor American manners through a cloud of blue smoke. Unfortunately, the pond is strictly off-limits to dogs, tourist or otherwise, so Ella must amuse herself, like the rest of countless visitors to Paris, with posing for snapshots in front of, underneath, and behind one of the world's most enduring symbols of human ingenuity.

Now, I don't mean for a second to suggest that Ella Konik is more visually impressive than the Tour Eiffel. Nor would I dream of implying that Ella Konik is more photogenic than one of the prime photo ops in the northern hemisphere. (Although, yes, she is pretty damn cute.) I must merely report the facts, like any quasi-journalist ought to.

Which are these:

- While the majestic and magnificent and marvelous Eiffel Tower looms above a sea of camera-toting tourists, Ella sits down not two hundred meters from the legendary landmark.
- Instead of snapping photos of the four-legged obelisk, everyone wants to pet the four-legged cotton puff.
- Approximately 197 people request a souvenir snapshot of my very personable mutt wearing a fake Hermès shawl. No one asks this of the Eiffel Tower.

I myself get a picture of Ella with about twenty-five Italian tourist hands upon her fur. She appears to have been mistaken for a lucky talisman, or an antidote to arthritis. (I also take a few pictures with the Eiffel Tower in the background, because, you know, it's there.) The Italians—and the English, and the Japanese, and everyone else crowding around the dog—ask me the usual questions: What's her name? How old is she? What breed is she? I answer by rote and nod appreciatively at their compliments and expressions of adoration. The Eiffel Tower casts its shadow behind us all, piercing the sky and standing sentinel over Paris. I look at my dog, my beloved mutt who's been everyplace with me this summer. She's in France, beneath the Eiffel Tower. But she might as well be curled up beneath the piano in our living room, or in the lobby of the Meurice; she might as well be in California, or beside the Berlin Wall.

It makes no difference to Ella. She displays the same equanimity in Antwerp as Austria, Prague, or Paris. Everywhere.

I'm a human being, and therefore I'm supposed to be a lot smarter and cleverer and more sophisticated than a dog with a brain the size of an orange. But if I could feel as Ella does, at home every place I greet the day, maybe being a dog might not be so bad.

A quick "bonjour" to the denizens of Damme, Belgium

Being chauffeured in DeHaan, Belgium

Chapter 14

Before traveling to Europe with Ella, I was unaware that there was such a thing as the "Belgian Riviera." I knew from high-school geography class that Belgium shares with Holland an extensive seacoast, which marauding armies have enjoyed invading through the centuries. But the concept of a *Riviera,* where indolent people with too much money keep third homes and yachts, didn't seem to me to be an appropriately Belgian phenomenon. Chocolate and sprouts and NATO wonks, yes. But a sublime refuge for the European jet set? *Mais non.*

Mais oui. As I've learned throughout our journey together across Europe, Ella Konik can find joy almost anywhere, even on scary trains at Parisian carnivals. She's most delighted, however, to be someplace where there's warm water in close proximity to sand. (Which makes her like a large number of American tourists, who prefer to vacation in Hawaii and Key West than, say, Buffalo or Omaha.) I was made to understand—chiefly by my knowledgeable Belgian companion—that one of the world's most perfect examples of this topographical confluence was less than an hour's drive from the diamond markets of Antwerp. I was made to understand that the Belgian Riviera is a superb place for a man and his dog to commune with Nature.

From October 1 through March 14, it probably is too. For the other 164 days of the year, however, it's a brutal tease, a cruel prank, more sadistic than setting loose a committed dieter in the local Godiva outlet. From March 15 through September 30, when it's warm and sunny enough for anyone to care, dogs are expressly forbidden on Belgium's precious seaside beaches.

This is very sad, because we're in Knokke, the St. Tropez of Belgium, in July. Everyone in the country, it seems, goes to Knokke for their summer holidays. Since the town is so close to the main population centers, Brussels and Antwerp, whenever the sun shines (which, in Belgium, is hardly ever), UV-ray-starved city dwellers pile into their Renaults and invade the beaches.

The town, I notice immediately, is filled with *chiens* (all on leashes), including a surfeit of Pomeranians and Pekinese and all the other toy breeds favored by people who have arrived at a certain station in life. Among this effete crowd, Ella, who is neither diminutive nor purebred, looks like an interloper, a hick from an endive farm who came to Knokke on a bus tour. She's not the kind of animal one can scoop under an arm or stuff in a beach bag. Visiting Belgium's most revered beach, where tiny changing huts on the sand cost only slightly less than a Nob Hill apartment, is going to call for some delicate maneuvering, if not outright subterfuge.

At one of Knokke's many seafood restaurants specializing in freshly caught swimming creatures, I point to Ella, who, as usual, is napping on the floor beside our table. "Can you explain the beach policy?" I ask the trilingual waitress dispensing steaming bowls of mussels and bottles of crisp white wine. "Are dogs really forbidden?"

She smiles apologetically. "The authorities, they're very strict," she reports. "The fine is two or three hundred euros. The police drive around in Jeeps at all hours, looking for dogs."

"Quelle horreur!" I exclaim in a tone of (only slightly) mock indignation.

"Well, people don't clean up after them properly, I suppose," the waitress says. "It's a pity."

I nod understandingly, already hatching a plan.

After dinner, around ten P.M., the light is still good, dusky and mysterious. The sky turns pink and purple, and the wind blows harder as the tide goes out, leaving more than a hundred meters of smoothly packed sand between the Knokke boardwalk and the surf. Night begins to slowly descend, and the beach, inundated with sun-worshippers during the day, is nearly deserted. Its only inhabitants now are millions of invertebrates: mussels and oysters and crabs, whose shiny shells flash in the sand. By now, most of the town's residents and visitors are gathered around dining room tables, sipping cognac and telling stories, or preparing for bed, rubbing soothing cream on their parched shoulders. I peer down the coast as far as I can see: no Jeeps—or any other motorized vehicles—in sight.

We stroll along the coast road toward Holland, away from the town center with its art galleries and boutiques and ice-cream shops, away from the fancy condominiums lining the shore. Sandrine says that if we were to walk for forty minutes or so we would cross into the Netherlands, where, she assures me, there's no prohibition on canine beachgoers. (Or anything else, for that matter. But that's another story.)

With each passing minute, the tide recedes farther in the direction of America, and the North Sea wind howls so fiercely that you can hardly hear yourself shout—unless you have the hearing of a white Lab-greyhound mix. When I can no longer see another human being in either direction, I give my mutt the signal to run free.

"Come on, Ella!" I shout, sprinting onto the beach. "Come on, girl!"

Ella dashes across the sand to the sea, pausing only to harass a few startled seagulls taking a nap. She runs as though she were a puppy again, the tiny bundle of energetic white fur I met more than nine years ago in Runyon Canyon. The sea is her restorative fountain of youth.

Insulated by the whipping wind, as though I were in a protective vacuum, I dance and leap and shout. Ella swims and barks and chases; she sniffs and digs and jumps, abandoning herself to sheer doggie joy. She's suddenly no longer an old lady worn out from traveling, from hot streets and vibrating floors and changing time zones. She's a rambunctious mischief-maker at the seaside, cavorting with her silly old companion on an endless beach, her favorite playground in the world.

The wind picks up her normally floppy ears and stands them straight. She looks like an albino German shepherd. The muscles of her flank, which are oblong and beautiful like a Thoroughbred horse's, twitch and flex beneath her fur as she prances in the sand. I don't think I've ever seen my dog so happy. Whatever pains Ella once suffered have been washed away by wind and water. She's delirious.

I watch her frolic on the Belgian beach. How I dread the day when I'll have to say good-bye to my best friend. Everyone who's ever owned a dog knows how these magical creatures quickly evolve from mere pets and pleasant distractions to fully vested members of the family. They're our four-legged sons or daughters or siblings. We care for and fret over them as though they were parents or offspring. People who dislike animals don't comprehend the dog lover's devotion. They innocently wonder, "What's the big deal? It's just a dog."

Those of us who share our home with dogs can't comprehend such a benighted viewpoint. To us, the love and the transcendent light a dog brings into the world are a very big deal, indeed. Ella Guinevere is an extraordinary animal unlike almost any other I've known. But in many ways she's just like every other dog on earth: They *all* radiate goodness into our frequently evil world. They all make us humans smile—and cry and laugh and sigh. They all make us *feel*. And for that we should be eternally grateful.

As I throw sticks of driftwood and empty oyster shells into the shallow surf, a wave of profound happiness ripples through me: I've given my dog, my best friend, a moment of pure and exalted fun. If only for a few minutes, I've made her young again. And for that, a three-hundred-dollar fine seems a worthy price.

On this chilly summer evening, no Belgian patrolmen appear

out of the dusky light. But if they did, I'd like to think they would note the unabashed joy occurring on their restorative beach, and they would drive on.

* * *

There is a golf course not far from Knokke, in another Belgian seaside town called Damme (like Jean-Claude, from whom the locals take great pains to distance themselves: *"Eee eez 'ow you zay? En embarussmount, yes?"*). This golf course, hidden within an intricate maze of dykes and cow pastures, is not on any of the Top 100 lists published by golf fetish magazines. It doesn't host major championships—or minor ones, for that matter. Hardly anyone in Belgium, let alone everyone outside of Belgium, has even heard of it. Yet the Damme Golf Club, on Belgium's Riviera(!), is, in my humble estimation, one of the greatest places in the world to play the game of golf.

This is why: They let dogs on the course.

For many years—ever since I realized Ella was better behaved and showed more consideration and etiquette than the average cart-driving, titanium-club-wielding hacker—I longed to play golf with my dog. It seemed so natural; what is golf but a four-hour walk in the park accompanied by a dear mate? Ella, like most dogs, loves nothing more (well, besides fresh meat) than to be outside, sniffing grass and scampering at her dad's side. A round of golf and a walk with the dog: What a perfect marriage of activities, I thought.

Well, in the litigious United States of America, proprietors of golf courses have come up with a million reasons to keep dogs off their turf, and most of these reasons begin or end with the word "lawyer." I've found one tiny pitch-and-putt in Los Angeles, down the street from Hef's Playboy Mansion, that allows players to bring leashed dogs on a tour of the course, a fleeting eighteen-hole journey that takes approximately forty-five minutes. Bona fide "championship courses" open to the public simply don't allow cute mutts, well behaved or not, to befoul their pristine fairways.

This is not the case in Scotland, where even on the putatively sacred grounds of the Old Course at St. Andrews, dogs are gladly welcomed. Likewise, I've played on courses in Ireland, Wales, and England where the companionship of a dog during a round of golf is seen not as a great affront but a highly civilized enhancement. Other countries seem to appreciate the wisdom (and simple fun) of taking one's hound along for an afternoon's diversion. Alas, not mine.

But today Ella and I are in Belgium, one of those "other countries" that allow Man's Best Friend to accompany him during a go at Man's Most Vexing Game.

And I'm in heaven.

When I rang up the club secretary a few days prior to our arrival on the Belgian coast, I inquired about bringing my mutt along for a round, expecting, as usual, to be told regretfully that "policies" didn't allow such a thing. But in this case, the lady said yes, sure I could bring my dog. People did it all the time. She wasn't concerned that I intended to have my mutt visit the club; she was concerned that I had an up-to-date handicap card to prove I knew how to play golf. I hung up the phone, mildly shocked. Was that it? Was there no catch, no secret provision about which I had failed to ask?

Apparently not. When I enter the pro shop of Damme Golf Club, with Ella at my side on a *very* short leash, no one makes the least bit of fuss. (They just want to see my handicap card.) After collecting my greens fee and wishing me well, the ladies in the office bid me good luck and point the way to the first tee.

I'm still thinking someone wearing an official beret is bound to stop me and tell me there's been a terrible misunderstanding, that dogs are allowed in the *parking lot* but not the actual golf course, and what am I, crazy? *Do they let dogs on the emerald links back in the States? So then why, Monsieur, would you presume that they are welcome in Belgium? Because we're a smaller country than you? Honestly, Monsieur, the nerve!*

But no. All we get are smiles and nods and polite *bonjours*. I'm still mildly shocked, and more than a little apprehensive as I approach the first tee at Damme. Golfers everywhere suffer from a malady known as "first-tee jitters," a condition whose symptoms include quickening of the breath, perspiration on the palms, and a general inability to duplicate on the first hole what has been done a thousand times on the practice range. First-tee jitters can be particularly noxious when playing with strangers or in front of onlookers. The average duffer deals with the side-effects of FTJ (slices, hooks, and feeble pop-ups) with a ready arsenal of sarcastic, self-deprecating commentary along the lines of "Oh, that was impressive! Hey, has anyone seen my palsy medication?"

There isn't another human soul near the first hole this morning at Damme Golf Club. Yet I've got FTJ worse than ever. I'm about to slap my golf ball into the distance, sling my bag over my shoulder, and tramp off into the freshly mown fairway—*with my dog!* "Do you believe this?" I say to Ella, who, apparently, is immune to first-tee jitters.

I position my mutt on the right side of the tee; she looks in the direction of the fairway, as though she understands which direction I'm supposed to be aiming my shot. I make a few warm-up swings on the left side of the tee and then take my stance.

Ella has seen me hit golf balls numerous times at the Griffith Park driving range, where everyone knows her and likes her (except for the once-every-couple-of-years occasions when she chases a squirrel into the practice field, in the line of fire of dozens of startled hackers; then she's in trouble). The small-caliber rifle sound of clubhead meeting Surlyn doesn't startle her. Nor does the rapid whip of a swinging golf club alarm her; she knows to stay out of the way. To Ella, nothing about what I'm doing this morning is out of the ordinary, except for the strange mumbling emanating from my lips.

I'm literally talking myself through my first shot. I'm so nervous I have to consciously remind myself how to get the club back into hitting position.

Then I look over at my pal of eleven years, the friend I've always wished I could have join me for a round of golf. She's sitting motionless on the first tee, waiting, watching, wondering, lost in her thoughts (whatever those might be). She's entranced by her senses. Ella breathes in the fragrant air and listens to the birds and sees something small and animate scampering across the grass in the distance. She's doing what all we duffers who don't play golf for a living ought to do: enjoy being outside with a cherished companion, feeling the good ground beneath your feet and the bracing air on your cheeks. My dog doesn't know the first thing about swing-plane and interlocking grip and weight transfer, or anything else about making proper swings. But she seems to know the ideal way to play golf.

I drive my ball down the fairway, sigh with relief, and suggest to Ella, "Let's go for a walk." She jumps up excitedly and goes to my left heel, dragging her leash along the short grass, sniffing every inch of turf she can get her nostrils on.

We're officially playing golf. Together.

I don't see any players ahead of or behind us. The solitude—it's just me, Ella, and the wildlife—enhances my impression that I've been set down in an enchanted paradise by an omniscient puppeteer, or that I'm in an arboreal fugue state. On some holes I talk incessantly to my companion, telling her what a good girl she is, what a talented heeler she is, and facetiously pinning responsibility for my errant shots on her hairiness. But for long stretches we play in silence, listening to the birds and the trees and the sky.

When we arrive at a green, I instruct Ella to lie down beside it next to my bag, since she's no good at tending the flag. On some holes, when she gets bored of waiting, she insists on standing at my side while I putt out, and one time, when I roll in a lengthy one, she walks over to the hole and peers inside it, investigating where my ball went.

We walk together through meadows and forests, in the sun and in the shade. And only once, when I see some invitingly tall grass to the side of the fourth hole and invite Ella to "go make potty," does she leave my side.

Eventually we catch up to a threesome ahead of us, who invite me to play through. They are Frenchmen on holiday, I discover, and they appear utterly unimpressed to see a dog on the golf course. They do, however, chuckle mildly when I instruct Ella to walk *around* the putting surface to get to the next tee and she mistakes my hand motion for a signal to "roll over."

We see five other human beings during our round at Damme, three of them members of the maintenance crew. Everyone waves and smiles, and we wave and smile back.

When Ella is thirsty, I let her drink from some of the ponds and lakes that frame the golf course. When she's intrigued by a herd of cows grazing behind one of the greens, I let her research. And when she becomes obsessed with a flock of geese and ducks standing on the banks of a shallow river, I let her chase them into the water and then have a brief swim among the honking and quacking birds, who aren't shy about voicing their displeasure. By the end of our round, I'm pretty sure Ella thinks the Damme Golf Club is the coolest place she's ever been.

I know I do. In between hugs and kisses and rambling monologues and silent meditation and leisurely strolls on the grass, I hit some golf shots, all of which seem irrelevant, despite the fact that I'm supposed to be playing golf. Focused on everything but the quality (or lack thereof) of my shot-making, I post one of the best scores of my career.

Even if I had shot 100 over par, my day at Damme would still rank as the finest round of my life. I want this day to never end, for Ella to be my friend forever, for this feeling of Yes! Yes! *Yes!* to never go away. I discover a lot of nice things this morning on the Damme golf course, some of them goofy, some of them profound, and some of them both. The most important thing I discover playing golf with Ella at the Belgian seaside is that, although it doesn't happen nearly as often as we expectant human beings wish, dreams sometimes really do come true.

* * *

Venice has gondolas. Vienna has horse-drawn carriages. And various Asian cities Ella Konik will never visit have rickshaws.

De Haan, Belgium, has a slow-moving family conveyance called the *quistax.*

A quistax is a quadracycle that seats as few as two or as many as six passengers. You guide it as you would a car, with a steering wheel that controls the front tires. (There's also a three-wheeled version that looks like a child's tricycle on steroids.) Quistaxes have no gears. If you want to go faster, you pedal harder. If you want to slow down you implement a hand brake. Some quistaxes have baskets in the back where you can put stuff, like portions of smoked eel; most have a little bell on the handlebars to warn pedestrians of impending collisions. There are quistax rental shops all round the town of De Haan, whose name, inexplicably, means "The Cock," despite being a near homonym for "The Hen."

De Haan is down the coast from Knokke, the last village of note before Oostende, where the ferry departs for England and where the local golf club also welcomes dogs on the links. If it had casinos, saltwater taffy stands, and showrooms featuring performers whose other big annual gig is warbling for Jerry's Kids, De Haan would be the Atlantic City of Belgium, only about a hundred times smaller. There's a nice boardwalk and lots of restaurants and hotels, and, of course, a plethora of quistaxian amusements. De Haan is a tourist town, but a charming one.

The most fun thing to do here is hire a quistax, put your dog in the middle seat, and storm around the main drag pretending you're Lance Armstrong.

Concurrent with our journey across Europe, the biggest event in cycling (and one of the biggest events in all of European athletics), the Tour de France, has been ongoing. Every afternoon, the race is broadcast live on a panoply of different channels, in several different languages. (In Belgium it's possible to get race commentary—*"Oh, he's truly suffering now!"*—in as many as six languages at once, though I usually opt for the English version, unless I'm in the mood for snide French insinuations about American performance-enhancing drug use.) Lance Armstrong, the inspirational cancer survivor and professional masochist—he is said to have a larger appetite for pain than his big-thighed competitors—is winning again this summer, as he has the past three times, and as the Tour draws nearer to its conclusion on the Champs-Élysées, I tune in intermittently to see how my compatriot is doing.

This is how Ella and I become familiar with the words *peloton* (large group of skinny guys wearing mirrored sunglasses and really tight shorts) and *poursuivants* (same as above, only in a smaller pack and not as far behind Lance Armstrong as the *peloton*). Whenever we go for a walk and Ella gets a little ahead of me, I announce that I'm officially a *poursuivant* and that she will soon be dragged back into the *peloton*. "If you were a purebred, hundred-percent greyhound, you could win the Tour de France," I inform her. "But you're just a stray mongrel."

In De Haan, pedaling around town on a quistax, I announce to Ella that I'm currently in possession of the leader's yellow jersey (despite the maroon sweater I'm wearing to fend off the North Sea breeze). "If you want to catch Lance Armstrong, you're going to have to work harder, Madame Peloton!"

Ella doesn't help pedal. Instead, she assumes a regal, sphinx-like pose, with her hindquarters on the middle seat between me and the *poursuivant* from Belgium, Sandrine. She rests her front paws on what would be the top of the dashboard, were our cycle an automobile. It's like this that we cruise around De Haan: two Tour de France hopefuls pedaling their quistax mightily, with an unflappable white dog doing her best impersonation of a hood ornament.

I ring the bell way more than necessary and talk to Ella as though I were a French sports commentator. She generally ignores me and concentrates on looking cute for the Dutch and German tourists who want to take her picture.

I feel like I'm a little boy again, inventing adventure games with my neighborhood playmates. We were so good, when we were young, at make-believe. Anything was possible if we could imagine it. Rolling around De Haan, on the Belgian Riviera, in a quistax, with my American doggie, I'm discovering all over again what I knew as a child and what we all somehow forget after we become adults. I'm learning all over again at the Belgian seaside what Ella seems to have understood instinctively ever since she was old enough to walk.

Playing with a friend is good for the soul.

HOTEL

Ella contemplating the fetid charms of Amsterdam's Singel Canal

Chapter 15

Ella Guinevere Konik is ready to return to her house in Hollywood. She's ready to go back to her garden and back to her brother the cat, back to barking at the mailman and running in between the legs of visiting neighbors. She's happy, but she's tired. (And so am I.)

We both look forward to the familiar comforts of our own bed and own bathroom and own everything else. We look forward to the simple pleasure of staying in one place, of feeling anchored. As Frank Sinatra sang on his album *Come Fly with Me*:

It's oh so nice to just wander
But it's oh so nice to come home!

Ella has seen more in the past month than most American dogs see in a lifetime. The friends she's made and the smells she's smelled and the forbidden foods she's eaten will all dance in her memory until the end of her life (assuming dogs actually have that kind of memory). She's traveled on and in almost every imaginable conveyance; she's been welcomed into sacred precincts generally refused to American mutts; she's given love in eight different languages, only one of which she understands. And most important, she's spent almost every hour of every day of every week with her dad, the highly flawed human being with whom Ella can find no fault. It's been a fabulous time.

Soon we'll be home together, back to workdays in the office, back to volunteer visits to nursing homes and cancer wards, back to jolly games of ball in the backyard. And all this European stuff, the dining together in restaurants and wandering into stores and all the rest, will be a coveted memory. Ella will go back to being an American dog living by American rules.

For now, though, for a couple more blissful days, she's in Amsterdam, the final stop on our European journey. And during our last hours together abroad, life seems as though it can't possibly get any sweeter.

Amsterdam is a wonderful city for dogs. To park a car on public streets costs about twenty-six dollars a day, so there are relatively few automobiles a pedestrian hound must avoid on her walks around town. Residents here mostly commute on foot or by bicycle. The stone streets traversing the interior canals have wide sidewalks, and unleashed mutts can sniff as they amble without fear of being plowed over by a Vespa or any other threatening thing with a motor. Above all, in Amsterdam, the prevailing attitude toward dogs—and just about everything that inspires disapproval in less libertarian places—is acceptance and tolerance. In a city where the coffeehouses legally sell hashish and marijuana, and where the prostitutes on public display are a genuine tourist attraction, the presence of dogs in hotels, restaurants, and shops barely registers among the egalitarian populace. The inhabitants of Amsterdam pride themselves on their liberties; they're too busy enjoying life to make restrictive rules about dogs.

Even if you're one of the people who think the 1960s had too much hair and not enough bathing, the hippie ethos of peace, love, and altered consciousness has its fleeting charms, particularly in a world torn asunder by religious hatred. It's hard to be uptight in a city where people behave as though the Beatles never broke up. Since getting and being stoned is a common part of Amsterdam culture, visitors of all classes, colors, and nationalities come to the capital of the Netherlands to let themselves go, to enjoy some temporary bohemianism. Even American dogs.

Ella Konik's rule-breaking, borderline anarchistic, anti-establishment activities include eating innumerable things off the street, in direct contradiction of her daddy's authoritarian dictums. I try to explain to her that snatching an old pizza crust off the ground in Amsterdam could easily have some unplanned hallucinogenic effects.

The longer I'm in the Netherlands, however, the less convinced I am that ingesting hash would be so terrible. Before arriving here, I had no intention of getting Ella high on anything but camaraderie. But seeing all the happy, carefree people blissfully lounging at sidewalk cafés beside the tranquil canals, smiling and singing and reciting poetry, I'm tempted to let her sample a small piece of "space cake" so that she might enjoy visions of dancing squirrels and trees that bear fruit the size, shape, and color of medium-rare porterhouses. Alas, I would never forgive myself if she should have a "bad trip." So I give her fries with mayonnaise instead—which, to Ella, is just as glorious as any barbiturate.

Though I resolve myself to shelter Ella from Amsterdam's drug scene—and that's not easy—I figure she's old enough to experience the city's renowned red-light district, where independent contractors display their wares in floor-to-ceiling windows. Walking through this carnival of sex with a dog creates an entirely different dynamic between seller and buyer than when one is an unescorted bachelor. Having Ella at my side strongly suggests I am not a potential customer, and therefore the performers and relaxation therapists who devote much of their promotional time to casting come-hither glances at anyone who walks past their window can drop the act and behave like everyone else we meet, albeit with less clothing. The denizens of Amsterdam's red-light district love Ella as much as all the other people we've encountered in Europe who don't charge by the hour. They wave and smile and ask to pet her, and Ella doesn't mind one bit, though she occasionally suffers a sneezing fit brought on by clouds of cheap perfume.

A lady of the night clad in a microscopic white bikini with lacy trim and white thigh-high stockings motions excitedly at me and Ella as we pass her window. I smile and wave politely. The entertainer, quite possibly an entrepreneurial Russian émigré, gestures frantically, pointing at herself and then at Ella. I indicate through sign language that I'm not interested in purchasing what she's proposing, whatever that may be. She shakes her head in exasperation and points again at Ella, then herself.

"Ah! I see," I say, forgetting she can't hear me. "You match!" I pet Ella's white fur and the lady pets her bikini. We both point back and forth at the dog and exchange thumbs-ups. Then I hustle Ella down the street, just in case I've completely misjudged the situation.

As we walk, I explain to Ella what just happened. "You two ladies were both wearing white. Only she's wearing more lipstick and you don't wax yourself." Ella wags her tail and pretends to understand what I'm saying.

In front of one thriving burlesque theater, Ella attempts to drink from a salacious fountain in the shape of a giant phallus. (A group of English tourist ladies recognize this moment as a tremendous opportunity for souvenir photos.) Rolf, the theater's Dutch proprietor, strongly suggests that the fluid emanating from the fountain's orifice is not exactly potable, but that he would be delighted to get the pretty girl some fresh water from within his establishment. He rushes inside the theater and returns with a drink, smiling warmly. As potential clients review posters listing the many live stage spectacles available at this bawdy emporium of naughty entertainment, Ella laps contentedly at a beer mug, oblivious to the moral turpitude around her. Indeed, Ella is utterly unaware of this thing we call "morality." Nudity and lust and pleasure are not concepts that offend or frighten her. She just wants everyone around her to be happy—and not to skimp on the affectionate scratches behind her ears.

A dog's view of the world is reductively simple—probably too simple to answer the questions the human mind conceives—and elegantly concise. Dogs, it seems to me, believe everyone should be free to do with their bodies what they wish, eat what they want, and love who they may. Dogs don't care to legislate private behavior or dictate desires. They see society dialectically, as either Good (people who are nice) or Evil (people who aren't). We humans know nothing is ever that clear, that there's a murky gray area between the polar extremes, and our constant arguing and fighting and warring over our disparate interpretations is what supposedly "elevates" us above simpleminded canines. (Well, that and our conditioned shame about urinating in public.) In peculiar old Amsterdam, however, Ella's live-and-let-live philosophy somehow seems to work not only for her but for the residents and tourists alike. Everyone is too busy enjoying themselves to worry about persecuting someone else for having different desires.

I do not mean to suggest that Ella Guinevere Konik can change the course of history, or even have much noticeable effect upon it. But seeing her be herself, her true unfettered self, in Europe this summer, I sense that she unconsciously brings something helpful and healing to our human hearts.

Ella is like comedy. Comedy cannot permanently alter the world—at least not as effectively as brave science, bold literature, and well-defined abs. But comedy can bring disparate human souls together in the shared communion of laughter.

We human beings have wildly different beliefs about religion and politics and justice, sex and love and kindness. But we *all* can laugh. Not everything is funny to everyone simultaneously (although a man in a dress seems to work for about 98 percent of Western civilization). Sometimes, despite our philosophical and moral differences, we "get it" at more or less the same moment. It's during these occasions of universal pleasure that, no matter our deeply ingrained conflicts, human beings can hold out hope that maybe our ultimate destination isn't self-immolation. Maybe we'll end up solving our problems with humor, cleverness, and grace.

Ella makes people laugh. And smile. And feel. Like most dogs, she has the astonishing ability to inspire humans to feel good about being alive. She can alchemically make something out of nothing, turning ennui and despair into hope and joy. No, Ella Konik isn't going to reinvent the world. But by merely being a really good dog, she helps make it an infinitesimally better place.

For that I shall always be grateful.

* * *

Amsterdam is often called "the Venice of the North." Any chamber of commerce with a glimmer of marketing savvy would like to be associated with the magical city of Marco Polo, and so almost any place that has water running through its borders is prone to compare itself with Venice, no matter how tenuous the connection. Amsterdam, I think, can make a legitimate case for being the lowland version of Italy's tourist magnet. Dozens—hundreds?—of operational canals sluice through the city, bearing houseboats, barges, and an inexorable procession of tour vessels, steered through narrow bridges and around tight corners with the precision of Michael Schumacher behind the wheel of his Ferrari.

Like Venice, Amsterdam's canals are both seductive and filthy; indeed, the houseboat toilets empty directly into the murky water, and the canals must be "flushed" into the sea once every day or two through a system of dykes.

Unlike Venice, Amsterdam is not home to a battalion of gondoliers, singing or otherwise.

But this doesn't mean the dreamy tourist enthralled by the languid peacefulness of the still waters can't do something romantic and relaxing upon Amsterdam's canals. He can always hire a canal bike.

These floating bicycles-built-for-two are made from molded plastic in the shape of a jumbo Jet Ski. You sit down in them as in a chaise longue, low enough so that you can reach overboard and almost touch the canal water, which is said to give a rash to anyone who immerses his arm in it for more than a few seconds. Like De Haan's quistaxes, these intimate watercraft are powered solely by pedaling. If you want to go faster, you pedal harder; if you want to stop, you pedal backward. Steering is tricky. A hand rudder in the center of the boat gets the canal bike pointed in the general direction you want to go, but, as in most boats, every steering correction occurs after a brief delay. So most inexperienced canal bike pilots end up riding in a distinct zigzag pattern.

Well, at least I do—especially since every time I see a big tourist boat bearing down on me I swerve wildly to one side—and then I swerve wildly again to avoid crashing my floating cycle into the stone walls lining the canal, not to mention moored houseboats and other innocent tourists out for a leisurely paddle. Plus, I have the added challenge of navigating Amsterdam's canals with two passengers on board: a Belgian woman with a camera and an American mutt with a waterfowl fixation.

Once upon a time, before six weeks of experience in Europe, I was scared to ask foreign merchants and proprietors if I could take my (very well behaved and very well educated) doggie with me into their store/shop/taxi/restaurant/horse-drawn carriage/hotel/gondola. Now I'm brazen. When I rent the canal bike at one of the many canal bike marinas around Amsterdam, I ask the man in the kiosk not if I can take my dog on the boat but if he'll take a photo of us before we depart. (The answer to both questions in Europe, I've learned, is bound to be yes.)

Ella gets on board the canal bike gingerly, like an acrobat testing her high wire. She can feel the water swaying beneath her feet, and she immediately understands that Dad's latest adventure with her doesn't involve the usual four wheels. She gets herself situated between me and Sandrine, in the middle of the front seat, very near the handle that controls the steering. (Every time I want to go to the right I have to nudge her heavy thigh with the back of my hand.) Our canal bike is all white, with red lettering spelling out on the side the name of the company that owns it. Wearing her jalapeño collar, Ella matches our vessel almost as well as certain red-light district impresarios.

After she gets accustomed to the gentle rocking of our ungainly craft, Ella feels confident enough to rise from her prone position on the seat and explore the bow. She keeps her back paws on the passenger seat and places her front paws on what would be the engine lid, if our little boat had a motor. She's like a gigantic mascot.

We pedal around Amsterdam like this for hours, stopping to admire pretty alleyways, and to listen to musicians performing at the waterside, and to rest. Ella stands watch, searching the horizon for signs of winged creatures. When we encounter families of ducks and mud hens, I must forcefully dissuade my little avian investigator from plunging into the canals to pursue the objects of her inquiry. She looks back at me to make sure I'm serious. And then she cries softly when she realizes I am.

"Don't worry, Ella," I reassure her. "Soon you'll be home with your squirrels. You can harass all the wildlife then." When I say the word "squirrel" she cocks her head and surveys the canals, searching for a waterlogged rodent doing the backstroke.

We see Amsterdam from the inside out. We're tourists, yes. But we're explorers too, finding the secret nooks and surprising sanctuaries the landlubber never sees. Sandrine and I sing songs. Ella takes naps. I wave to people on houseboats tending to their plants.

We three float past our hotel, on the Singel, the innermost of the canals. I can see the street Ella and I traverse each morning on the way to her pee spot. It looks unreal and artfully constructed, like a movie set.

Has my dog, my sweet American mutt, really done all the things I recall her doing? Has she truly been all the places I remember? Or is this all a figment of my imagination, the fantastical by-product of too much hashish smoke wafting through the Dutch air?

I study my Ella as she stands watch on our canal bike. Her nostrils flare with each inhalation she takes. The air is like a book to her; she reads it with her nose. Her ears twitch with every peculiar sound echoing off the water. The hum and crackle of everyday activity is like a symphony to her; she hears the music of unseen life in frequencies and colors I can only imagine. Her chocolate eyes, fringed with demure blond lashes, sparkle in the sun. The choreography of human interactions is like epic theater to her; she views our species' two-legged perambulations with a mix of concern and amusement, not sure if what she's witnessing is comedy or tragedy. (Of course, it's often both.) And though Ella Guinevere Konik exists in a state of mild confusion, never fully comprehending the odd constructs of the human mind, she seems to understand me and my fellow men and women better than we often understand ourselves.

She's just a dog. This I know. But she is my friend too, my best and truest friend. She harbors nothing in her heart for me but everlasting love. We're in the Netherlands today. Next week we'll be back in the United States of America. And one dark day we'll have to say farewell forever.

When the time to part has come, I will remember Ella Konik standing upon a canal bike in Amsterdam, and crossing the Charles Bridge in the Czech Republic, and watching soccer in a Belgian pub. I'll remember her adventures all over Europe, adventures we shared together. And like every lucky man who has ever had a dog to light his life, I'll know that for a too-brief magical time I was truly blessed.

Vigilantly patrolling for squirrels beneath the aloe in her backyard

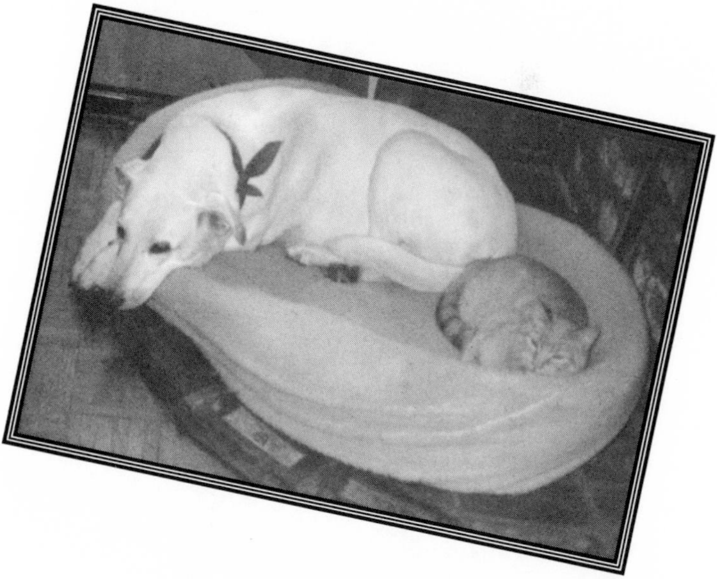

Ella and her brother Sammy the cat,
supervising from her office bed

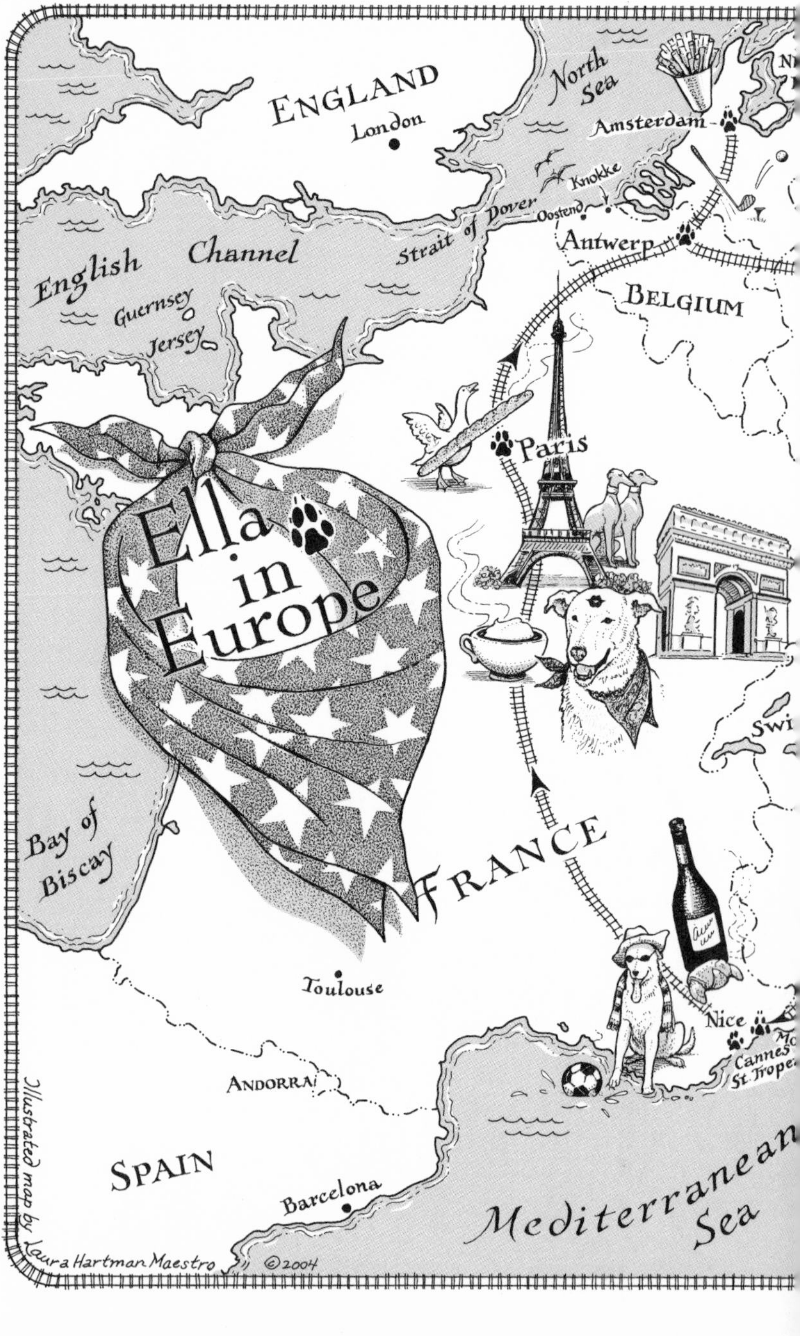
ENGLAND
London
North Sea
Amsterdam
Knokke
Oostend
Strait of Dover
Antwerp
English Channel
Guernsey
Jersey
BELGIUM
Paris
Ella in Europe
Swi
Bay of Biscay
FRANCE
Toulouse
Nice
Cannes
St. Trope
ANDORRA
SPAIN
Barcelona
Mediterranean Sea
Illustrated map by Laura Hartman Maestro ©2004